D1590022

Forgotten Voices of Mao's Great Famine

FORGOTTEN VOICES OF MAO'S GREAT FAMINE, 1958–1962

AN ORAL HISTORY

ZHOU XUN

Yale
UNIVERSITY PRESS
New Haven and London

Yale University Press books may be purchased in quantity for educational, business, or promotional use. For information, please e-mail sales.press@yale.edu (U.S. office) or sales@yaleup.co.uk (U.K. office).

Set in Gotham and Garamond type
by IDS Infotech Ltd., Chandigarh, India.
Printed in the United States of America.

Library of Congress Cataloging-in-Publication Data
Zhou, Xun, 1968–
Forgotten voices of Mao's great famine, 1958–1962: an oral history / Xun Zhou.
p. cm.
Includes bibliographical references and index.
ISBN 978-0-300-18404-4 (alk. paper)
1. Famines—China—History—20th century. 2. Food supply—China—History—20th century. 3. China—Population—History—20th century.
I. Title.
HC430.F3Z467 2013
363.80951'09045—dc23 2013015473

A catalogue record for this book is available from the British Library.
This paper meets the requirements of ANSI/NISO Z39.48–1992 (Permanence of Paper).

10 9 8 7 6 5 4 3 2 1

I dedicate this book to my grandmother,
a survivor of the Great Famine

Contents

Acknowledgments

First of all I thank the survivors whose courage and generosity helped to make this book possible.

This book is part of a bigger project undertaken in collaboration with my colleague Frank Dikötter at the Faculty of Arts, University of Hong Kong. Between 2008 and 2010 we received a research grant from the Research Grants Council, Hong Kong, and a research grant from the Chiang Ching-ko Foundation in Taiwan. These grants allowed me to carry out essential research for this book, which I acknowledge with gratitude. I also thank the Sino-British Trust for a pilot grant in 2007 that enabled me to fly to China to conduct interviews. My deepest gratitude goes to Frank Dikötter, for he has given me valuable suggestions and encouragement throughout my research. Without his support this book would not have been possible.

During the course of my research I have benefited greatly from conversations with Gao Wanling, formerly of Renmin University of China in Beijing, and Cao Shuji at Shanghai Jiaotong University. Cao Shuji also helped me greatly during one of my research trips to Anhui province. My friend Jiang Anxi, a freelance filmmaker based in London and Beijing, has given me much help and useful insights as well as constant support while I was researching this book in China. I am also grateful to Anna Lora-Wainwright, an anthropologist at the University of Oxford, for introducing me to a number of survivors in northern Sichuan who appear in this book.

I also wish to thank Sander Gilman at Emory University in Atlanta for the enthusiastic and steadfast support he has given in the course of writing this book. He kindly read a draft version and, as always, his useful comments were much appreciated.

My heartfelt thanks go to my friends Julie Kleeman, the former chief editor of the Oxford English-Chinese Dictionary, and Father Edmund Ryden, S.J., as well as Rachel Barrett. They have spent many hours carefully reading the manuscript and have made many invaluable comments for improvement, particularly with the English language.

While I was writing, several people read portions of the manuscript, or listened to my ideas, or made insightful suggestions. They are Gerard Lemos, the former acting chair of the British Council and the author of *The End of the Chinese Dream* (2012); Paul Thompson, the British sociologist and oral historian, formerly of the University of Essex; Poppy Sebag-Montefiore, a freelance British journalist and filmmaker who has spent many years in China; Frances Wood at the British Library; and Stephan Feuchtwang at the London School of Economics and Political Science.

In the middle of writing this book, I had a road accident and was hospitalized for over six weeks. A number of friends, as well as my family, helped to take care of my ten-month-old son and encouraged me to finish writing. These friends are Gail Burrowes, Vivienne Lo, Jiang Anxi, Harriet Evans, Louise Edwards, Nancy Holroyd Downing, and Sander Gilman. I am very grateful to all of them.

I am grateful to the School of Humanities, the History Department, the Centre for the Humanities and Medicine, and the Hong Kong Institute for the Humanities and Social Sciences at the

University of Hong Kong, and the Department of History at the University of Essex for providing me with the environment and essential support needed in order to continue my research and complete this book.

Finally, I wish to thank Yale University Press for its commitment and enthusiasm, and in particular its assistant editor Christina Tucker, manuscript editor Phillip King, and former reference editor Vadim A. Staklo for their crucial assistance.

Forgotten Voices of Mao's Great Famine

Map of China in 1959

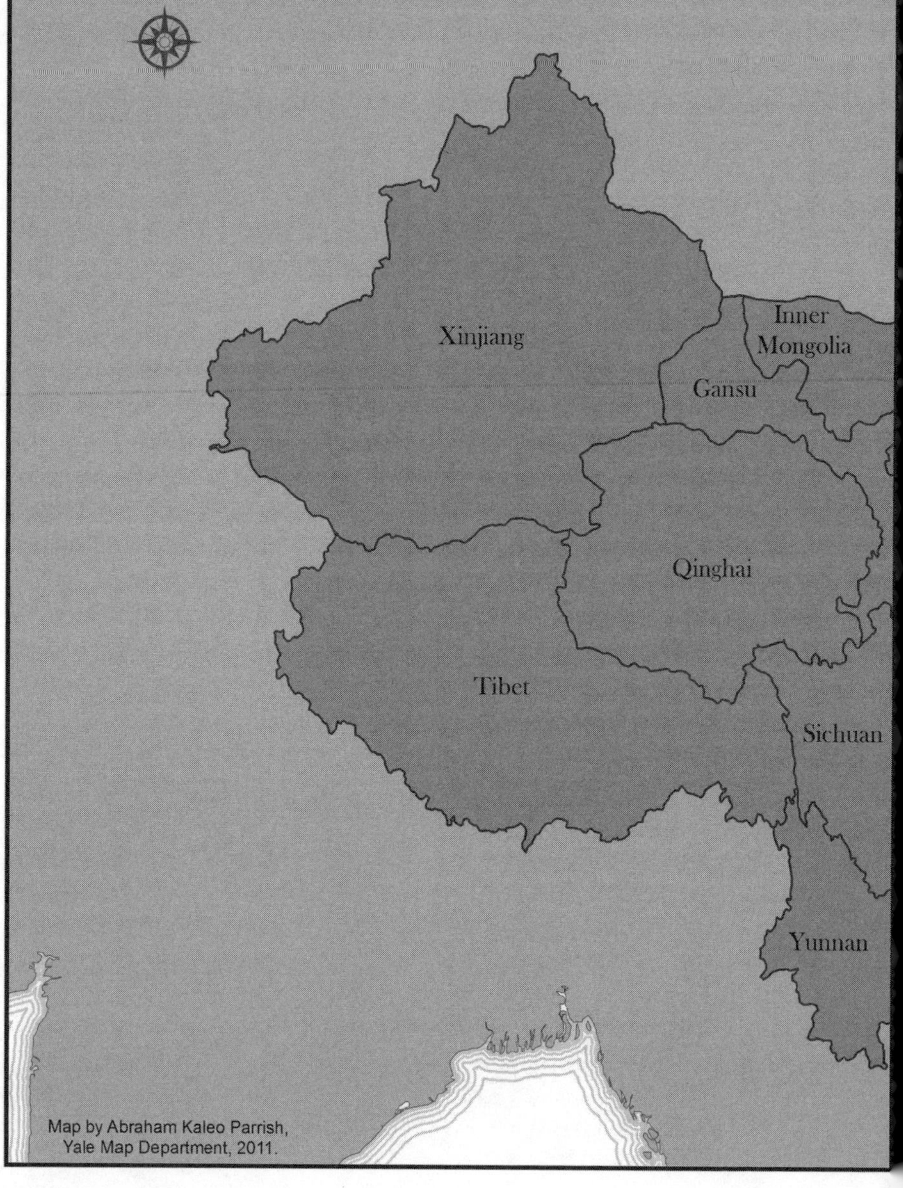

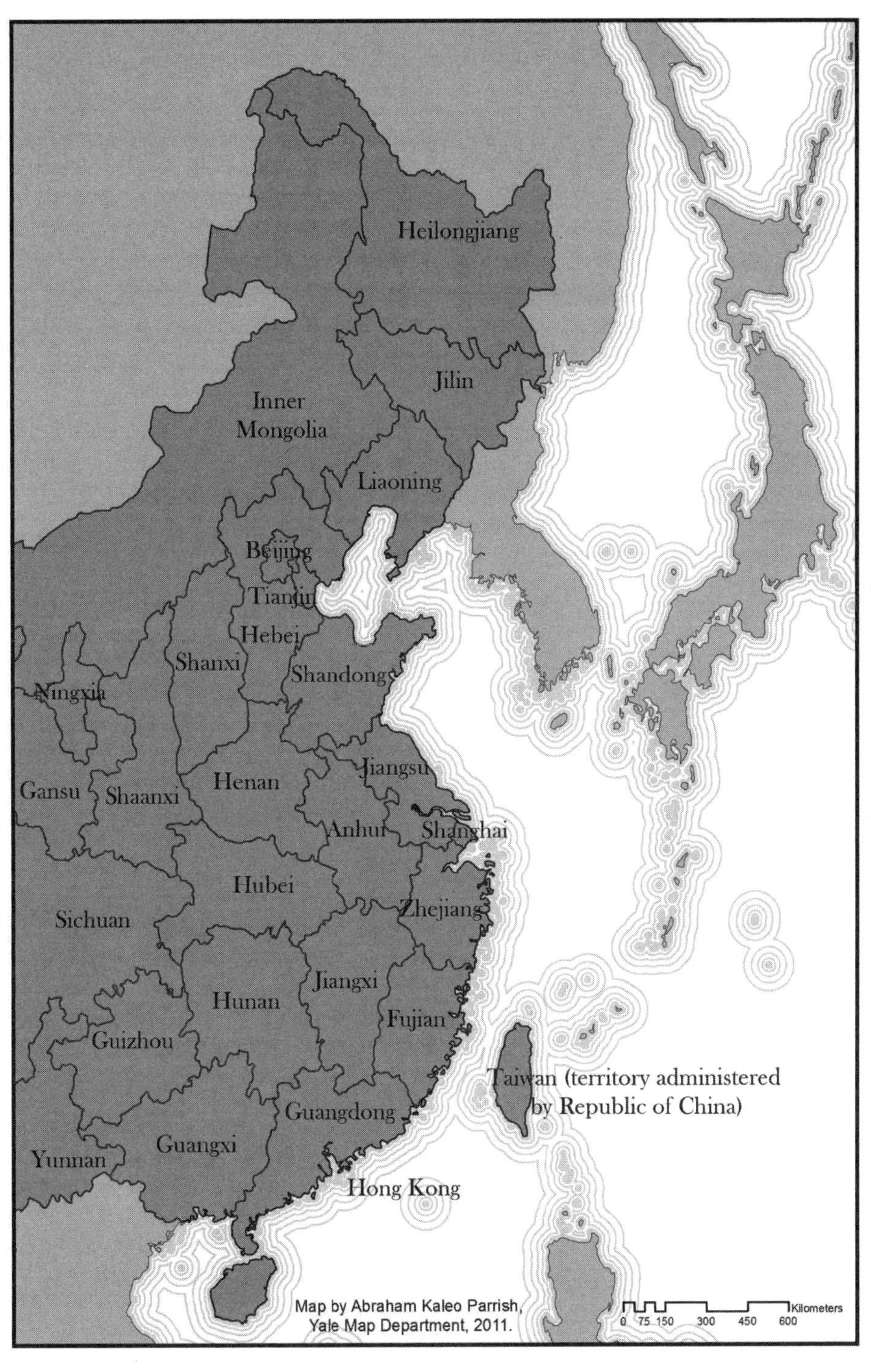
Heilongjiang
Jilin
Inner
Mongolia
Liaoning
Beijing
Tianjin
Hebei
Shanxi
Shandong
Ningxia
Jiangsu
Gansu
Shaanxi
Henan
Anhui
Shanghai
Hubei
Sichuan
Zhejiang
Jiangxi
Hunan
Fujian
Guizhou
Taiwan (territory administered
by Republic of China)
Guangdong
Guangxi
Yunnan
Hong Kong
Map by Abraham Kaleo Parrish,
Yale Map Department, 2011.
0 75 150 300 450 600
Kilometers

Introduction

I was born at the height of the Cultural Revolution, one of the most violent periods in modern Chinese history. My mother gave birth to me while bullets were flying around outside the hospital window. At night my family slept under the bed to avoid being shot by machine guns.

My mother told me that during her pregnancy she craved some green chilies, but the shops were empty and no street vendors were allowed. After I was born, my grandmother paid an extremely high price on the black market to secure some eggs for my mother so that she would be able to produce enough milk to feed me.

When I was a child, my family had very little. I never starved, but food was something very precious. Everything was rationed in those days, including salt. Our daily diet at the time consisted mainly of stale corn imported from Cuba. It tasted sour and disgusting. I used to detest mealtimes. For me the height of luxury was cooked rice mixed with a lump of lard, soy sauce, and MSG. While trying her best to indulge my craving for rice and lard, my grandmother also scolded me for not understanding what real hardship was about. She used to tell me stories from the time of the Great Famine, how one of my great aunts died of starvation because her grandson had stolen all her food rations, how my uncles used to fight over a bowl of watery porridge, and how my youngest aunt always screamed for the biggest bowl. She did get the biggest bowl, but the amount of food in it did not increase.

In September 1976, Mao died. Very quickly, things started to change. My home province of Sichuan, in southwestern China, was one of the first to release land to individual farmers. By the end of the 1970s Sichuan recovered its reputation as the "Land of Abundance." Food, once again, became plentiful. By the time I left China in 1988, the problem was no longer food scarcity, but the amount of waste. Lard, the luxury food of my childhood, is now perceived to be harmful to one's health.

After I left China, I found a new home in London. Yet despite all the years, my childhood experience in China has never left me. Today, however, returning to China leaves me feeling like a stranger. It seems that the China I grew up in is gone forever. Just as most of the old buildings have been torn down, so too the past has quickly been erased. What is presented in the state museums corresponds little to what I experienced and heard as a child. As a historian of modern China, I feel a strong urge to record the past experiences and memories of those who are still alive before they too pass on and it is too late.

I decided to begin with my family. In spring 2006 I accompanied my eighty-year-old grandmother on a visit to her home village in northern Sichuan. By the time we reached the nearest shanty town, the road had disappeared. The only way into the village is up a hill, and just a small muddy path led the way. "Oh, dear me, still the same, still so poor," my grandmother sighed. In the end I left my grandmother sitting in the teahouse at the bottom of the slope, and I climbed up to the village barefoot. Nestling inside a beautiful bamboo grove, the village felt tranquil and timeless. What a huge contrast to the fast-changing life in Chinese cities.

I talked to a few villagers, and they all seemed content with the very little that they have. "Life is so much better now" they told me, "we no longer have to starve." Then they told me stories of how they used to endure hunger and hardship. "The worst was the three difficult years between 1959 and 1961 when there was a terrible famine, and many people died of starvation." "The three difficult years" is the local expression for the time of the Great Famine under Mao. Listening to their stories, I realized how little I knew about this area of China's recent past, and what a horrendous time it had been.

After I returned to my home city, Chengdu, Sichuan's provincial capital, I visited the provincial archive. I was shocked by what I read there. Between 1958 and 1962, nearly 12 million people in Sichuan—the land of abundance—died of starvation.[1] For the next four weeks I sat in the archive reading secret documents full of horrific details about how people were deliberately starved, tortured, and beaten to death, and how people had resorted to eating human flesh to stay alive.

Over the next four years, I traveled across rural Sichuan, as well as other parts of rural China including Henan, Anhui, Shandong, Hebei, Shaanxi, Jiangsu, Yunnan, Guizhou, Gansu, Guangdong, and Guangxi to interview famine survivors and to try to read as much archival material on the subject as I could. Often, after a few hours listening to people's gruesome accounts of how they survived the famine, and after spending day upon day looking at the archival materials, I fell into silence. I didn't want to talk to anyone about what I had heard and read. I knew that if I did I would break down, and I would never be able to carry on with the project. I struggled. While I engaged with the famine survivors, I also learned to distance myself from their world. In order to keep my calm, and so that I could continue to face conducting more interviews the following day, at night I would read *Laozi* and the *Arabian Nights* to take my mind far away from their tales of the devastating famine. It was a very solitary four years. In order to complete this project, I left London and my friends, and moved to Hong Kong, where I could be closer to mainland China. Fortunately, at the University of Hong Kong I worked closely with Frank Dikötter, and I could talk with him about my research and share some of the burdens, since we have a common interest in this subject.

It was a very difficult few years. Midway through my research, I left my former job in the School of Oriental and African Studies to relocate to Hong Kong University. Then there were my parents. They lived through the most turbulent years under Mao, and my father's parents were purged and died because they were born to landlords' families and had worked for the former Nationalist government. Quite understandably my parents did not want me to touch such a sensitive topic. But the biggest obstacle was trying to get access to the archival material. Since the Great Famine is still a taboo subject in China, all material on the topic is deemed "sensitive." The courage of those who survived the famine gave me the strength to carry on with the project. Through perseverance over the years I was able to piece together many of the "official" accounts from contemporary documents rarely, if ever, seen before. By painstaking work in small and large archives throughout China I was able to gather a fuller story of the famine. A cross-section of these documents has been published as *The Great Famine in China, 1958–1962: A Documentary History* by Yale University Press in 2012.

This has also been the most blessed four years in my life. On many of those long and lonely journeys into rural China, I was helped by countless strangers. A number of people gave me rides on their scooters so that I could catch the last bus to the next destination. On one trip to Henan province in central China, one family insisted on feeding me after my interview, and bought me a bus ticket to the train station. On the streets of Beijing I met many migrant workers who willingly took me back to their villages and welcomed me into their homes. Their parents and elders in the village shared with me many heartbroken stories of how the radical collectivization had robbed them of everything; how in order to achieve Mao's Great Leap Forward they were forced to sacrifice their homes, their pots and pans, as well as their lives; how they survived the Great Famine by enduring extreme hardship. To stay alive, they stole, they cheated, they sold their children, they ingested worms, and some even ate human flesh.

The Great Leap Forward (1958–61) was Mao's dream for leading China into a Communist Utopia—"a great, powerful, prosperous and virtuous socialist state, ultimately a Communist society." Like all utopian projects of the twentieth century, it was doomed to fail. It emphasized industrial development at the expense of agriculture, which led to a devastating famine throughout China that lasted more than three years, claiming millions of lives. It also led to mass destruction of agriculture, industry, trade, and every aspect of human life, leaving large parts of the Chinese countryside scarred forever by man-made environmental disasters. To a large extent, the destruction of the Great Leap Forward continues to exercise an influence on everyday life in the countryside to this day.

Traveling through the Chinese countryside, I was often struck by the level of poverty. Fifty years after the famine, the lives of those who survived have improved very little. In 1958, the rural population in China was forced to sacrifice homes and possessions in order to build socialist collectives, but today many survivors of the famine are still left without homes, health care, and sometimes food. It may be hard to believe in today's China that there are still a fair number of people suffering from starvation.

For many living in the remote rural villages, the economic boom of the cities is simply beyond reach. On a number of my trips, the modern highway suddenly disappeared into dust. In particular, my trip to a small village in Luliang county, Yunnan province, in southwestern China, made a deep impression on me. Luliang is about 135 kilometers northeast of the provincial capital Kunming. This is one of China's major tourist routes, served by a brand-new national highway. It took me just two hours by bus from Kunming to Luliang county. The next part of the journey into the village was only 10 kilometers, but it took me over an hour to get there. The narrow road was so bumpy that at one point I thought my heart was going to leap out of my chest. The villages along the way looked poor. A number of old folk sat by the side of the road breathing in the dust while a few minivans passed by. China's modernization has brought these poor villagers nothing except filthy air.

Luliang holds a special place in the history of the Great Famine. Fifty-five years ago, wide-scale famine and death occurred there as a direct result of the Great Leap Forward. At the time, Xie Fuzhi was the Yunnan provincial Party secretary. Before joining the Chinese Communist revolution, Xie had worked as a carpenter. Later on he rose to become one of the top military figures of the Chinese Communist Party, and he was given the task of governing Yunnan in the early '50s. Situated in the far southwest, bordering Tibet, Burma, and Laos, Yunnan was considered one of China's most troublesome frontier provinces. It also had the largest number of ethnic groups. From the beginning of his tenure, Xie introduced extremely tough measures to tackle the widespread problem of opium use and trafficking and to rid the region of bandits. Xie's achievements made him a new star in the Party. After dealing with opium and bandits, Xie decided to address the next challenge: water conservation. Large-scale water conservation projects were an important component of Mao's Great Leap Forward, and Yunnan was at the forefront. In January 1958, under Xie's order, the provincial government engaged 90 percent of the local population to work on water conservation projects. Xie's goal was to fully irrigate more than 10 million hectares of land in Yunnan within one year.

To achieve this, hundreds of thousands of farmers in Yunnan paid a heavy price. They were forced to work for more than ten hours a day, sometimes all night long, at physically exhausting tasks with insufficient food. In February, a major outbreak of severe malnutrition-related edema was reported at Luliang's Xichong reservoir construction site, and a huge number of people died. The local cadre who reported the incident was denounced for undermining the Great Leap Forward. After that no one dared to reveal the truth. The situation quickly worsened. A major famine broke out and the death toll rose sharply. Soon edema and death became widespread in a number of neighboring counties, but anyone who dared to report the problem was purged as a Rightist. By August 15, at the height of the Great Leap Forward, some 169,000 cases of edema had been reported in Luliang and nearby counties, and nearly 24,000 people had died. Many families fled the famine. The crisis could no longer be denied, and on August 29, the provincial government in Yunnan finally admitted that a serious famine had taken hold. But it took more than a month for the news to reach the central government in Beijing, and by then another 20,000 people in Luliang and neighboring counties had been killed by the famine. At the same time 20,000 more also died of starvation in other parts of Yunnan province.

After reading a report of the Luliang incident, Mao wrote simply: "This is a good report. The Yunnan provincial government made a mistake, but they have realized that there was a problem, and they have dealt with the problem correctly. They have learned their lesson, and they will not make the same mistake again. This is a good thing: turning disaster into a blessing." At the same time, the Central Committee of the Communist Party in Beijing issued an order that everyone in the country should consume at least 2,500 calories a day.[2] Both Mao and the Party leadership ignored the crucial fact that there was a major outbreak of famine in the country and that a large number of people were dying. The food for 2,500 calories a day was simply non-existent. Not long after the Luliang incident, Xie Fuzhi was promoted to the post of minister of public security. Some years later Xie played an important role during the Cultural Revolution and was elected an alternate member of the Politburo.

The Luliang incident was the first major episode of mass death during the Great Famine period. However, no alarm was raised and the Great Leap Forward marched on. The famine worsened. During the winter of 1958–59, more and more people began to die throughout the Chinese countryside. By the end of 1959, death by starvation had become commonplace in many rural areas.

Today, although a large proportion of the rural population of Luliang remains poor, according to official announcements the area is now one of Yunnan's most prosperous granaries. "We don't see any of the prosperity, it's all lies," some villagers told me. "The cadres get all the glory and put all the cash and rewards into their own pockets, but we get nothing. Things have not changed much." Riding back on the dusty, bumpy road, the sheer discomfort forced me into agreement.

After my trip to Luliang, I knew that I could no longer remain silent. After spending several years working on this project, collecting nearly a hundred interviews, the time has come for the stories of the famine survivors to be heard. This book gives a voice to the people who lived through the famine. The people who gave these interviews are *lao baixing*, or ordinary folks.[3] The majority of them are illiterate peasants and none of them have had a public voice in the history of the Great Famine, or in the history of Maoist China, or in any kind of history.

The voices presented here come from all over China and represent a wide spectrum of ages, backgrounds, and social positions: from ordinary peasants to former grass-roots cadres. Some are mothers who watched their children die of starvation and could do nothing, others grew up as orphans after having lost their parents. They are not heroes, nor are they saints: many of them stole food in order to survive. They have not led remarkable lives, but it is their ordinary and imperfect life stories, in most cases full of misery and pain, and also their will to survive, that I find compelling.

I searched them out by location, through mutual contacts and by suggestions from others. China is a vast country. It would be impossible for any one person to go to every corner of the land and interview every survivor. I gave priority to Sichuan, Henan, Anhui, Shandong, Gansu, Guizhou, Yunnan, Hunan, and Guangdong: nine provinces that were among the worst hit by the famine. Furthermore, these provinces present a measure of geographical and political diversity. All nine of the provinces underwent similar and yet very diverse experiences during the time of the famine. I tried to make plans before each trip. Sometimes those plans did not work out, but this often paved the way for unexpected opportunities. On one occasion I had arranged to interview an old man in a small market town in western Sichuan, but when I got there his daughters raised objections to the interview. Disappointed, I took a stroll around the town and came across three women vendors. I started chatting with them. I asked them about their experiences during the time of the famine. In the beginning, they hesitated. One woman told me she could not bear to think about those times, that it was simply too painful. But after I stopped asking, they started to talk. The interview lasted two long hours.

I started my interviews with a set of questions, but quickly abandoned them. The more I listened, the more I came to appreciate that each individual survivor had a unique story to tell, and that I need not and should not tell them what to say. During many of the interviews I also noticed that many of the interviewees did not quite get the chronology in the right order or the names quite correctly. The value of these intimate testimonies is that they bring us closer to the everyday reality under communist rule, and offer us a window into what life was really like for a whole range of complex individuals struggling to survive the worst famine in history. They also reveal the coping strategies they adopted and their worldviews.

In recent years there have been a growing number of books and articles on the famine by historians and journalists, inside as well as outside China, who have managed to gain access to various archival collections, including my colleague and collaborator Frank Dikötter's award-winning book *Mao's Great Famine: China's Most Devastating Catastrophe* (2010) and Yang Jisheng's *Tomb Stone* (2012). But *Forgotten Voices* is the first book to give voice to survivors from throughout China, allowing them to reminisce about the horrors of the Great Leap Forward and the famine. Firsthand historical accounts of the life of ordinary people in China either now or in the past are extremely rare. The reasons are simple. Under Mao archival scholarship and oral history were undervalued. In contemporary China official censorship makes the situation even worse. For these reasons, in general terms, the historical literature on modern and contemporary China needs far more primary sources and firsthand accounts. It is the biggest gap in the current literature on China. This work is the product of a pioneering approach to the writing of the history of the People's Republic of China through the use of new oral and archival evidence.

Following the publication of this book, the transcriptions and recordings of the original one hundred interviews will be made available in an oral history digital archive online. This resource will provide readers with the original materials I have collected as well as encourage other researchers to undertake further wide-ranging oral history projects in contemporary China.

The one hundred interviews run to a total of about two hundred hours in length, and the transcripts contain more than four hundred thousand words. Clearly, not all of this has made it into this volume. Some exclusion has been necessary to avoid repetition, and because the book aims to reflect a diversity of experiences.

I have concealed the identities of the people interviewed for this volume in order to protect their privacy and for political considerations. But I have not altered their stories. I have tried to present each individual voice as it really is, without making any judgment on whether their statements were accurate in every way. I believe that these are their stories, and that they should be allowed to tell them as they wish. As with all human stories, they are a more or less truthful way of reflecting the enduring realities of human life.

In the middle of writing this book, I had a terrible road accident, which left me in a coma for two weeks. When I woke up, I was confronted with the challenge of how to survive my trauma physically and emotionally. Lying in a hospital bed, I remembered those survivors of the Great Famine, including my own grandmother.

Their resilience in enduring terrible suffering, degradation, and cruelty, and their courage in telling their stories with great dignity gave me much strength to overcome my personal tragedy. There have been many sleepless nights as I wrote this book. I would be woken by the voices of individual survivors. "There are many things that still disturb me about what happened during those years of the Great Famine, but I shall take most of those things to the grave with me," says one voice. Such statements remind me of the urgency of memorializing the forgotten voices of Mao's Great Famine. Unlike the history of the Holocaust in Europe, in China there is no collective memory, no public monument, no museum, no remembrance day, and no mention of the Great Leap Forward Famine under Mao in any school or history textbook. There are a few people alive today who know about this chapter of China's recent history, but it is important that the past is not forgotten as the survivors of the famine gradually pass away. The world must know about the pain and suffering they endured. Hopefully, their experiences of the past will provide lessons for the future and help to prevent the type of fanaticism that killed millions in China from happening again.

1

The Tragedy of Collectivization

People's Communes are big, and they are public: Lots of people, a vast area of land, large scales of production, [and] all activities are [performed] in a big way. [They] integrate government [administration] with commune [management] to establish collective canteens, eliminating private plots. Chickens, ducks, and young trees in front of, and behind, the houses are still private. This, of course, will not exist in the future. . . . With a surplus of grain we can implement the supply system. . . .

In ten years time commodities will be abundant, the standard of morale will be high. We can start Communism with food, clothing, and housing. With free food in the collective canteen, that's Communism.

—Mao Zedong at Beidaihe Conference, August 19 & 21, 1958

Before the early 1950s, private land ownership formed the basis of agriculture in China. However, the growing population contributed to an escalating land shortage problem, and the lack of land subsequently became directly linked to poverty. In 1943, Mao Zedong, the new supreme head of the Chinese Communist Party (CCP), proclaimed agricultural collectivization as the only way to eliminate rural poverty, and he stipulated that collectivization should be the CCP's long-term goal. In 1949, at the end of the civil war, which had lasted ten years, the

CCP finally defeated the Nationalist Party (KMT) and took control of the entire mainland. Despite its initial victory, the new Communist regime was anxious about the risks of descending back into civil war. Although the KMT had been driven off to the island of Taiwan, it continued to present a threat to CCP rule. Though victorious, the CCP was also haunted by the fissiparous warlord years and the risk of internal insurgencies and breakaway movements. To consolidate their grip on power over such a vast country with many divisions and to prevent any backsliding into Nationalist resistance and a further outbreak of civil war, Mao Zedong and the CCP leadership rushed to develop and implement a new Communist economic and social orthodoxy. To enforce agricultural collectivization in the countryside was part of the process that Mao saw as integral to building a new socialist consciousness among China's mass population.

Despite the bloodshed and catastrophic results that had accompanied the rapid collectivization initiated in the Soviet Union by Joseph Stalin in 1927, Mao was not content with the speed of the initial stage of collectivization in China. He wanted a fully socialist agricultural system established throughout the country, and he wanted it fast. In the summer of 1955, he pushed forward the leftist economic policies of the "Socialist High Tide" in the Chinese countryside to speed up the process of incorporating individual peasant families into agricultural cooperatives. Once it was launched, the campaign of agricultural collectivization swept through the country like a whirlwind. A number of provincial and local cadres embraced it with unprecedented enthusiasm. This became known as the "Little Leap Forward." The pace of agricultural collectivization was astonishing, and it proceeded even faster than Mao had anticipated. By 1956, virtually all agricultural households in rural China had been organized into farming collectives.

The initial success, however, did not satisfy Mao. He wanted an even greater Leap Forward to ensure the Communist writ ran across all aspects of life in the country. He subsequently revived the slogan "More, better, faster, and more economically," and it became the rally call in this campaign to modernize China rapidly. His push to go further forward was also a response to the setback of his leftist economic policy or the "Socialist High Tide." In the latter half of 1956, a number of CCP leaders, including the premier Zhou Enlai, were concerned that collectivization was progressing too fast. They opposed a "blind advance" (*jizao maojin*) and called for a slowdown. This displeased Mao. In June 1957 he launched the Anti-Rightist Campaign and put Deng Xiaoping in charge. The campaign's primary target was the so-called "bourgeois rightists," non-party members who had responded to Mao's call to criticize the Party on all manner of topics but whom he decided had gone too far. More than half a million people were labeled "bourgeois rightists" and were soon disposed of.[1] Thereafter Mao seized the initiative to relaunch the idea of a leap. In January 1958, at a meeting for top Party leaders, Prime Minister Zhou Enlai was pressured by Mao into making a public self-criticism for his part in encouraging "right deviationist conservative thinking," for trying to persuade Mao to halt the earlier version of the Great Leap Forward. Alongside Zhou, a few other leaders were also criticized for the same reason. Any voice opposing collectivization was silenced. Until this point, it had seemed that all the top leaders were working together. A few months later, in spring 1958, the full force of the Great Leap Forward was unleashed, with Mao at its helm.

Another motive behind the Great Leap Forward was the rivalry with the Soviet Union. Referred to as the "Big Brother" by the CCP, the Soviet Union served as not only a model for the new Communist

China, but also the target of its envy. Like Communist leaders elsewhere during the same period, the CCP leaders had always been in psychological thrall to the events in the Soviet Union. The death of Stalin in 1953 created an opportunity for the CCP but also increased uncertainty over Soviet economic aid. Mao saw rapid collectivization as a means to make China self-reliant. On May 17, 1958, two days after the Soviet Union had successfully launched the third Earth satellite *Sputnik 3*, in a speech at the second session of the Eighth Communist Party Congress, Mao told the Party that China should emulate the success of the Soviet Union, and shoot a few "sputniks" into orbit. "Ours must be bigger and heavier [than the one launched by the Soviet Union]. They must not look like the satellite made in the United States. It looked like an egg." In the same speech, Mao also criticized the Stalinist interpretation of orthodox Marxist theory of economic development and boasted that China would overtake the Soviet Union and be the first to achieve true Communism.[2]

People's Communes were officially inaugurated in August 1958 as an essential component of the Great Leap Forward. Mao believed that a socialist system of agriculture, or the People's Commune, would bolster agricultural productivity, stimulate rural markets for industrial products, and divert sufficient workers and funds toward the acceleration of China's industrialization. The policy of "walking on two legs" was launched.[3] In Mao's view revolutionary zeal and cooperative effort would transform the Chinese landscape into a productive paradise. His goal was to overtake the United Kingdom in steel output within fifteen years and turn China into an industrial powerhouse. By then Mao would figure as not only the supreme leader of the CCP, but also the leader of the world Communist movement. By the end of 1958, according to an official estimate, nearly 99 percent of the peasant population had joined a commune.

Approximately 26,000 communes had been set up, with an average of 5,000 households within each one.

The general image projected of 1958 is of the entire country united in rapturous enthusiasm for the Great Leap Forward and that by the end of the year steel, coal, and industrial output had seen a huge boost, even as the production of grain and cotton had also increased considerably. It looked as if the Communist dream was on the verge of becoming a reality in the Chinese countryside. The original goal of fifteen years was cut to five. The reality was very different. For the majority of China's rural population, this was a terrible time. Private possessions were collectivized; household furniture became the property of the communes; pots and pans were smelted to make more steel; individual houses were burned down to make fertilizer. In some areas family graveyards were destroyed to make way for communal farmland, and the bricks from private graveyards were removed to build collective canteens or nurseries. In a frenzy of collectivization, even mothers' sewing needles and children's diapers were confiscated and turned over to the communes.

The radical collectivization in China turned out to be as bloody and violent as it had been in the Soviet Union. Unlike in the Soviet Union, however, where collectivization led to a civil war between the state and the peasants, in China Mao pitted all individuals against one another. He called this "mass struggle," or a "bottom-up" approach, in contrast to the "top-down" approach of the Soviet Union. During the Land Reform and the Campaign to Suppress Counterrevolutionaries in the early 1950s, the CCP leadership urged local cadres to "not fear executing people" and to punish those who were too lenient and practiced peaceful land reform.[4] From the latter half of 1950 the mass class struggle against "feudal" landlords and counterrevolutionaries was rapidly implemented throughout China.

The Korean War (1950–53) and the imagined threat presented by "counterrevolutionaries," such as landlords, was incorporated into the official nationalist discourse. Its deceptive power inspired millions in China to turn extremely violent against these real or imagined foes. As Hannah Arendt famously argued, "The sad truth is that most evil is done by people who never make up their minds to be good or evil." In Communist China during the Land Reform, encouraged by the state, countless individuals became engaged in violence against their next-door neighbors or strangers on the street.[5]

For some, the practice of violence became a habit and they needed no intellectual rationale for their behavior. In Yunnan province's Zhanyi county, seventy people were tortured to death within twenty days during the Land Reform in 1951. One landlord was beaten to death simply because a villager wanted his trousers. In China's southwest, 13,590 people committed suicide by July 1952 in fear of the torture, humiliation, and executions. In Zhejiang province's Zhuangqiao township, one percent of the total population was tortured to death during the Land Reform.[6] In northwest Guizhou province's Wuchuan county, with a predominantly Miao and Gelao population, a seventy-year-old local landlord, Zhang Baoshan, was tortured to death during the Land Reform in 1951. His son Zhang Ren'an was later hanged after his unsuccessful attempt to seek revenge for his father's death. Afterward, some villagers chopped off Zhang Ren'an's tongue and penis, and burned his body. The rest of the family was also arrested and brutally tortured by local cadres and villagers.[7] An estimated 1 to 4 million people were killed during the first years of the regime, and an additional 4 to 6 million were sent to forced labor camps where a huge number eventually died.[8]

A few years later, between 1955 and 1956, during the initial stage of collectivization, poor peasants were once again urged to struggle against "middle" and "rich" peasants, as well as "counterrevolutionaries" who opposed collectivization. Although this phase of collectivization seemingly was relatively easy, it did encounter a huge amount of opposition. Violence was used to whip those unwilling individuals into joining collectives. Many also became victims merely because they happened to be born into the "wrong class." From 1958, during the period of radical collectivization, terror and repression were extended to a much wider population, and the level of violence intensified. Mao conceived of the People's Commune as an environment without legal safeguards, which operated strictly as a military organization. His view was that "We should be a bit rough—it shows we are being truthful."[9] In some parts of the country, this meant that violence could be practiced with little or no restraint. Endless "struggle" meetings also provided opportunities for venting personal revenge and for other selfish pursuits. Local cadres used their positions of power to extract as much benefit for themselves as they could, while punishing anyone they disliked or with whom they disagreed. To survive, peasants fought against peasants under the People's Commune, and in some cases even family members fought one another.

In the pursuit of Mao's utopia, unleashed by totalitarianism, families and homes were destroyed and many lives were sacrificed. Those who survived these tragic years still remember the period with horror, great pain, and a "bitter taste in their mouths."

Marching into Radical Collectivization

Qiu Wenhua lives in a small village in southern Henan's Pingdingshan region, central China. On the eve of radical collectivization Qiu was only nine years old. Henan province, today home to the highest number of serial killers in China, is often said to have been the cradle of Chinese civilization.[10] It had had a predominantly agrarian economy and it found itself at the forefront of radical collectivization in 1958. Qiu recalls:

> In 1959 I was still at school. Every day we had to listen to things like mass production of iron and steel, the Great Leap Forward, and to uphold the "Three Red Flags" [the Party's general line, the Great Leap Forward, and People's Communes]. I had no idea what they meant. Men and women, all the agricultural laborers, were told to go into the river to dig sand because someone said the sand in the river had a high iron content. Only old people and children did not go. There was no one at home to harvest the crops that year. They were left to rot in the field. . . .
>
> At the time we were told that we had entered into Communism, and there would be no more private housing. The day before that happened we were still living in our own house, but the day afterward our house was turned into a granary for the collective. After that we had to move from one place to another on a regular basis. There was no peace in those days.
>
> In our village, there were no other activities except for denunciation meetings. . . . All "rich" and "middle" peasants were denounced. . . . We ate in the collective canteen at the time. Every day before sunset we had to attend denunciation meetings. Only after the meeting were we allowed to have something to eat. People were regularly beaten at those meetings. Sometimes they were forced to kneel on a stool or on coal dregs. No one dared to disobey. In those days even

> if you did nothing wrong, the cadres would still find something to trouble you with. Many people were denounced for nothing.
>
> Life was very bitter for us and for most of the villagers. Only cadres had a better life. They had good food to eat. Ordinary villagers were desperate for something to eat. Even tree leaves were hard to find. . . .
>
> No one dared to oppose it when we were merged into the People's Commune. I remember someone said something like: "The People's Commune is good but the fields are full of weeds." That person was denounced as a "bad element." Afterward no one dared to say anything anymore. We had to follow everyone else and join the commune.

In China's far southwest, Mao Xiansheng lives in a hilly village in Renshou county, south-central Sichuan. Sichuan is another one of China's biggest agrarian economies. During the Great Leap Forward, Sichuan was one of the last places in China to become fully collectivized, but once collectivization took hold, there was no turning back. "Renshou" means "benevolence and longevity," and today the county is known as Sichuan's granary and the home of the sought-after loquat fruits. Yet while interviewing for this book, I visited Renshou several times to speak with survivors, and I found it a rather backward place. Halfway to Mao Xiansheng's village, I had to step out of the bus and walk because there was no bridge over the river. I set out early in the morning, but by the time I reached Mao's village it was after midday, and Mao was having his lunch. When he heard that I had arrived, he put down his bowl of noodles and came out to greet me. His house was rather shabby and dark, but he told me things were a lot worse fifty years ago:

> It was on October 1, 1958, when our area merged into one People's Commune. We were forced to move out from our home and to live communally. Our house was burned down because the commune needed more land to grow crops. Suddenly we had nowhere to live. In the end we moved in with other families, several families crowded into one room. . . . Furthermore, our pans and pots were taken away since we were not allowed to cook at home. At the People's Commune we could only eat at the collective canteen. Everything was collectivized and we had nothing left in the end. . . .
>
> Most collective canteens had over one hundred people. We had food to eat in the very beginning, but soon thereafter the food ran out. . . . In our canteen there were more than three hundred people and there was never enough food to feed all of us. . . . As the food ran out many people were sent away to help develop industry. Only a few less capable persons or those who obeyed the cadres were allowed to stay to do agricultural work. All the rest were sent away because the cadres found them difficult to manage. So in 1958 most crops died. We watched the rice plants die in the field when they were still young, but there was nothing we could do.

Zhu Erge's village in Jianyang county is just north of Mao Xiansheng's. I was told the area had a very high death toll at the time of the famine. Today the place still feels incredibly remote. The rapid modernization in cities seems to have had no effect on the rural tranquil life of Zhu's village, even though it is only about fifty-five kilometers southeast of the provincial capital, Chengdu. From the village bus stop to Zhu's home up in the hills there is only one small, narrow road. The only way to get up there is to walk or ride a motor scooter. With some help I found a man who was willing to give me a ride for a modest fee. On the way I was told that on a rainy day it's impossible to get up to Zhu's home as the road turns into a mud pit. To get out or get back in can be very hazardous. As I listened I looked up to the sky and was very thankful for the fine sunny weather that day. When I finally got to Zhu's house, he and his wife welcomed me with big smiles. When I asked him about the time of collectivization, his smile disappeared. He told me:

> The cadres were real tyrants in those days. They went around houses smashing up everything without any hesitation. . . . Wardrobes and beds were broken into pieces and burned as fuel. . . . At the time, what did our home look like? I tell you something that the Communist Party did: they took away all our pots and pans to make iron and steel . . . and they even destroyed our stove. They went as far as pulling down the four walls of our house in order to make fertilizer. There was no chemical fertilizer at the time. It was thought that old earth had a rich chemical content and therefore made good fertilizer. In our village in those days most houses were built with old earth. They were all pulled down. In the end all of the houses stood empty with nothing left but a few pillars. What could we do? If one of the houses happened to fall down on someone's head, it was just their fate. What did the government care?
>
> In my family eight of us crowded into five rooms, and none of the rooms had any walls. [Laughs] . . . Even our beds were taken away. Ordinary people like us could do nothing about it.

I ran into Chef Yan by accident at a street market not far from Sichuan's provincial capital of Chengdu. He made a delicious lunch for me and my companions. After the meal I went to thank him and started a conversation with him about the Great Famine and collectivization. He told me his home was down south in Sichuan's Ziyang county. He was only a child when radical collectivization was launched at his home village.

> After collectivization we were forced to live communally. . . . My father, I, and my brother lived in one room, and all the women in our family lived in another room. It was in a big house. Apart from us, there were also many families from other brigades. We belonged to No. 5 brigade. No. 7 brigade was high up in the mountains, and conditions were really harsh for them, so they moved down to stay with us. Some landlords, rich farmers, and all those who did not boast a good family background were forced to live with us too. They all crowded into our farming brigade.
>
> Our own house was torn down. Villagers were ordered to pull down houses at night, and then the wood was used as fuel. Nothing was left. Our house had no floors, nothing. Everything was removed. The only things we could take with us were our clothes, our bedding, and the mosquito nets. We put everything into a trunk, and took the trunk with us, but the rest we left behind.
>
> My father was such an obedient man. I only ever heard him saying that this was the government policy. He told me that "we will have a canteen soon, and we will have to live together with others. We must move out of our home, as it will soon be pulled down. We will be moving into a big

> house with others." That's what he told us. [Before that] he had been asked to attend a meeting regarding the matter.

A year after my interview with Yan, an anthropologist friend of mine introduced me to Li Anyuan, a quiet man from a small village in Langzhong county, northern Sichuan. My visit was in April. Li's village was surrounded by fields of beautiful yellow rapeseed flowers. I was told this is one of the most prosperous villages in Langzhong, as it is close to the main road. Li's dark old wooden house, covered in dirt and straw, looked very messy. There was no sign of prosperity here. Li, dressed in a dark blue Mao suit, was friendly but cautious. Watching me being attacked by mosquitoes, he felt sympathy for me. This sympathy led to trust. As he helped me to fan away the mosquitoes, he told me how in 1958 he and his fellow villagers were simply told to join the commune. It was compulsory, and they were not given any choice.

> Join the commune? It was the Party policy to join the commune. At a meeting, the cadres made a public announcement informing us that we were to form a collective canteen. Each brigade had to build a public stove. They took tables from each family to kit out the canteen. We had to eat together. People who lived far away were relocated in order to be closer to the canteen. They had to move in with other families. . . . However, the landlords and rich peasants could not join the collective—they had to find their own food. But how could they find any food, when they no longer had any land? . . .
>
> The canteen collected food from individual families. I did nothing to oppose it—I had to do whatever the cadres above

me told me to do. . . . My family was classified as "middle" peasants. People like us had food at home. When we had our land we could harvest between five hundred and two thousand kilograms of rice a year. During collectivization, all our food was taken away by the canteen—that was the policy. We were not even allowed to cook at home. The cadres sent people to destroy our stove and took away our wok. There was no way to continue living a normal domestic life.

Besides our food, our land was also taken away. . . . Under the commune, everything belonged to the collective. Pigs were also taken away from individual families and were regarded as common property. In those days everything belonged to the collective—we hardly owned anything for ourselves.

Individuals who kept barns containing pigs and oxen saw these buildings torn down during the Great Leap Forward. Even people's houses were demolished and the building materials were used to make fire torches. These were needed so that people could continue working through the night. There was no other firewood to burn in those days, so people's houses looked as good a bet as any. Anything that could be burned was used to light the fire.

As soon as the grain was harvested, we handed it over to the government. Any food we grew was immediately collected by the government. We used to work all night long harvesting grain, but the next day it was loaded onto a truck and taken away. It was sent away to pay off the country's debts—debts to the Soviet Union, or that's what we were told.

We were not permitted to grow any vegetables ourselves. In those days if we were caught selling two eggs, we would be accused of taking the capitalist's path. No one dared to do any business or to make any money.

Farther south from Langzhong, in a small village in Chongzhou county, just north of Chengdu, I visited Jiang Shunliang, a middle-aged man with strong hands and a handsome face. Jiang was only five years old when radical collectivization came into force, but he remembers his parents' frustration and confusion on the eve of the event.

> It was in the second half of 1958 when the collective canteen was introduced in our village. The canteen was opposite our house. In the beginning each brigade had one small canteen with about eighty people. Not long after, all small canteens were merged into a big one. More than one thousand people ate at the big canteen. . . . Life was very harsh and bitter in those days. An adult laborer was only given three hundred grams of rice to eat after working all day. . . .
>
> [At the time] I was still very young. I was at primary school and I did not understand what was going on. . . . Even my parents had no idea what was going on or what was happening to our society. They were only peasants. They did not understand what Communism was all about. Suddenly our house was emptied out, the walls were torn down, and private possessions were taken away. My family had some antique wooden furniture with beautiful carvings. They were my mother's dowry. These were all taken away and smashed into pieces to feed the furnace. I don't know what my parents thought at the time, but I guess there was nothing they could do—it was the government policy. No one dared to ask why. In those days every family used copper bowls to wash their

> faces. These were also taken away and used to make iron and steel. Iron and steel were being smelted everywhere throughout the countryside.

As the train took me eastward to Hunan in central China, I heard much the same story from the survivors there. In Junshan, by the shore of beautiful Dongting Lake in northern Hunan, I met Wang Deming at a bilharzia clinic, and he was sitting on the bed in a crowded ward. Local people call bilharzia (also known as schistosomiasis) "snail fever." This water-borne infection can cause lifelong debilitation. Wang told me that a huge number of people in his village are suffering from this deadly disease, and the collectivization in 1958 was partly to blame.

> Collectivization began in the 1950s. It must have been in '56 or '57. In 1958 all the collectives were merged into the advanced People's Commune. Everything was collectivized. Individual houses were pulled down. . . . We were tasked to pull down houses every day. I had to do it. In those days I had to do whatever the cadres told me to. If I dared to disobey their order, I would be beaten up. Some people were even beaten to death.
>
> Those of us whose houses were not pulled down lost the right to live in our own home. Our home was given to two different families in our brigade, and we were forced to move in with the Ye family. There was no logic to the way families were moved around. Everything was very haphazard in those days.
>
> The order to pull down houses came from above. They told us the cement from old houses can be turned into good

> fertilizer. Overnight all the houses were pulled down. The cement was thrown into the pond to make compost. We could no longer drink the water. Since there was no well or other water source, those who did drink the water got infected with bilharzia. . . . Since we had no money and there was no food to eat, I went into the lake to pull up some lotus roots, and to fish for fish and shrimp. That's how I got bilharzia.

From Hunan I moved south to Guangxi province. Chen Xiansheng was born into a merchant family in the beautiful city of Guilin. After collectivization the family lost its entire fortune. Gradually his family moved to Hong Kong to start over again.

> I was born into a family of merchants who owned a pharmaceutical factory in Guangxi. In 1956 the factory was taken over by the government. In 1958, during the time of the Great Leap Forward, all of our other private possessions were also collectivized. The iron door of our shop was taken away and fed into the furnaces to make steel. Even the iron chairs in our house and the stools in our garden were taken away as scrap metal to make steel. . . . They went around every house searching for metal items. Besides doors, chairs, pots and pans, they even took away metal locks. The locks were smashed into pieces and smelted. Radical collectivization was as bad as religious fanaticism.
>
> I was in a school in Nanning at the time. There was no classroom. We had to carry our own stools to a temple each day. The temple was converted into classrooms. It was the same story all over Nanning. In our school backyard we built furnaces for making iron and steel.

> We were taught many lies in the school. In 1958, lies spread like the wind all across China. The news and all our books were full of false claims—big, empty claims. I was in Grade 5 at the time. I remember that our textbook had a story of a model farmer, Zhang Qiuxiang. In Zhang Qiuxiang's village there were two acres of corn fields. Drought was a big threat to the crops. Every day Zhang walked two kilometers to a small river to collect water to irrigate the fields back in his village. According to the book he carried two hundred buckets of water each day. The corn fields were saved, and he became a model farmer. I was only a Grade 5 student at the time. I told my teacher Zhang that the story couldn't be right. I said to him: "Our math teacher, Mr. Ye, taught us that a person could only walk five kilometers per hour at most. To carry back two hundred buckets of water would take a person four hundred single trips. Each return trip adds up to four kilometers. Two hundred return trips equals eight hundred kilometers. How is that possible?" Teacher Zhang smiled wryly. He said to me: "What's written in the book is fiction."

Xushui in northern China's Hebei province is a flat little county with nothing much to see. Today more than 100,000 workers from its agricultural population have deserted their home villages and emigrated elsewhere to seek a better fortune. I came here because at the time of radical collectivization Xushui boasted of having produced China's first "sputnik field." In October 1957 the Soviet Union successfully launched the first earth-orbiting artificial satellite, *Sputnik 1*. This was seen as a great victory for the socialist camp. As the Great Leap Forward came into full force, Mao pushed to launch "agricultural sputniks" in the Chinese countryside. In April 1958,

China's first People's Commune, Chayashan, in central Henan, was born. It was called the "Sputnik Commune." In August that year, Xushui county in Hebei province was reported to have produced China's first "sputnik field." Following Mao's command and Xushui's model, "sputnik fields" were set up throughout rural China. "To shoot sputniks" became an expression for achieving astronomical agricultural gains and steel production figures. On my visit to Xushui I could not see any traces of the "sputnik field" but I found a little museum in memory of Mao's visit to Xushui in August 1958. At the time Xushui was a small county of 300,000 people, but Mao as well as other top leaders in China were deeply impressed by the speed of collectivization here. Mao wanted Xushui to be the inspiration for the entire country. In September 1958, according to the *People's Daily*, the official voice of the Communist Party, Communism was becoming a reality in Xushui. To enter into the Communist promise, however, entailed Lao Tian's family and their fellow villagers living on nothing.

> I don't remember much about what happened in 1958 except that my first child was born that year and we began to eat at the collective canteen. The collective canteen lasted for three years. Sorry, I was wrong: my first child was not born in 1958. He was born when the collective canteen ended. I was still single in 1958 and I lived with my parents. . . . My parents were in their sixties and they had to do farming work in the field. Those who did not work had no food to eat. Only those who were seriously sick were allowed to rest. Very young children who could not work were sent to the collective child care center. The food was never enough at the canteen. We were usually offered a bun or two with a

> bowl of water. At most we got to eat five hundred grams of food a day. That's not enough for an adult laborer who has been working all day in the field. I remember we licked the bowl inside out every time when we finishing eating. The buns were made of a mixture of corn and bark. Only very occasionally we got buns made of corn only.
>
> . . .
>
> We could not even live a normal life in those days. To make iron and steel the cadres confiscated all metal tools from every household. I remember that they didn't allow my mother to keep even one sewing needle. For years we had no needles to use for repairing our clothes. There was only one sewing needle going around between several families, and we were always in a long queue to borrow that needle. . . . One other thing is that many villagers were even deprived of the chance to go home at night. Most of the time we had to work at night, so we slept in the fields or by the furnace. Only occasionally were we allowed to go home.

My trip to Luliang county in Yunnan province in the southwest of China was memorable. This was a "pioneer" county at the time of the radical collectivization, but there is nothing romantic about this backward little rural county today. Standing in the middle of a road, watching geese and ducks crossing alongside a hand-pulled two-wheel cart, it felt as if I had been brought back more than a century ago. In 1958, Luliang was one of the first areas in China where massive famine and death by starvation occurred. Zhu Daye, a villager from Luliang's Aishipu village, is now in his eighties. His hearing and sight are deteriorating, but he still has a clear memory of the day when the People's Commune was formed in the area.

> With the People's Commune, it was not just a case of private land becoming communal—even the chili was removed from individual homes and handed over to the collective canteen. If we wanted to have something to eat, we had to sneak into the canteen to steal. . . . On the day when the commune was formally inaugurated, all individual families handed over their food. They left it on the public ground. But by the evening, all the food had disappeared. The cadres had divided the food up and taken it to their homes. Everyone knew about it, but no one dared to say anything. . . . Many houses, especially mud houses built fifty years ago, were pulled down to make fertilizer. Villagers were given a small room as a temporary shelter. . . . Besides food and housing, all the domestic animals were also collectivized. . . . In those days every village was allocated a food collection quota. If one village had not enough food, the village cadres would go to another village to try to collect some food there to make up the amount.
>
> Occasionally they encountered resistance; a number of old ladies refused to hand any food over. Cadres were under a lot of pressure in those days. If they could not meet the government quota, they'd be punished. So they often lied.

In other parts of the country, such as Langzhong county in northern Sichuan, even dead souls were not allowed to rest in peace for the sake of collectivization. Villager Wei Dexu from the northern Sichuan hills remembers that at the time he was sent to work on a special project.

> One thing we had to do in 1958 was to "flatten graves and turn them into farming land." Usually graves were built

> to look like little hills. We were ordered to destroy them at night, and to turn them into farming land. We then planted mulberry trees over the top of them. . . . You see, in those days burial was regarded as an old custom, and it was not allowed to be continued.
>
> . . . At the time, life was really difficult. Ordinary people were not allowed to cook at home, and they had to eat at the collective canteen. I don't know where the order came from, but anyway we were not allowed to light our own stoves. Cadres came to our kitchen and blocked our chimney. The chimney was the only thing that belonged to us in those days. The rest, including the courtyard, was all public. Even the walls belonged to the collective.

With radical collectivization people not only lost their homes and private possessions, normal family life was also destroyed, as in Hebei province's Xushui county, where villagers were not allowed to go home to rest. In northern Hunan, Wang Deming, the bilharzia sufferer, says the level of disruption was much the same in his village of Junshan:

> In 1958 we were merged into the People's Commune. We were forced to live and eat together. We also ate together from one pot. A prime laborer like me only managed to eat 200 grams of food at each meal. Sometimes we got even less than that, 150 grams or 100 grams per meal. Even then the canteen manager had no qualms about stealing the food from right under our noses. When that happened, we ate next to nothing. Life was incredibly difficult in those days, but still we had to carry on working as usual. The work

> tended to be very tough, with both men and women sharing the same amount of hard work. Our workloads were very heavy in those days. Men and women had to live separately. Women were sent to transport earth for building the dike. Even grandmothers were made to work. Often women had to bring children with them to work. Even in the winter months we had to carry on building dikes and the canal. Those were very tough days.
>
> At the commune we were divided into brigades, which were the basic working units. In 1958 the commune opened a union factory. Individual carpenters, iron makers, and tailors were merged into the union factory. After the autumn harvest of 1958, the strongest men were also sent away to work in the factory. In the factory men were instructed to come up with technical innovations, and to develop needle-roller bearing technology. A whole lot of nonsense!

Fifty years later, the situation has not improved much for Wang. Along with many of the farmers in the area, he has been suffering from the parasitic disease bilharzia. Although China declared the successful "control" of the disease through the elimination of the snails that carried it in the late 1950s, in reality the extensive Great Leap irrigation projects only compounded the problem. The resulting illness is chronic. It can damage the sufferer's internal organs and even lead to death. Wang is now bed-bound, and he receives little help from the government. Life is difficult for him and his family.

South of Junshan, in Hengyang in central Hunan—the home region of Mao Zedong and Peng Dehuai—Wang Wenchun, an ex-soldier who was severely disabled in the Korean War in the early

1950s, recalls that the situation was not any better in his village under radical collectivization.

> In the People's Commune, everything was collectivized. This was known as "equalitarianism and indiscriminate transfer of resources." Even people were collectivized. Farmers from over here were transferred to another village; farmers from that village were transferred over here. Families lived apart as husbands were sent away to work elsewhere. . . . It was in 1958, the movement for mass production of iron and steel began. Villagers were sent to different places. Women stayed at home to carry on the farming work, but men were sent away to support industrial work. I was sent to a Youth Farm at the time. It was far away. . . . In those days we had to follow the order. . . . When we were told to leave, we had to. The People's Commune determined what we did and how we lived. No one dared to disobey. If we did we'd be beaten up and deprived of food.

West of Hunan in a small village in Sichuan province's Peng county, Pan Zhenghui was an enthusiastic "Great Leap Forward Worker" at the beginning of radical collectivization. Now, in her eighties and enjoying a good life with plenty of Mahjong and cigarettes, she has no feeling of nostalgia for the period.

> When I think about collectivization, I feel very angry. We worked together as a collective, but in the end there was no food to eat and nothing to wear. . . .
>
> When the Great Leap Forward started, I was sent away to work in Ya'an.[11] I was recruited by the government to be a

"Great Leap Forward Worker." Why? In those days, factories needed workers, and peasants in the countryside were sent to support the factories. I had a child who was just a few months old at the time, but I left him at home and went to Ya'an by myself. The child subsequently died [Laughing]. I was young. I just let things go. I don't think I cared very much. In those days, young people like me cared for neither our elders nor our children. We did everything we were told to do. We were full of revolutionary zeal. That's how it was.

As a "Great Leap Forward Worker" in Ya'an, I worked seven days and seven nights without leaving the furnace. When I could not carry on any longer, I put some Tiger Balm on my temples. When my eyes started to close, I even rubbed Tiger Balm into my eyes. But I still dozed off. For a whole week I did not leave the furnace. Even when I felt like I was ready to drop, I had to keep going. There was no other choice.

. . . I worked very hard in those days. I am not an articulate person, but as long as I took the lead by working hard, I didn't have to worry about words. . . .

I joined the Party when I became a "Great Leap Forward Worker." But in 1961, while I was living in Ya'an, I received a telegram from home to say that my mother had a tumor growing in her stomach. It was a big tumor, weighing about six kilograms. She was due to have an operation at the hospital in Chengdu. I asked for leave, but it was turned down. The refusal made me very angry. My heart was very troubled. But I tried once more, and this time they gave me leave for fifteen days. After I had returned home, I decided to stay at home. My husband advised me to return [to Ya'an] but I told him: "No, I am not going back there!" Because I

> ran away from my duties, I lost my Party membership—I was accused of betraying the Party.
>
> Later on I was invited to rejoin the Party, but I refused. I told them: "Oh no, I have already betrayed the Party, I am not going to rejoin it." [Laughing] "I have forsaken my privilege."

Having destroyed normal family life, the People's Commune was reorganized as a military organization. In some areas such communes were run in a system similar to that of a Gulag.[12] Militarization was seen by Mao as a vital aspect of life in the People's Commune. "Arm the militia and assemble them into big collectives," he said at a Party conference on August 17, 1958; "in six years time every fourth person in the country should have a gun, one billion guns in total. Everybody will be given ten bullets, and everyone must fire all of the bullets."[13] Xushui county in Hebei province under the Party leadership of Zhang Guozhong, a ruthless military man, was the first in the country to turn every farmer into an armed militiaman. Lao Li, a healthy-looking canteen worker in his seventies, was still in his teens at the time. He remembers the time clearly:

> I have never had any schooling. Not even one day of schooling! During the Great Leap Forward period I worked in the fields, every day and every night. After finishing agricultural work in the fields, at night we were called out to produce steel.
>
> I also joined the local militia. I felt great about it because I learned to play with guns. You know, we peasants had never had any toys in our entire life! In the militia, although we were not given bullets, we were allowed to take the guns

> anywhere we liked, and that made us feel ever so proud and handsome!
>
> I had a lot of fun as a militia member. I was invited to many meetings and was treated as someone important. But I have to say those meetings were very boring and exhausting. Usually they were held late at night when others had gone to bed. One of our duties was to punish landlords and rich peasants. We told them to shut up. I think it did them a lot of good to keep their mouth shut. In those days people who spoke too much often got themselves into trouble, especially those labeled "bad elements."

With the chairman being the prime advocate, farmers throughout the country were quickly organized into battalions and platoons. In the southwest, in Sichuan province's Renshou county, Mao Xiansheng and his fellow villagers were reorganized into military units.

> The commune was run like an army—we even wore uniforms. Every night we had to guard the crops, and during the day we studied military theories. Our village belonged to Zhangjia district. But after the People's Commune, Zhangjia district was dissolved and reorganized into a battalion. . . . At the time I was appointed as the head of a squad and my duty was to guard the crops.
>
> Militarization was Chairman Mao's idea. Every morning the cadres had to get up early to exercise. Farmers carried diggers and marched around. That was called militarization. We were organized into companies, platoons, and squads. I was a platoon leader. A platoon had about thirty people. It

> did not last long. After 1959, we were reorganized again, and the military units were dissolved.

Next to Sichuan is the frontier province Yunnan. At the time Yunnan's Party secretary was Xie Fuzhi, a man well known for his tough measures to outlaw opium and control bandits in the early 1950s, after the Communists took over the region.[14] Under him villagers were treated no better than opium criminals and bandits. Zhu Daye from Luliang county recalls the harsh military regime in the People's Commune.

> The People's Commune was run like an army. I was a carpenter at the time. I had to go to work where the cadres told me to go. If anyone dared to disobey orders, he'd be interrogated by the commune at nighttime. We lived and worked like an army with very strict discipline. We had to work day and night without a break. If we wanted to take a rest, we had to ask for permission. If anyone failed to turn up to work, they were deprived of food. On our way to work every day, the cadres stood by with a bamboo cane in their hand. If anyone was slow in walking, they would use the bamboo to beat that person. In our village about 90 percent of the people were beaten.
>
> . . .
>
> The cadres had the power to accuse people of anything and to arrest people for no good reason, while they themselves enjoyed tremendous privileges. They could eat as much food as they wanted in the canteen. No one dared to say anything. I remember that during those years no family produced any new babies except for the families of cadres,

> because there was no food to eat. Villagers were regularly beaten or scolded because they were caught stealing food. It was different for the cadres. The head of our brigade could go to the canteen to eat anytime and anything as he pleased.

Far from Luliang, I visited Wang Daye in Puxi, a small town located in Jimo county in the southwest of the Shandong peninsula bordering the Yellow Sea. He was a village cadre at the People's Commune. Jimo is a relatively wealthy area in eastern China, rich in natural resources. For generations the local farmers were sustained by the fertile agricultural land and the nearby sea. But this all changed with radical collectivization in 1958, as Wang Daye told me:

> In 1958, the two natural villages here were forced to merge into one People's Commune, and we all had to eat in the collective canteen. Everyone except the elderly was sent to work up on the hill. We slept in a temporary shelter made of dried sorghum stalks. It was huge, everyone slept in it. . . . The People's Commune was like a military organization—anyone who refused to follow orders would be punished. People were regularly deprived of food.
>
> Food, animals, and seeds all belonged to the commune. There was no proper system of distribution. If one brigade had no food to eat, they took food from another brigade, since everything belonged to the commune. No one wanted to do any work in those days, because there was no incentive. Even if you worked hard, you wouldn't necessarily receive anything for your efforts. By the end of the year nothing was harvested, and yet there were always so many things to do. We often had to work day and night.

> The political situation was very tense in 1958. America imposed an embargo on us. Chairman Mao said we had to be self-reliant, and we had to produce huge quantities of iron and steel. Houses were pulled down, and wooden items were fed into furnaces. Pots and pans were smelted to make iron, but in the end the iron we produced was useless and had to be thrown away.
>
> By 1960, the situation had become really bad over here. There were about four hundred families in our two natural villages, and more than two hundred people had died. That's 10 percent of the total population. The bigger the village the more deaths occurred.

The People's Commune Was No Bridge to Communism

As in Jimo, elsewhere in China the People's Commune was far from the Communist paradise depicted by Mao and the official propaganda at the time. While most of these communes were certainly big and public, as Mao had envisaged, not everyone was treated equally, and peasants were regularly exploited. Farmers sweated day and night, but their hard labor was in vain. The planned economy and collective farming proved a total failure, leading to disastrous results. Under the commune, brutality and starvation were the two most common experiences of a majority of the peasants.

Deng Xiansheng was eighteen when radical collectivization took hold in his hometown of Dongguan in Guangdong province, just across the border from Hong Kong. The locals spoke Cantonese, but this had to change with collectivization. All had to learn Mandarin. In 1962, Deng joined the mass exodus and escaped to Hong Kong, where he now lives.

> In 1958 the People's Commune was established. . . . I was just a young man, an ordinary farmer. I knew nothing about Party politics. . . . One thing that happened in the commune was the eradication of illiteracy. Everyone had to study Mandarin. Even old grandmothers had to learn to read and write. At their age, how much could they take in? The more they were forced to learn, the more confused they became. . . .
>
> Before the commune, grain was distributed to individual families, and half of it was used to feed the pigs and the chickens. Almost every family kept pigs at that time. By the time of the commune, however, since everyone had to eat in the collective canteen, there was no food left at home. The pigs became so thin that there was hardly any flesh left on their bones. I never ate any pork during those years.

Back in Sichuan province in southwestern China, Pan Zhenghui, the woman from a small village in Peng county who lost her membership in the Party because she wanted to visit her terminally ill mother, introduced me to her neighbor Lei Huazhen. Lei is a handsome woman and unusually tall for an inhabitant of Sichuan. She had nothing good to say about the People's Commune and collective farming.

> When collective farming was imposed in 1955, all private land was confiscated and became common property. We were divided into farming brigades and each brigade contained several families. We worked together, but individual families were allowed to keep the food that they grew. A few years later, in 1958, the collective canteen was introduced,

and the People's Commune was established. The situation deteriorated.

At the commune, we ate together. There were nearly a hundred families eating in the collective canteen. We all moved to live together in one big courtyard. We worked collectively, lived collectively, and ate collectively.

Our daily task was to "make fertilizer by burning the soil." We dug up perfectly good soil and put it into boxes. We then moved those boxes on to one plot of land. We were told to set fire to some grass in a little hole and pile up all the boxes with soil on top. After we had burned the soil, we spread it evenly and smoothly all over the field. It was such hard work, so exhausting. I really don't know whose idea it was.

Besides "burning soil," we were also told to "kick the soil loose." In those days the soil in the field often came in big chunks. After an ox had plowed the field, we had the task of kicking the big pieces of soil with our feet so that they broke into smaller chunks and became loose. In the big collective, there were always plenty of jobs, one after another, all day long, and day after day.

After we had worked through the day, we still had work to do at night, at least until midnight. There were days we had to work all day and all night, especially during the harvest season.

Farther south, in Sichuan's Jianyang county, Zhu Erge recalls how collective farming led to nothing but lies in his village.

At the time everyone was told that they had to take part in the Great Leap Forward. Over here we joined the big

> collective. It was called the "Sputnik Commune." People had to work together and eat together. In those days, hardly anyone did much farming. . . . The majority of the farming land was deserted. There were only a few crops by the roadside. . . . "Roadside farming" was a mere ruse for fooling the government investigation teams. The government sometimes sent officials into rural areas to make inspections, so the local farmers would put on a show to dupe them. Even by the roadside, only the patch of land closest to the road had crops growing on it. . . . [Laughs] However, it was reported that several thousand kilograms of wheat and five thousand kilograms of sweet potatoes had been harvested. The higher the figures, the better, but of course the numbers were exaggerated.
>
> The order for collectivization came from above . . . just like the orders do now. The government issued official orders, and these were passed down to the provinces. The provincial government then passed the orders further down to the grassroots levels. At the bottom, all we could do was follow the orders—no one dared to resist. Even if people didn't like the orders, what could they do? In those days, no one dared to challenge the officials. No one dared to resist even when the cadres knocked down our walls to make fertilizer. . . . The cadres were so fearsome. For instance, one day some four or five year olds in our village went and picked some peas in the fields, and they got caught. The local cadres tied them up and threw them down into a dried-up old well in order to frighten them. . . .

Wang Shiyong from Shehong in northern Sichuan was fourteen when radical collectivization was launched in his home county; he too says the People's Commune and collective farming were disastrous.

> The People's Commune sounded like a good idea, but in reality life was very hard. People were starving in those days. The policy was extreme left. The "Wind of Exaggeration" was out of control. Production figures were inflated five times or even more. It was lies such as these that caused the problems. Production figures were invariably high, and yet peasants in the countryside were suffering terribly. The amount of food being produced did not match the figures being reported. As a result, peasants had to work day and night. During the night shift, people cheated. When the cadres came, everyone started working, but when they left everyone stopped straight away and would go and rest. Even when there was no work to be done, no one was allowed to get any sleep. After a while, people began to get ill. No work was getting done, and no one had any strength left to do any work. Day by day things got worse and worse. By the end of the year little food was harvested, and there wasn't enough to go around.
>
> I remember that in our farming brigade some cadres tried to pocket the peasants' food rations. Every time the food came in, the cadres always took away some for themselves. The head of our farming brigade and the storekeeper in particular pocketed most of the food. In the end ordinary peasants like us only managed to drink watery congee from the canteen. The soup was mostly water, and our stomachs would quickly swell up like balloons, but just a short while later we would become hungry again. There was nothing we

> could do. All we could do was to try to survive on water and vegetable soup. Many people became ill. Edema was very common. . . . A few people died of starvation. I was still young, and I never tried to find out what was going on. To be honest, how could I have understood?

Wei Dexu, the man who was sent to flatten graves during the radical collectivization, is now his mid-eighties. He lives high up in the mountains in Tufangshan village, Langzhong county, in northern Sichuan. In the 1930s this was a "Soviet base" for the Communist Red Army, and one of the first places in China to complete the "Land Reform." But the Communist Liberation brought little benefit to the locals. Today the village has only one post office, which also serves as a bank. Because it is so high up and so rural, it is badly served by transportation. The general population of the area is extremely poor. A majority of the villagers have barely any spare clothes to change into, and can only just about get enough to eat. Although life is not great for Wei and his fellow villagers, he still thinks it's a lot better than it was under radical collectivization.

> I was in my forties at the time. The work was very hard. We had to work at night, and our work was in the mountains, so we had to carry fire torches with us. The night shift usually lasted for several hours, and we couldn't go home until we were told to. If we left early, the cadres would cut down our food portions. [Laughing]
>
> People were forced to work day and night, but still hardly any crops were produced. The problem was that even though everyone went out to work, most of the time they weren't really working. In fact they did as little work as possible.

Even after meals and tea breaks they kept on resting. If officials came to inspect, everyone had to work at night, and it was only then that people really worked hard. How can you expect things to improve when the situation looks like that? That year we produced nothing except a few silk worms.

At the time, life was really difficult. Ordinary people were not allowed to cook at home, and they had to eat at the collective canteen. I don't know where the order came from, but anyway we were not allowed to light our own stoves. . . .

Life in the collective canteen, oh dear me, it was terrible. As for the food, I can barely mention it. . . . Most of the time all we got to eat was a bowl of sweet potato leaves. That's all. I don't know how I managed to survive all those dreadful years. . . . Oh I can hardly bear to talk about it. Corruption was fairly common in those days. The serving spoon could "read" people's faces.[15] The government ration should have been divided by the number of people, but the cooks in the canteen often pocketed the food. Each mealtime, the canteen rang a bell, and as soon as it sounded we started queuing up for our food. We lined up like ducks in one straight line, one after another—that's how we received our food portions. Those who had good relationships with the cook received more solid food. When it was his or her turn to be served, the cook would use the spoon to give the pot a good stir, whereas the rest of us would only be served a spoonful of watery stuff. It was a kind of greenish liquid, and it was basically undrinkable. The green color came from the wild vegetables it was cooked with. We also ate noodles made out of hemp plants. Normally we used hemp to make rope. To make noodles, we would cut the roots of the plant into long silvers. We also ate the bark of the parasol and loquat trees.

That was the situation, and it lasted for several years. People died of edema. I watched them die. In our area there were over twenty people who died of starvation. It was terrible. Their legs completely swelled up. Looking back now, I can safely say that if the canteen had lasted another two years the disaster caused would have been unimaginable.

In Li Anyuan's village, which is about forty kilometers down the mountain from Wei Dexu's, the situation in the commune was just as appalling.

In the commune things were pretty awful. Misconduct among local cadres happened all the time. Day and night we were forced to grow vegetables, or to gather fertilizer. Even in the middle of the night, we had to work. Lots of the things that we did turned out to be a complete waste of time. For instance, we were told to dig up perfectly good soil and pile it up over a net. We would then light a fire to smoke out the soil. We were told that this was how to make fertilizer. Every night the local cadres shouted at us to get us to go to work. If we did not go, they would not give us any food to eat. A number of people were deprived of food.

At the time there was the so-called "Wind of Exaggeration." Local cadres talked up the amount of food being produced. In reality there was never as much food as they claimed. In those days, it was cadres' job to exaggerate the amount. How could they become a cadre otherwise? Exaggeration was the general trend of the time. From the commune to the county,

> the "Wind of Exaggeration" was blowing apace. How could those cadres at the grassroots level do otherwise?
>
> Some local cadres were selfish, and they regularly abused their power. For instance, the storekeeper used to pocket food before it ever reached us. When it came to serving food in the canteen, those who wielded the serving spoon got up to all kinds of tricks, so the cadres always ended up with double portions. The cooks always served themselves more solid food. Some people complained about things like that, but what could ordinary people achieve by complaining? You might be worse off the next time. They might only give you water the next meal because of your complaint.

Down south in Sichuan's Jianyang county, Zhang Ershu was only thirteen at the time, but the harsh life in the commune left a deep impression on him.

> In the countryside the situation was dismal at that time. If you said something to upset the brigade head, he'd denounce you immediately. In those days the cadres punished people by whipping them with bamboo sticks. They also broke tiles into small pieces, and forced people to kneel on them. There was no black or white situation—everything was at the mercy of the cadres. I remember that once our brigade killed some ducks, and the head of the brigade asked us children to pluck the duck feathers. Some of the children pulled out the ducks' tongues, cooked them up, and ate them. Because of that their whole family was punished and deprived of food.
>
> In those days we ate at the canteen. Every day we received four hundred grams of wheat porridge . . . but after the

> canteen manager had helped himself to what he fancied, there was usually next to nothing left for ordinary farmers. The porridge was mostly water, occasionally with a few cabbage leaves. When it spilled onto the floor, the liquid would soak right through. Even the dogs didn't bother to lick it up.

Although Zhang Ershu was originally from Jianyang, he now lives in the deep mountains of Liangshan, bordering Yunnan and Sichuan in China's far southwestern corner. Travel into Liangshan was difficult. The overnight train took me only to Xichang, a town famous for its beautiful Qionghai Lake and for being China's satellite launching center. From Xichang I embarked on a six-hour bus journey to Heizhu in the mountains. The bus set out at six in the morning in bright sunshine, but halfway into the mountains we ran into a snowstorm. The bus stopped. Eventually I managed to persuade a truck driver to take me, promising in return that I would buy him the most expensive cigarettes we could find in Zhaojue, the little town next to Heizhu. When we finally got to Zhaojue, it was already in the afternoon. A local primary school teacher met me and took me to her father's little shop, where I met Zhang Ershu and Hushu. Like Zhang Ershu, Hushu was also a migrant to Liangshan. His home village was in Wangyang in Sichuan's Renshou county, now a relatively rich fruit basket for the region. Although life in Wangyang appears to be much more comfortable than in the deep mountains of Liangshan, Hushu says that after radical collectivization he could never face returning to his hometown.

> In our rural countryside life was incredibly tough in those days. We were treated worse than animals. At the time we

> were called out to work every day, but they fed us very little food. Day and night we had to work in order to achieve the targets set by the Great Leap Forward. Eight hours of hard work were not enough in those days. We continued working into the night by holding torches. . . . People's houses were pulled down and burned as fuel to feed the furnaces. They were forced to live on the street or in the fields. That's the Great Leap Forward. . . . There was no food to eat. Ninety-five percent of villagers got edema. You could see people drop dead while walking.
>
> . . .
>
> I was seventeen or eighteen at the time, and I was still in school. Watching families break up and people dying, I decided to quit the school. I joined the army and came to Liangshan. We were sent here to suppress the [Yi] uprising.[16] The uprising in Liangshan started in 1957. [After it was put down, Liangshan was turned into the Yi Autonomous Region.] I have been living in Liangshan ever since. It's been more than fifty years. See what happened to me in the end? My retirement salary is only 750 yuan [the yuan is the primary unit of Renminbi, or Chinese currency] per month. I fought for the Communist Party with blood and sweat in those days, but what did I get in the end? Nothing!

While Hushu says his life under radical collectivization was worse than that of animals, Zhang Yeye from a small village in Lushan county, not far from Qiu Wenhua's mentioned earlier, in southern Henan, compared radical collectivization to slavery. The day I visited Zhang Yeye, it was snowing. I was badly dressed for the cold weather, and there was no heat in the house. As I shivered through the entire interview, Zhang Yeye smoked tobacco to keep himself warm. The tobacco he was smoking was so harsh it made me wonder whether I'd die from the smoke first or the cold. Two years later, when I visited Zhang's village again, I was told Zhang Yeye had passed away from lung cancer. The news depressed me. After I got back I played my interview with him over and over again. His words depressed me even more.

> After we merged into the big People's Commune, our situation changed completely. . . . From the day we joined the commune, it was like going back to slavery again. Why do I call it slavery? Because in the commune we lost all our freedom. We had no individual liberties whatsoever. The cadres were like slave owners. If they did not want you to live, you would not live. . . .
>
> What kind of society was that? Even if I wanted to have a haircut, I had to go to the head of the farming brigade to ask for a haircut coupon. . . .
>
> We had to work all the time. Even when it snowed, the cadres told us that government officials were coming to make inspections and that we had to take off our clothes to work. That was in the winter, when it was snowing. But they still forced us to take off our clothes because of the government inspections. Isn't that slavery? If you refused to take off your clothes, they would scold you and call you names in order to humiliate you.

Huang Mama, a short but tough looking woman from a small village just west of Chengdu in Sichuan, recalls that the cadres in her village too were real tyrants.

> At the collective canteen, the cadres shouted at people, and they also knocked people around. People with a strong mind often got bashed up. The cadres used to beat people up if they did something wrong, but they also beat people up if they simply didn't like them. Once the storekeeper in our commune attacked his stepmother in public because he claimed she wasn't his real mother. He yelled at her and ordered her to stand in front of everyone during the mealtime. Then he started to hit her. His stepmother was a handsome woman—tall and strong. After he humiliated her in public, she went home and took some poison. First she swallowed some matchsticks, but that didn't kill her. In the end she hung herself inside a well. Her tongue was hanging out. It was an awful spectacle to behold.

More Failed Promises

According to Mao, in the People's Commune there would be no more poverty and there would be free meals, clothes, shelter, and health care for all. But for most peasant families this was certainly not true. Li Anyuan, the villager from northern Sichuan's Langzhong county, who lives in a wooden house covered in dirt, told me that his family was classified as "middle" peasants in the early 1950s after the Land Reform. Initially they managed to make a reasonable living with the few acres of land they owned, but during radical collectivization they lost their land and anything else they owned. Their life was to change.

> What I dared to think in those days? Everything was so strict then that even if I had thoughts there was no way

that I would dare to oppose government policy. No one dared to oppose it. I did feel that life was not as good as it had been. That much was obvious. Anyone with any sense could feel that life was not quite right at the time. I resented it a little. Of course I resented it, everyone did. But what could I do? If my children died of starvation, I had to let it go, there was nothing I could do. Some people whinged a little. There was no food to eat so of course people were not pleased, of course people complained. But the majority of people just waited to die. What else could one do? Anyone caught opposing the government would not be allowed to live.

. . .

After collectivization, life became very difficult for my family. My wife was in very poor health, so we suffered from a shortage of labor. I was the chief laborer in my family. I did all kinds of heavy duty, from the early morning until the sky turned pitch black at night. How long could one go on like that? All that work, but for a full day's toil I only earned myself a few work points. Every year we ended up owing debts to the collective. They kept an account, and if we couldn't pay back all the debts within one year, then we had to pay them back the year after. It all added up, year after year. It took my family six or seven years to pay back the debts we owed. Every year the farming brigade deducted our annual food ration against the amount that we owed. My family always ran out of food, and my children were constantly crying out in hunger. But I had to leave them to cry. In those days even if they died of starvation, no one was too concerned. After all, who could care for them?

Farther up in the mountains, Barber Feng's village, badly serviced by transportation, is much poorer than Li Anyuan's. Fifty years after collectivization, the Fengs still live in very miserable conditions. The day when I interviewed him, he tried to dress up for the occasion, but he did not have a clean jacket to change into. A bowl of plain noodles was the best he could get to fill his stomach. His children are working in towns and cities, but the money they make is used to pay off the debts the family owed to the commune years ago.

> When the collective canteen first started, every family was instructed to hand in all the food they had, but my family did not have any food to contribute. We had less than ten kilograms of food at home, so we didn't turn it in. We did not get away with this. At mealtimes, when we should have received two bowls of food, we would only get one.
>
> If we turned up in the canteen a little late, they'd refuse to give us any food at all. If we didn't go to work, they'd deduct our portion of food. At the time, food was served in bowls, and my family was supposed to get two bowls every mealtime, but sometimes they refused to give us even one bowl. They said that as we had not worked, there would be no food for us. The hardship we endured at the time is indescribable.
>
> During the time of the Great Leap Forward, I was the barber for the collective. I cut hair for the villagers, and the collective took in the money that I made—all of it. The bookkeeper for the collective was responsible for collecting the money. . . . I was the only barber in this area. . . . I traveled around from village to village, and cut hair for farmers. . . . When I was traveling, I ate with villagers but I had to pay for the food that I ate myself. Occasionally someone took

pity on me and fed me for free. Sometimes, sensing the difficulty that I was in, they gave me food to take home for my family as well.

At the time we were given food according to the work points we earned. There were nine of us in my family, most of whom were children and elderly people. Two members of the family suffered from poor health. They could not work, so the entire family depended on me. Nine mouths looked to me only. . . . Life was so difficult at the time, it's hard for me to describe.

Since then we have been consistently in debt to the commune. We have had to pay back our debts every year, year after year.

We were completely penniless at that time, so much so that we could barely clothe ourselves. The clothes that we wore were indescribable. If I tell people now, they'd laugh at me. We wore the sackcloth that was used to make mosquito nets. It was very thick. We had no money for soap, so we never cleaned the fabric.

There was no place for us to live either. Nine of us, we lived in one big straw shed, which was terribly run down. The roof was full of holes, and we couldn't afford to buy straw to patch it up. We didn't even have a table. When it rained, the water just poured in. We would have to put on our straw hats and rain capes.

In the end I made a request to the village head. I told him that as my children were growing up, washing and pissing had become a problem for us, so I asked him if it would be possible for us to build a toilet. He refused. Later I built an extension myself in secret.

Cadres told us that the hardship we suffered was all because of the number of children that we had. At the time however, there was no contraception. If we gave birth to a child, we had to bring him or her up. We could not kill the child. One of my children died of hunger during the famine. He was only a baby. There was just no food—the canteen manager wouldn't give us any. He said that there were too many of us, and that we didn't do enough work. . . . My wife had no milk to feed him. Without milk and food, how could we keep the child alive? So he died.

When my oldest son [was old enough] to work, the person in charge of recording the work points deliberately mistreated him: if he did six points worth of work, he was given only four points. The head of our farming brigade was the type of person that Mao once warned us about: a "crook"—a "political crook." He cheated his way to becoming the head of our brigade, and then he gave his brother the task of recording work points. Anyone who didn't have a good relationship with him would be mistreated by his brother: he'd deliberately miscalculate that person's work points.

The head of the brigade, the political crook, took everything into his own hands. He was heartless. If we had any money of our own, he would take it away from us. What's more, the bookkeeper was the crook's running dog. He used to accuse me of not turning in the money I earned for cutting hair. The money was taken by the collective, and I received nothing, but he insisted that I give him several thousand yuan.

Party members? In those days, there were only a few good Party members; the rest were dreadful. If you let them eat

> your food, they might stop making trouble for you, and let you off the hook. If you had no food to offer them, they'd look for all kinds of reasons to harass you. They'd take apart whatever you said. That's what Party members were like in the rural countryside. They were only concerned about how to get food into their mouths. They only cared about themselves. Nowadays, Party members are even worse.

Another promise was that the People's Commune would relieve women from heavy domestic duties so they could enjoy more freedom outside their homes. But for many women radical collectivization actually produced the opposite result. I met Bai Daniang in a small market town just west of Chengdu, in the southwest of China. It was a sunny morning when I came across her sitting against a wall and petting rabbits in a basket. Her face was creased by life's hardship. When I asked her about life in the People's Commune, for a moment she looked at me in silence, and then she began to speak:

> In those days, we ate three meals a day at the collective canteen. We had to run as fast as we could to make sure we got something to eat. If you were slow you got nothing. Let me tell you, people like me who had children, we had to go home to get the kids dressed first, so by the time I arrived at the canteen, the staff had already put the lid back on the big pot, and they refused to serve any more food. They would tell me off, saying, "Why don't you come earlier?"
>
> I had to go to work very early in the morning before I could get back home to get the children dressed, so how could I get there any earlier? They refused to give me even old cabbage, or just carrot leaves. So I starved until

lunchtime. How desperate! You see how tough my life was? At the time, my children were all sent to different places: one was in kindergarten, one was at school, and the other was in a preschool class. Each of those places had a separate collective canteen, so in my family we were assigned to four different canteens. By the time I had taken my children to their separate canteens, I couldn't get anything to eat for myself. Normally I only managed to eat one meal a day.

At the canteen children only got one spoonful of food for each meal. Adults like us were supposed to receive two spoonfuls of food, but it was mostly liquid with old cabbage in it. Occasionally there might be some sweet potatoes, but the cadres and canteen staff had usually eaten those for themselves the previous night. People like us who had to work in the fields had the worst deal of anyone. In fact, it was us peasants who dug up the sweet potatoes from the field and brought them to the canteen, but in the end, we were lucky to get any of it, while the cadres and canteen staff ate their fill. In the evenings, cadres from the big production brigade often cooked the sweet potatoes up in a wok and filled their stomachs to their hearts' content. The next day, only a little would be left for ordinary farmers like me. Those who ran very fast might get to eat two pieces, but the portions were tiny anyway. Normally our bowls were filled with nothing but liquid. You see how miserable life was then, but we could do nothing except to endure the misery.

Lei Huazhen, the tall and handsome looking woman I came across in the same village where Pan Zhenghui lived in Sichuan province's

Peng county, was also a young mother at the time of radical collectivization. She says life was very tough for her as a mother:

> [In the People's Commune] we worked day and night. We never managed to go home to rest before midnight. During harvest season we didn't get any rest at all. After working all day, we had to harvest grain all night long. I had to leave my children at home. The older ones looked after the younger ones. [At the time I was breast feeding my son], and every day at lunchtime I ran home to feed him. Once I finished the feeding, I had to put the baby down and run to work. When I went home after work, his nappy was always wet. . . . I had to learn to be reckless in those days. I suffered terrible back pain because of the hard work. Life was terrible in those days.

Su Wanyi is a sixty-five-year-old woman living in a small village in Pengxi county, northern Sichuan. She is a simple illiterate peasant woman who attributes all the bad things that have happened to her to "fate." Su's former husband was a Party cadre for the village. He abused his power and chased after young women in the village, leaving Su to look after their children and do all the hard work for the family. Su received no help from the commune.

> My life has been very hard. My husband had an affair with someone else in the town, so he left me. I was left at this home on my own. . . . There was hardly any food to eat in those days. Even when I was pregnant I could not get anything more than a handful of rice plus some vegetables to eat. . . .

> During the Great Leap Forward, life became worse. Because I stayed at home to look after the children, they deducted my work points. In the end I had to walk a long way from here to another village to work. It was dreadful. I worked all day long, seeding, plowing the fields or growing vegetables. After work all day, I had to look after my children. There was nothing to eat in those days except for some sweet potatoes. The canteen served mostly sweet potatoes.
>
> . . .
>
> My whole life is full of hardship. After all the children had grown up and formed their own families, my unfaithful husband came back [because he was dying of cancer]. His mother was still alive then. No one in his family called a doctor for him. He died in less than a hundred days. I was left on my own. I cried for many days. I don't know why I cried. I should have been relieved after his death. He left me not long after our marriage.

Contesting

Not everyone meekly followed orders or subsided to fate. People contested collectivization in different ways, sometimes with clever tactics, sometimes by simply arguing with local cadres. Chan Daoching and Qiaoer's families came from entirely different backgrounds. Chan's family was from a coastal village in Fujian province's Fuqing county, southern China, where all the families had overseas connections; Qiaoer's was from a rural mountain village in Shandong province in eastern China. Both families refused to comply with the orders under the People's Commune. I first became interested in Fuqing because while living in London I constantly met undocumented illegal immigrants from there. These people told me that migrating for a better life has a long history in Fuqing. Like many villagers, Chan Daoching left his native village with his wife and children in 1976 to seek a better life elsewhere. Today they live comfortably in Hong Kong. He says that although radical collectivization took place relatively earlier in Fuqing, many villagers did not simply follow the order as elsewhere.

> When my father died I was only five. My uncle in Indonesia promised to look after me and my mother so that my mother would not have to remarry. As a widow, my mother felt powerless in the family. My uncle in Indonesia wrote the local cadre a letter and sent him valuable gifts, saying that we had bought our land through remittances from overseas, not by exploiting peasants. My other uncle's eldest son then married a powerful local cadre's daughter by offering the family an imported bicycle and a sewing machine sent from my uncle in Indonesia. These gifts kept my family out of political trouble.
>
> Many people contributed their metal utensils to the collective furnaces, but I refused. I had a good excuse—I said that my uncle in Indonesia would be angry if I did not keep our metal utensils for him. In my school many students came from families with an overseas connection, and they all used the same excuse. In the end the school had to purchase raw iron material elsewhere.

Although Qiaoer's family in a mountainous village in eastern Shandong province had no overseas connection or any goods to bribe the local cadres, they did not simply give way to them.

> After we joined the commune, anything with iron in it was taken away and used to make steel and iron. Each family was left with just a wok. We were so poor at the time—we had no furniture, and just a wok and a few tools. My parents argued with the cadres because our livelihood depended on the few things that we owned. We needed the agricultural tools to do farming work—we needed diggers when we went out to dig the wild herbs. We relied on all those tools, but still they took them away from us. It was not possible to keep anything.

A Pipe Dream

I met Liushu in a small shop in Wengong district, Renshou county in south-central Sichuan. He is an upright man who uses words sparingly. After a few exchanges, he told me he is a local cadre, and he supported the Communist Party most of his adult life. When I asked him what he remembers of the radical collectivization, he says it's a "pipe dream."

> At the time, we were told that the speed of change was too slow, and that in order to achieve Communist goals more quickly, China needed a Great Leap Forward. . . . In 1958 the whole country took part in the Great Leap Forward, and the People's Communes were formed. Individual farmers were required to join the commune. [We were told] that "today we establish socialism, and tomorrow we wake up in Communism." That was the situation. I remember how over here in Wengong, about ten thousand people gathered together for a meeting. We were listening to a speech by Li

Jingquan, who was the Party secretary of Sichuan province at the time. Li was already in his fifties then, and his voice was crackling, and he coughed a lot. In the speech he told us to establish the People's Commune and collective canteens.

In order to build the People's Commune and the collective canteen, individual possessions were collectivized, including cooking utensils and bowls. . . . The situation was hopeless. The [Great Leap] policy was a failure that in turn affected productivity. That was under Mao Zedong's leadership. According to the policy, we should all have become prosperous together. But how could everyone have become prosperous at the same time? . . . It was not possible in practice. It was nothing but a pipe dream, without any hint of practicality about it.

2

Endless Campaigns and Political Pressures

> In the transition from capitalism to socialism, there are still anti-socialist elements hiding among the people, e.g. the bourgeois rightists. With regard to the problems of these people, our solutions are essentially the "bloom-contend" type of mass debate. Suppression applies only to serious counterrevolutionary saboteurs. When the transition is over and classes are eliminated, the politics of a country become purely a matter of internal relationship among the people. Even then, ideological and political struggles between men and revolutions will continue to occur; they will never cease. The laws of unification of contradictions, of quantitative to qualitative changes and of affirmation and negation will hold good universally and eternally.
>
> *—Mao Zedong, "Sixty Points on Working Methods," February* 2, 1958

Mass political campaigns were the predominant feature of Mao's reign. During the Great Leap Forward, endless campaigns were part of everyday life for China's rural, as well as urban, population.

In the autumn of 1957, following the Socialist Education Campaign for China's rural population and the Anti-Rightist Campaign in government work units, state-owned factories, the army, as well as cultural and educational institutions, Mao launched the Great Leap Forward. This brought further collectivization initiatives to the countryside and resulted in existing farming collectives merging into gigantic People's Communes, with an average of five thousand households per commune. Peasant farmers were mobilized to build Mao's grand water conservation projects, to construct backyard furnaces that were intended to boost China's steel production, and to "shoot sputniks" from the fields. The Pull Down the White Flag and Hoist the Red Flag Campaign was first launched in the People's Communes in August 1958 as a means of driving the peasant population to work harder and longer for their country. Those who followed the Party line and the orders given by the cadres were praised for their "socialist thinking" and were rewarded with red flags. Those who questioned the unrealistic production figures or indeed questioned anything at all were classified as having "unhealthy" ideas. They were denounced at public meetings and given a white flag, or in some local areas a gray or black one. In more severe cases people deemed to have "unhealthy" ideas were deprived of food and physically tortured.

At the end of 1958, as the reality of crop failure and widespread famine came more and more into conflict with Mao's vision of abundance, he began to put pressure on the local cadres. In February 1959, at a meeting for top Party leaders, Mao indicated his belief that the food shortages had been caused not by crop failure, but rather by peasants hiding grain. He maintained that the real cause for this was corruption at the local level, so he gave orders for the launch of the Rectify the Commune Campaign throughout the countryside.

Unable to meet the government quotas, the cadres at the provincial level turned on those at the next level down. As the old Chinese saying puts it: "The big fish eats the small fish, the small fish eats the little shrimp, and the little shrimp eats nothing but sand." At the grassroots level, the local cadres turned on powerless villagers. In Guangdong, in southern China, the provincial Party secretary, Tao Zhu, decided to begin his attack in Dongguan, one of Guangdong's "sputnik counties," by launching the Anti-Hiding Campaign.

Dongguan is geographically situated next to Hong Kong, which was then a British colony. The campaign ended in vain. After much searching and looting, Tao and his team found that the only things being cooked in the peasants' miserable pots were wild herbs. Despite Tao Zhu's initial failure to find any hidden grain, the Anti-Hiding Campaign developed into a series of nationwide crusades.

In the far southwest of China, known as "the land of abundance," the Sichuan provincial Party boss Li Jingquan was eager to please Chairman Mao Zedong. During the rigorous Anti-Hiding Campaigns, he continued to receive praise from top leaders such as Mao and Deng Xiaoping for Sichuan's generous provision of grain to the rest of the country, just as millions of Sichuanese people were dying of starvation or were being beaten to death. In the early spring of 1959, a serious food crisis hit Sichuan's countryside, but even this did not stop Li Jingquan from launching the Balance the Books Campaign throughout rural Sichuan. To "Balance the Books" was to match the ever-inflated grain production figures and to reach the higher and higher procurement quotas.

As violence permeated down through the bureaucratic structure, it became more extreme at each lower level, from the county to the communes, and then to the production brigades. On the ground, to "Rectify the Commune" was often interpreted as to loot the peasants' houses, and to rob them of the very last reserves of food they had, if any. If no grain was found, in some places peasants were punished with torture or with food deprivation.

When the Great Leap was propelled further forward after the Lushan plenum in late July and early August 1959, Party-engineered mass campaigns such as "Anti-Right Deviationism" turned into physical beating frenzies that spread across many parts of the country.[1] Anyone trying to speak the truth was denounced for "right deviationism." To make up for the forged production figures and the ever increasing procurement quotas, local cadres forced already enfeebled peasants not only to hand over their very last kernels of grain but also to work day and night in scorching summer and freezing winter on empty stomachs. Anyone who did not follow orders was punished. Many were beaten, and many were deliberately starved to death.

Famine worsened in the countryside, and eventually took more than 40 million lives. Meanwhile, in the People's Communes, about 3 million were tortured to death, and many more were killed through the deliberate withholding of food.

1958: "The Year of No Abundance"

The general image of 1958 was that it was the "year of abundance." But as I began research for this book, I quickly learned the reality was very different. In August 1958, Mao visited Xushui county in Hebei province, where he was impressed by displays of food everywhere. Zhang Gouzhong, Xushui county's Party secretary at the time, told Mao that too much food had been produced, and he planned to use the extra food to buy robots. Mao smiled but suggested that maybe Zhang should consider letting the peasants feast on five meals a day. The reality in Xushui was, however, quite different. Lao Tian, the villager from Xushui who told me that his mother's sewing needle was collectivized, remembers well what actually happened in anticipation of Mao's visit.

Once, Chairman Mao came to Xushui to inspect the Great Leap Forward. In anticipation of his visit, the county cadres built a two-story building to display our achievements. Later on the building was used as the Museum of the Chairman, but we peasants called it Mao's Temple.

On the day of Mao's visit, I couldn't see him. I only saw a lot of food set out everywhere. But the county cadres warned us: "Don't eat it!" The food was there to show Mao how good our life was.

The "Wind of Exaggeration"

Elsewhere what I heard shocks me even more. Suiping county in Henan province is an unimposing flat little county in central China. It became well known during the Great Leap Forward and in the history of the Great Famine because China's first People's Commune, Chayashan Sputnik Commune, is only twenty kilometers away from Suiping county town. Not only so, Suiping, situated in Xinyang region, was pushed by Lu Xianwen, the Party secretary of Xinyang region, to take the lead in radical collectivization. Harsh campaigns were launched, and villagers' homes were looted till there was no trace of food to be found. Ten out of one hundred villagers in Suiping were starved to death. As I was doing research for this book, I made several attempts to go to the Suiping county archive, but each time I was turned down. I was not even allowed to read the catalogue. Having traveled more than eight hours by train from Beijing and another hour on the local bus, I was determined not to waste the trip. I wandered into a small village in Yicheng district and met Liu Laoshi, a former primary school teacher. After I briefly explained my intention, this friendly old man told me how things began to go wrong right from the outset.

> China's first People's Commune was born in Suiping. In those days, collective farming sounded very inspiring. The People's Commune would be like the Paris Commune—it was a term I only encountered in books. No one had any experience of it. It was something new! To form a commune and to live communally sounded so novel, but there was no economic basis on which to achieve it. Exaggeration was inevitable. In Suiping, the "Wind of Exaggeration" was very prevalent. At the time, Chayashan People's Commune claimed to have produced 3,888 catties of wheat per mu. [One catty is 500 grams, and one mu equals 0.1647 acres, or 666 square meters.] Of course we did not believe it. But even if we didn't believe it we couldn't say anything. In those days, everything had to lean toward the left. No one dared to be accused of being too right. If you uttered anything that could be construed as leaning too much toward the right, you'd be purged.

Jia Daniang lives in the village next to Liu Laoshi's. Now in her eighties, she recalls how ordinary people suffered because of the "Wind of Exaggeration":

> The cadres exaggerated production figures. If they had not exaggerated to such an extent, things would have been better. They lied about the amount of grain being produced, and if we did not lie along with them, they beat us up. They then blamed us peasants for stealing the grain that was being produced. What could we do? There was no wheat growing in the field, so what could we say? They sent the strongest hands to make iron and steel, or to dig canals, so no one was

> left to attend to the fields. Added to that there was no fertilizer, so how could anything grow? In the end they blamed everything on us. They held meetings at night denouncing ordinary farmers. They even beat people up. No one dared to say anything at those meetings. Anyone who spoke up was beaten. Any cadres who did not exaggerate their successes were purged and lost their positions. Some cadres were denounced at public meetings for telling the truth. They were accused for not setting upright examples.

East of Henan is Shandong province. Jimo county in the southwest of the Shandong peninsula was known for its extreme leftist policies during the time of the Great Leap Forward. There the "Wind of Exaggeration" blew fearsomely. When the actual food production figures did not match the projected targets, ordinary peasants were forced to squeeze out every last kernel of grain to account for the made-up figures. I ran into Li Dabai while I was interviewing Wang Daye, the former village cadre from Puxi, who appeared in the previous chapter. Li lost his father in the famine. Now in his late seventies, he was twenty-four years old at the time of radical collectivization.

> The head of Jimo county was extremely left in those days, and the "Wind of Exaggeration" was blowing like crazy. Take our brigade, for example. The cadres exaggerated the amount that was being produced, and forced us to hand over every last grain to account for their claims. In the end there was just nothing left. Not only that, the cadres also forced us to hand over food that had been kept in reserve to support those building the dam. The order for building the

> dam came from above. We were told that building irrigation works would boost productivity. I have no idea whether it helped productivity or not, but anyway we were left with nothing to eat. That was in the winter of 1959, the worst winter ever.

As mentioned before, Wang Daye was a small cadre of the same village at the time. He was subject to his superior, and he told me the Party secretary in his commune was a real hardliner.

> In the commune, the Party secretary was the boss—he was the one who gave the orders. All other cadres in the commune were frightened of him. Anyone who disagreed with what he said was given a white flag. People with white flags were treated like prisoners. They had to carry them with them everywhere they went. Then they were sent to other brigades to be purged. The cadres didn't allow them to stay in their own brigades, because they figured that people in other brigades, not knowing them very well, were less likely to take pity on them.

The "Wind of Exaggeration" was spreading across China. Chishui in Guizhou province is a remote county of China's southwest. Sandwiched between Sichuan and Guizhou, and with the Chishui River running through it, Chishui is strategically and commercially important for the region. In 1935, Mao led the Red Army across the Chishui River four times to escape the assaults of the Nationalist army. The incident made Chishui a Communist "Red base." To maintain its Red legacy, during the Great Leap Forward the local Party head, Wang Linchi, used up all local resources to build grand revolutionary halls and theaters. Wang did not want to be left behind on the production figures either. High up in the mountains, Chishui is famous for its lush bamboo groves, but it has very limited farming land. Under Wang, bamboo forests were destroyed to make way for irrigation pipes and terraced fields. At the same time the farming population was diverted to build Wang's grand projects and to make iron and steel. Jiang Ayi, a retired grandmother in her late seventies, told me that she was working in a government administration department at the time of the Great Leap Forward. Her job required her to go to work in the rural countryside on a regular basis. She tells me what she saw there:

> With the advent of the Great Leap Forward, the People's Communes had grown vastly in size. Sometimes one entire township became one commune. In those days a large number of laborers had been relocated for the purposes of making iron and steel. Our area was very poor in mineral resources, but the government insisted that we must produce iron and steel. In the end it was a waste of time, and agriculture suffered as a result.
>
> In order to meet the government targets, cadres in the countryside had to exaggerate the amount of grain being produced. The competition was fierce between communes and between brigades. For example, one commune reported five thousand kilos of grain per mu, another reported six thousand, and the third reported seventy-five hundred. If any cadres reported less, they'd be in trouble. The honest ones were sent off to be reeducated or to do hard labor. In those days, the armed militia stood by in the fields forcing people to work.
>
> The plot of land that was supposed to have produced five thousand kilos of grains was in fact in Tiantai township, where

I was the administrative head. At the time, the deputy head for Chishui county was Shi Yongsheng. It was Shi who announced the five thousand kilo figure at a county meeting. Afterward Chishui County News called me up and asked me where this plot of land was. Shi had not advised me [in advance], so I had no idea. Later in 1959, during the Anti-Right Deviationism Campaign, I was removed from my position as the administrative head. I was charged with suppressing production figures. They were going to send me back to my home village to attend public study meetings, but I didn't want to go. I knew that in my home village the methods of punishment used were very brutal. Fortunately the policies started to turn at that point and I was very lucky to have escaped that awful fate.

The "Wind of Exaggeration" plus the craze for making iron and steel took up most of the agricultural manpower, and agricultural production suffered very badly as result. Very little food was being produced by the end of 1958. By 1959 and 1960 almost nothing was being produced. In our county more than thirty thousand people died.[2] Some brigades had fewer than a hundred people left in them in the end. Tiantai township was the worst. When I was the administrative head there, I came across incidences of suicide every day [due to the hardships]. Often I could see people collapsing and dying while they were out walking.

Next to Guizhou, in Sichuan province, I learned the situation was just as severe under the provincial Party secretary there, Li Jingquan. In central Sichuan's Renshou county, Mao Xiansheng, the villager mentioned in the previous chapter, tells me that people were regularly beaten up if they did not falsify production figures.

> In those days people could be beaten up simply because their production figures were lower than others. For example, if someone reported one thousand catties of grain being produced per mu, and then someone else reported twelve hundred per mu, the person with the lower figure would be beaten up while the person with the higher figure would be spared. In the end people had to make up the figures. Normally one mu of land could only yield about four hundred to five hundred catties of grain, but the figures would be inflated to up to five hundred kilograms. In order to fulfill the government targets for cotton production, families would have to tear up their winter quilts and take out the cotton. So in winter people would freeze. No one dared to voice any kind of opposition. If the quota was not met, people would be beaten up. Besides physical beatings, cadres would also punish people by forcing them to kneel on a stool or hanging them up. Sometimes cadres even punished people by pulling out their hair. Once I saw someone's hair being pulled right off.

Farther south from Sichuan and Guizhou, in Yunnan province's Luliang county, Zhu Daye too tells me the devastating consequence caused by the "Wind of Exaggeration."

> During the Great Leap Forward period, the "Wind of Exaggeration" was widespread. Take agricultural work for example. Everyone tried to cheat his or her way through in those days. Instead of pulling weeds out by hand, someone came up with the idea of using wooden boards, but that way they killed more young crops than weeds. No one did

much work—people just pretended that they were working. Those who cheated always "finished" their work first, and they would get the red flag. The honest hard-working ones were always the last to finish. Production suffered terribly as a result. There was very little food produced by the end of the year. In 1958, the whole brigade produced only thirty-five thousand kilos of grain—that's not even enough food to feed all the families for the year. And that's the so-called "Great Leap Forward."

Yang Yingpei was the deputy county head in Luliang at the time. At a meeting in the provincial capital Kunming he reported to the provincial government on the food crisis in Luliang. He told them that many people had died of starvation, and that others had fled from the famine. After that he was denounced as a rightist and was removed from his position.

. . .

When government procurement targets were not met, the officials above pressurized the cadres down at the next level. Local cadres were often disciplined if they failed to meet government targets. To avoid getting into trouble, they had to exaggerate the amount that was being produced. The bigger the lie, the more honor they would receive.

Irrigation Projects

In addition to the "Wind of Exaggeration," the endless water conservation projects turned out to be another damaging ordeal. These half-baked undertakings were not only financially costly, but they also took many lives. Zhu Daye and his daughter were sent to help build the Xichong reservoir in Luliang county, one of the failed water conservation projects of the Great Leap Forward. The two of them were lucky to have survived, as thousands lost their lives at the construction site. More than fifty years later, the horror of what happened still haunts Zhu Daye:

> The Xichong reservoir was a Great Leap Forward project. At the time, many people were sent to construct the reservoir, but only those who were formally employed by the project got food provisions there. Many villagers who were sent there informally to provide support had nothing to eat. Their food rations were back at their home village. The work was very hard. People worked from six o'clock in the morning till six o'clock at night. Even on a snowy day, it was just the same. There were no exceptions for sixty-five-year-old grandpas or ten-year-old girls. Many people died at the construction site. I remember someone from our village was so exhausted that he didn't even have the strength left to chew his food. No one took care of him and he died not long afterward.

Like the Xichong reservoir in Luliang, the Banqiao Reservoir Dam in Suiping county, Henan province, in central China, was another famous Great Leap project. Initially built in the early 1950s, the dam was expanded in 1958 after Tan Zhenlin, then the vice premier in charge of agriculture, ordered that dam building should extend into the plains of China. The chief hydrologist for the dam, Chen Xing, opposed Tan's order and warned that it would lead to waterlogging and alkalization of the farmland. Chen was dismissed from his job and purged for "right-deviationism." The expansion project went ahead. In 1961 problems with the dam's water system started to become apparent. In that same year the central China plain suffered severe flooding, waterlogging, and alkalization, damaging more than 750,000 mu of farming land and causing 640 houses to collapse. The problem did not end there. Fourteen years later, in August 1975, an even worse disaster happened: the dam collapsed during heavy rains, killing more than 85,000 people and flooding twenty-nine counties covering more than a million hectares of farming land. The disaster was gradually reported by some environmental activists in China and abroad, but little is known about how many lives were lost at the construction sites between 1958 and 1961, and the hardship endured by the millions of farmers who built it. During my trip to Suiping, I constantly came across villagers telling me the horrors caused by Banqiao Reservoir Dam. Jia Daniang, the elderly woman mentioned earlier, was one of the many workers who toiled at a Banqiao Reservoir Dam construction site.

> I was sent to construct the dam. My responsibility was to transport sand. In the evening we all slept on the cold ground. I couldn't sleep at all. In those days, those who were seen as having done good work were given red flags, and those who were seen as having underperformed got black flags. We all had to work hard to follow the example of those who got red flags. Even when we had no strength left, we still had to work, or otherwise we'd be denounced at the evening meetings, and be given the black flags.

After saying goodbye to Jia Daniang, I ran into two of her fellow villagers, Chen Daniang and Zhang Mama, who also worked on the dam construction site at the time. Chen Daniang recalls what it was like at the construction site:

> I was also sent to dig canals [for the Banqiao Reservoir Dam]. Almost everyone had to do it. You can't imagine how crowded it was—it was like there were "oceans of people." No one was left behind at home to do the farming work. On the construction site we lived in a big tent. It was winter and it was snowing. We had to carry on working even in the snowy conditions. At night the ground was frozen because of the heavy frost. We were given some soup to drink. Afterward we had to carry on working until midnight. We worked from five in the morning until midnight. In the summer we also had to work under the blazing sun.

At this point, Zhang Mama eagerly nodded her head and joined in telling me what happened:

> The construction work was very tough. Every day someone would get sick. We all looked as thin as ghosts. But still we had to carry on working. If anyone stopped working, they would be beaten up. A number of people were beaten to death.
>
> No one died of hunger on the construction site though. They could not let people die of hunger, because they were afraid that the government inspection team would find out. So if anyone became ill, they just sent him or her back to the village. Many people died soon after returning to the village.

While all of this was happening in Suiping, the situation was not any better down south in the neighboring central province of Hubei. At the time, Meng Xiansheng was a student in Wuhan, the provincial capital of Hubei. Wuhan is central China's major industrial city and transport hub through which the mighty River Yangtze runs.

Wang Renzhong was Hubei's Party secretary at the time. In 1956, he accompanied Mao on his swim across the Yangtze, and was yet another ardent supporter of the Great Leap Forward. Wang did not want Hubei, situated next to Henan, to be disgraced by its northern neighbor. In August 1958, a few months after the Chayashan Sputnik Commune claimed that it had achieved a production rate of nearly two thousand kilos of wheat per mu, in Hubei's Macheng "China's Number One Field" was born. Here the production figures went through the roof: Macheng claimed to have produced more than ten thousand kilos of grain per mu of land. Wang Renzhong was overseeing the proceedings. Hubei was taking the lead in the race to the Great Leap. To produce high yields, thousands of irrigation canals had to be constructed. Ordinary farmers in Hubei paid a heavy price for it, as Meng remembers:

> On the way back to Wuhan I decided to visit my mother, who was working on a construction site for irrigation canals. When I passed the construction site, I saw hundreds of male peasants working half naked. It was a bitterly cold winter day so I was really taken aback to see this. I asked one of the peasants why they were working half naked and he told me that the cadres did not allow them to wear anything on their top halves. The logic was that people had to work hard if they didn't want to freeze to death.

Mass Production of Iron and Steel

Another major campaign during the Great Leap Forward was the mass production of iron and steel. Again, millions of farmers worked day and night in the freezing winter and under the blazing sun trying to reach the unrealistic government targets. Many more lives were lost. In southern Henan's Lushan county, local newspapers boasted that Lushan's steel production had reached more than ten thousand tons per day during the month of August 1958, but Qiu Wenhua from Dinglou village, the villager whose home was turned into a collective granary as mentioned in the previous chapter, recounts what happened to him and his fellow villagers in striving to reach this astronomical figure. He was only nine at the time.

> In order to meet the government targets for iron and steel, we worked extremely hard. Both men and women had to contribute toward the production of iron. I went along with others to the Helong River to dig sand [for making iron]. The weather had already turned bitterly cold, but we had to stand in the icy water for our work. By the end of the day our bodies were covered with blisters from the cold.
>
> We were not paid for the work. In those days we ate communally—that was Communism. At each mealtime the commune sent us some food. We worked twenty-four-hour shifts. Some people fell asleep and fell into the river. There were guards watching us. If they didn't like what they saw, they would beat us up. . . . They would tie people's heads to ropes. Then if anyone fell asleep, they'd pull the rope and the skin of the person's head would be ripped off. That's how they stopped people from falling asleep.
>
> A number of people also starved to death while digging the sand. Every meal we got just one sweet potato that weighed about a hundred grams. We had to carry on working even if we were starving.

North of Henan, in Hebei province's Xushui county—Mao's model county for the Great Leap Forward—furnaces could be found everywhere. On my visit there, a number of villagers told me that at the time the whole county looked like a giant iron foundry. I also learned that, to satisfy Mao's expectations, Xushui's local Party head Zhang Guozhong, a former military man, ran the place like a gulag. Peasants worked day and night in an attempt to meet impossible targets. Many died subsequently. Lao Tian, the villager who earlier told me about Mao's visit to Xushui, was still quite young then, but like everyone else in Xushui, he was forced to join the ranks making iron and steel.

> [At the time] no one dared to challenge the authorities. The village cadres told us, "Don't ask any questions! Just do as you are told!" Even if we had understood that the method used could not possibly have produced any iron or steel . . . no one dared to challenge the authorities. I remember that once some county cadres came to our village to inspect the furnaces, which had not been built according to the standard required by the county. They arrested our village Party secretary and put him in prison. After that no one dared to make any comments. Actually, all the leaders were very frustrated. They had no good techniques for producing steel, so they just forced us to work harder. The more frustrated they were, the more pressure they put on us to step up our work.
>
> In those years, starvation was not the only hardship. We were even deprived of sleep. Sometimes we could not sleep for eight or nine days on the trot! It was very inhumane! I felt so tired back then. Sometimes I would fall asleep while I was actually hammering at the iron pieces. I remember on

a winter day I was tending to the furnace at midnight, and I was so tired that I really couldn't hold out any longer. I so desperately wanted to go to sleep. At that moment I couldn't have cared less if I ended up being punished. I said to myself that even if they were to give me the death penalty I really didn't care anymore. So I went into the room next to the furnace, and I saw two people sleeping there already. I didn't know them well but they looked like cadres. I slept next to them. When I woke up I discovered that the two of them were dead! The ventilation in the room was appalling, and the room was heated by burning charcoal. They must have died of suffocation.

Anti-Hiding Campaign

As huge numbers of farmers were diverted into iron and steel production and water conservation projects, only very few women and elderly people were left to do agricultural work. By the end of 1958 hardly any food was produced in the Chinese countryside; acres and acres of fields were left wasted. The news of a country-wide famine began to reach the central government in Beijing. It conflicted with Mao's vision of abundance for the Great Leap Forward. Since the chairman was always right, it was the ordinary farmers who ended up paying the price. By the beginning of 1959 a nationwide Anti-Hiding Campaign was launched in which cadres toured the peasants' homes searching for "hidden grain." Often the grain confiscated from peasants' homes ended up in cadres' or canteen staffs' back kitchen. Anhui in central-eastern China, southeast of Henan and east of Hubei, is another of China's big agricultural provinces. At the time, Anhui was under the Party leadership of Zeng Xisheng, a longtime follower of Mao and ardent supporter of the Great Leap Forward. I met Wang Qibing, an amiable man always wearing a shy smile on his face, at a small village in Chaohu, central Anhui. His house was close to the road, and the gate to his courtyard was wide open on the day of my visit. I walked in and asked whether I could talk to him about what happened during the Great Famine. He invited me to take a seat in his front room. As I was sitting down he asked me: "You mean the time of extreme hardship?"[3] Before I had the chance to nod my head, he went on telling me what happened in his area during the Anti-Hiding Campaign.

> At the evening meetings the cadres tried to trick people by insisting that individual families had being hiding food at home. People got scared, so they reported on each other. The cadres went around searching every home. If they found any grain, they would take it away. . . . At the time everything belonged to the collective, and individual families could not own anything at all. . . . All food was supposed to go to the collective canteen, but often at the canteen food disappeared mysteriously. It was stolen by the canteen staff. So many villagers died of starvation in our village. Yulin and her sister lost both their parents. The two sisters survived by going around begging and stealing. One of the sisters was blind, and the other was retarded.

Far away in Sichuan province in the southwest of China, the provincial Party boss Li Jingquan, a man with a thick, harsh Jiangxi accent, was another hardliner. The Anti-Hiding Campaign was carried out very stringently under his direction. Chen Gu from Pengshan county in central-south Sichuan is a very talkative woman.

I ran into her by accident in a small market town not far from Pengshan. In the beginning I did not intend to interview her because she looked rather young to me. But I was wrong. After she heard me talking to another lady nearby, she eagerly joined in. Although she was only a little girl at the time she remembers well what happened during the Anti-Hiding Campaign in her village:

> The cadres went around searching out every family home for food. If they saw smoke coming out from any of the houses, they would go over and confiscate the wok and any food. They then took any food they found back home. . . . The cadres' homes were always full of food—they never suffered from starvation.
>
> Someone in our village was so hungry that he stole some wheat one evening. . . . He got caught, and the cadres hung him up and beat him. They even pulled off his trousers. It was heartbreaking to watch.

In central Sichuan's Jianyang county, Zhu Erge, the friendly man whose family home lost its four walls at the eve of radical collectivization, recalls the Anti-Hiding Campaign was just as bad in his village:

> No one was allowed to light a fire at home or to cook at home. The reason was that some people were stealing food and taking it home to cook. So the cadres went around confiscating people's pots and pans, and destroying their stoves.

Farther northwest from Jianyang, in Sichuan's Peng county, cadres from Lei Huazhen's village checked peasants' homes several times a day.

> We did not dare to steal or hide any food—people from the commune were going around checking on different houses several times a day. If you got caught, they'd take you and any food you had stolen to the canteen. They'd put you on a high stool, remove your bowl from the table, and deprive you of your portion of porridge.

Further Lies

Even as peasants were not allowed to keep any food, neither were they allowed to tell the truth about how people were starving. By late 1958, although Mao appeared to disapprove of the "Wind of Exaggeration," he was still insisting that the Great Leap Forward must speed up and that his vision of abundance must not be challenged.

Hushu, the man originally from Sichuan's Renshou county who now lives deep in the mountains of Liangshan, remembers that there was massive political pressure during the time of the Great Leap Forward, and people were compelled to lie:

> At the time you simply couldn't say that you didn't have enough to eat. If someone asked you, you would reply: "There is more than enough." No one dared to admit that they didn't have enough to eat. If anyone mentioned that there wasn't enough food, that person would be asked to stand up at the evening meeting. He or she would be accused of attacking the Party and would be given a dunce hat to wear. After the meeting, the cadres would march that person through the streets. There was no way anyone could come out of it alive. The policies in those days were very heavy-handed. You just

> had to follow what the cadres said. If you dared to challenge them, it was regarded as class struggle, and you would become the class enemy. You couldn't get away. In those years we lived under so much political pressure.

Those who did speak the truth were purged. I met Lao Yu through Hushu. Yet another migrant to Liangshan, this retired officer did not move there by his own choice like Hushu. He was assigned here by the government. Lao Yu had originally come from Fushun county in southern Sichuan. During the Great Leap Forward, Fushun was at the forefront: it boasted very high agricultural and steel outputs. The reality was very different. Between 1959 and 1962 this small county, famous for its ancient salt mining, had one of the highest death rates in the province, and the death rate in Sichuan was one of the highest in China. But the truth still had to be concealed, as Lao Yu tells me:

> In those days the cadres told us that we had to pay back our county's debt to the Soviet Union. They also told us that the famine was a natural disaster. Who would dare to say that it was a failure of the policy? No one spoke up. I remember in 1961 or '62 someone said something like: "How can you say the situation is good? How come I can't even buy toilet paper?" He didn't get away with it. He was punished and sent to do hard labor.

Terror

Across the country, there were countless accounts of people being punished for telling the truth or for challenging Party policies. Through endless political campaigns and denunciation meetings, people were terrorized and gradually silenced. Wang Lishi is a small but strong and outspoken woman in her eighties. Her house is next to Li Anyuan's in Langzhong county, northern Sichuan. Although now her son makes a good living working in Langzhong town, his wife dislikes her mother in-law, so Wang Lishi lives on her own and still grows her own food and vegetables. She tells me that she moved to this village a few years before the radical collectivization, after she got married. The only things that seemed to take place in her newlywed husband's village were political campaigns and meetings.

> Meetings—almost every day there would be a meeting. The cadres would hold a meeting even for a small matter. . . . Sometimes the meetings were in the evening, sometimes they were at noon. Even during the [hot] summer months, we would still be having meetings at midday. We had to attend those meetings after we finished working in the fields. There were just endless meetings in those days. We used to say that under Chiang Kai-shek there were endless taxes to pay, and under Chairman Mao there were endless meetings to attend.
>
> Then there was the Rectifying the Commune Campaign, during which we were given "socialist education." The campaign was intended to correct society and the work methods of the cadres. It was really tough. Damn it! People like me who were not cadres had to attend so many meetings.
>
> There were campaigns like that all the time. After rectifying the Party members in the commune, they would go on to purge the cadres. After they had done with cadres, they would start on the ordinary farmers. From one level down to the next, this just went on and on. Every night they called us

out to meetings. Only one or two nights when there was no campaign meeting could we get some rest. But the peace never lasted long. Soon, another campaign would begin. Every day different Party members, some of whom were also cadres, would be called out to "correct" their working methods. During the day, the meetings were mostly for cadres, but at night all farmers had to attend. At those meetings, we were required to speak. Every farmer was asked to speak.

Before the Rectifying the Commune Campaign there was the campaign asking people to "speak out freely." Some Party members and cadres spoke quite frankly. After that campaign, many of them, including some of the high-ranking officials, were accused of having said the wrong thing. They were then purged as rightists. This happened to some people over here too. The government first checked their family backgrounds and history, and then removed them from their positions. There was one person from around here who used to work in the Changxi court. During the campaign he spoke very frankly because he was encouraged to do so. He was told to speak out if he felt that something was not quite right with the system. But in the end he was accused for saying the wrong thing, and he was dismissed and sent to do hard labor in the countryside.

After the government dissolved the collective canteen, they also encouraged the people to "speak out freely." They told everyone to say whatever was on their mind. They said we should not be afraid. But the majority of the farmers didn't dare to speak out. A few villagers who had the guts did, however, speak out. They spoke about the fact that people had been given only 115 grams or 100 grams of rice per day to eat, and how people starved. I remember a number of people complaining that the ration of 100 grams of oil was not enough to even spread around one's ass, and that the clothes people were wearing were disgusting. A number of cadres spoke first, and they were followed by a few farmers. When people had finished speaking, they were taken to the big brigade to be denounced. Then they were beaten up.

Everything that was said at those meetings was recorded. The government officials then went through the contents of every statement very carefully. They made reports and used them as evidence against these people. Many of them were purged for having made the wrong comments. There used to be public denunciation meetings at the school down the hill. Everyone was requested to attend. The person who had complained that 115 grams or 100 grams of rice was not enough was interrogated with questions such as, "Why was it enough for everyone else but not for you?" But the truth was that no other farmers dared to come forward to say that they also thought it wasn't enough, although in secret many farmers agreed with him. Everyone knew that there was not enough food to eat, but nobody dared to speak out. Only those with the guts spoke their minds.

After one wave of campaigns, another would begin. Every time people were asked to speak out, but every time those who dared to speak out were purged. By the end no one said anything any more.

What kind of society were we living in? Oh, dear me! There were campaigns all the time, and loudspeakers everywhere. We were surrounded by propaganda. The atmosphere was so tense that no one dared to do or say anything.

In Anhui province's Dingyuan county, in central-eastern China, Huang Manyi remembers being nineteen and terrified by what was happening at the time.

> I don't remember much about 1958, except for the mass political campaign called the "Great Debates." I was so frightened in those days. There were constant arrests, and many people were tied up and tortured. At the time I was at school not far from our village. One of my teachers, an educated man, made some criticisms of the government. He called the Great Leap Forward a failure, and said that everyone was neglectful and hardly any grain had been produced. He also criticized the "Wind of Exaggeration," saying that it was doing a lot of harm to ordinary people, and he claimed that the collective canteen system had deprived people of the right to cook at home. He was sent to a labor camp for eight years.
>
> The life we had to endure in those days was worse than the life of primitive societies. We lived like animals. The local cadres and the policies here were incredibly unreasonable. The cadres could denounce you anytime, and they could deprive you of food at whim.
>
> In our area denunciation meetings were part of everyday life. From morning to night, there were just meetings all day long. My mother was denounced in 1958. The head of the brigade kept some chickens and ducks at the time. My mother made the comment: "How come he can keep poultry but nobody else can?" and she was denounced because of it.
>
> My second uncle's wife was eating wheat in the field when she got caught. She was denounced and tortured there and

then. It was very brutal—too brutal for me to talk about it. They accused her of sabotage, and they beat her until she died from her injuries. That was in the winter of 1959.

My eldest aunt died in a similar way. It happened on a snowy day. She was crawling along the road looking for something to eat. There was a field of wheat near the house. She went there and started grazing on raw wheat. After she was discovered, a large group of people were sent out to catch her. They denounced her right there. She was cold and hungry, plus she was badly traumatized, and she died soon after.

My younger brother was a timid boy. Once he went along with a few kids in the village to pick young rice plants in the fields. They hid the rice plants in their trousers. While they were tying their trouser legs, someone saw them. About five or six boys were caught. They were sent to a village far away and were detained there. I went to see the head of the brigade, but he ignored me completely. I ran around for almost half the night trying to look for my brother. By the time he was released, he looked so thin. While he was detained, they had treated him very harshly. . . .

My big brother once spoke out about the fact that there was a famine going on in the countryside, and people were regularly dying of starvation. Someone reported him, and a public meeting was held to denounce my bother. After that he was sent to Fujian [in southern China] to do hard labor.

Liushu, the man from Wengong district in Renshou county, central Sichuan, who called radical collectivization a "pipe dream" in the previous chapter, tells me that as a young man one of his tasks was to take the minutes during the many denunciation meetings. He remembers the time well:

> In the 1950s, the major campaigns included the Anti-Rightist Campaign and the Rectifying the Commune Campaign. . . . The Anti-Rightist Campaign began by asking people to "speak out freely." People were told to express whatever was on their minds. They were encouraged not to hold back in any way, but to express themselves freely. Some people were not happy with the government, and they spoke out without exercising any reservation. Later on it all got a bit out of hand, and many people did not get away with what they had said. . . . In fact, regardless of whether you had said anything or not, in those days as long as someone reported that they had heard you expressing anti-government feelings, you would be purged as a rightist.
>
> The campaign first started in the rural countryside, and it expanded into the government working units. Initially the government sent out teams to inspect conditions in the countryside. When they saw what was going on, some people spoke out critically. But afterward, when they returned to their work units, they were purged. . . .
>
> In the countryside, those who were purged were called "fourth-bad-class elements"[4] . . . they were denied the right to speak, and they were not even allowed to attend meetings. The rightists were treated in the same way. Those who were labeled rightists were sent to the countryside to do hard labor. One rightist was assigned to our farming brigade. He was a teacher, a head teacher for a school, and a very talented man. When he was sent to the countryside to do hard labor,

he was given the task of digging and transporting feces, but he didn't know what to do. Other farmers did the job very quickly, but it took him forever. When he tried to lift buckets full of feces over his shoulders he often dropped them and spread feces all over the place. He had probably never done anything like that before. He was an intellectual.

The Anti-Rightist Campaign was in 1957, and it was followed by the campaign to "Rectify Incorrect Working Styles." . . . At the time I was only a teenager, but I was given the task of recording the meetings. . . . I did have my own thoughts in those days, but my thoughts were not going to make any difference. What could I do? During the time of collectivization, I could see clearly there were no crops growing, but what could I do about it? They told us to plant one hundred catties of seeds per mu, and we all knew that nothing could grow that way. But what choice did we have? There was nothing we could do. If anyone spoke out, they would be getting themselves into big trouble. The "Wind of Exaggeration" was widespread, so what difference could we make? People were being denounced regularly for leaning toward the right. Some cadres even lost their jobs. . . .

In those days the local government behaved rather erratically. For instance, one day it might suddenly decide to denounce somebody. . . . During the denunciation meetings, the victims were told to stand at the front, and anyone who happened to say the wrong thing would be denounced in full public view. Physical torture was used at those meetings—people would be whipped. . . . When the "Wind of Exaggeration" was at its height, the cadres would beat people up. They hit people with sticks and whips. Some

> people got so badly injured that they would spit blood. Anyone who didn't go along with the "Wind of Exaggeration" lies would be beaten up by the cadres, so no one dared to oppose the cadres. . . . Even if there was nothing to eat, we still had to endure the hunger.

Li Anyuan, the old man from a small village in northern Sichuan mentioned in the previous chapter, recalls the brutality suffered by his fellow villagers as well as his own father under the political campaigns.

> A major campaign in those days was class struggle. We were told that it was fundamental to struggle. Farmers were frightened of it. No one dared to violate the orders from above—any slip-up and the consequences would be unimaginable. Some people suffered really badly.
>
> Cadres were fierce in those days. I guess they had to be fierce, or no one would follow their orders. They forced us to work hard. Of course we were afraid of them. How could we not be? They had the power to deprive us of food. In those days, the main forms of punishment included heavy fines or deprivation of food. If we had no food we'd starve. Of course we feared them.
>
> The worst were those cadres sent by the commune or the government to inspect local work. They used to beat people up. I remember one who was sent here by the government. He used to beat people really badly. If anyone disobeyed him, he would punish them with harsh physical beatings. In our village, for example, there was a girl called Zhou Yuzhen. She disagreed with him on one occasion, so this official held public meetings

every night to denounce her. Once [during the meeting] she fell asleep, so he ordered someone to pour a bucketful of urine all over her body, even filling her mouth with urine. That was in front of everybody. That's how it was in those days.

Sometimes the cadres went around the villages confiscating people's chickens or their quilts. This happened regularly to those who did not obey them. If they caught anyone picking sweet potatoes, that person would also get into trouble. Besides a heavy fine, they would denounce that person in public meetings. . . . Often in the evenings the officials in the commune would send the militia out to make inspections. If they caught anyone cooking, or saw smoke rising from any of the houses, they would deprive that person or family of their food rations.

During the Rectifying the Commune Campaign, my father was a cadre for the brigade. Even as a cadre, he was denounced. My father was illiterate, but he was an honest man. During the Chinese New Year, he allowed the canteen manager to give every family one kilogram of sweet potatoes. This was against the rule. Some Party members from our farming brigade reported it to higher-ranking officials, and my father and the canteen manager were punished as a result. The officials accused my father of serious misconduct. My father and the canteen manager were denounced during a public meeting. I watched them mocking my father, criticizing him for following the capitalist path. They also forced my father to wear the dunce hat.

Li Anyuan's seventy-five-year-old next-door neighbor Wang Lishi, the woman who moved to Li's village after her marriage as mentioned earlier, also remembers vividly the incident in which Li's father was purged for trying to help his fellow villagers:

> Just before the New Year the cadre of our production brigade gave each person five catties of sweet potato, so we could at least have something to eat for the New Year. But one of my sisters-in-law, a Party member, reported him to the big brigade. They held a denunciation meeting over there. It took place at night. They strung him up really high.
>
> After the meeting, we were told to hand over all the sweet potatoes we had received. Ordinary farmers followed the order obediently. . . . But cadres divided up the sweet potatoes handed over by the farmers and shared them among themselves.

Others, like Wei Zhengzheng, an unassuming peasant woman from a small village near Qianjiang, in central Hubei province, did nothing to disobey the orders of the cadres or to complain about food shortages. Her only "fault" was that she happened to be born into families with the "wrong" political background.

> My grandfather's cousin had a position in the Nationalist government, and in the 1950s he escaped to Taiwan. In 1958 some local cadres and militia members came to investigate the matter. They accused my grandfather of harboring evidence and assisting his cousin to escape. My grandfather denied it all. They strung him up and beat him. I was in the same room when it happened, and I was giving birth to my fourth child right at that very moment. I screamed like hell because of the pain of the delivery, and at the same time my

grandfather was also screaming at the top of his voice because of the pain of the torture. The incident left my grandfather completely paralyzed. They broke both his arms and thigh bones. He could not do a thing after that and we had to feed him every meal. In 1961 our house was destroyed by fire, and soon afterward my grandmother also died of illness.

Because of my family background, nothing good ever happened to me. I was constantly being denounced and punished with hard labor. I was never spared any of the bad stuff. The cadres even tried to persuade my husband to divorce me. They told him that he should keep away from a "black sheep" like me. But my husband refused. After that my husband was sent away to make iron and steel. They also sent him off to dig canals. They always sent him away to do the toughest jobs. Like us, my children also suffered a great deal in those days.

Mass Campaigns Against "Enemies"

Mao was known for his skills in mass mobilization. It was his means of controlling China's immense population. He was proud of it and he called it his most powerful weapon. Throughout the period of the Great Leap Forward, while most of the people in China were toiling and starving, Mao was constantly launching nationwide wars, against either the so-called four evils (sparrows, rats, flies, and mosquitoes) or the Nationalists in Taiwan. Wei Dengyu, a friendly old man from a mountain village in northern Sichuan—one of the poorest villages in Sichuan even to this day—remembers how peasants were forced to spend days chasing after sparrows. The "crime" of the sparrows, according to Mao, was that they consumed the grain.

The irony was that after the sparrows were wiped out, insects multiplied and consumed the crops in just the same way. Not only so, much of the manpower and time were wasted.

> There was the Eradication of the "Four Evils" Campaign. I can't remember the year exactly. I only remember that we had to fire rifles in order to chase away the sparrows. We were also organized into groups to shout at the birds as a way of scaring them away. We had to go deep into the mountains and line up one after another. Then we would shout out loud [at the birds]. Hearing the noise, the birds would fly away. But we had no idea what the end result was. I don't think we actually caught anything during the campaign to eradicate the "four evils." But it was quite fun, a bit like play.

In the autumn of 1958, while all of China was preoccupied with the Great Leap Forward, China's People's Liberation Army fired 450,000 shells at the Quemoy islands—then and now under the administration of the Taipei government—at a cost of millions of dollars, and incurring the loss of many Chinese lives. This is known as the Second Taiwan Strait Crisis. The conflict began in August 1958 when the People's Liberation Army began an intense artillery bombardment of Quemoy. It was Mao's war against the "American plot to divide China." At about the same time, radical collectivization of the Chinese countryside was formally inaugurated at a Communist Party Politburo meeting. It was decided that gigantic People's Communes would become the new method of economic and political organization in rural China. The goal was to turn China into an industrial superpower. The war against the "American imperialists" and Nationalists in Taiwan gave additional urgency to China's Great Leap. Before

October 1, 1958, in anticipation of China's National Day celebrations, ordinary people from all over Sichuan, as well as other parts of the country, were organized to join the march to "Liberate Quemoy." Wang Dezheng, a chatty man I have known since childhood, was fifteen at the time, and he was living in a small farming village outside Chengdu. He remembers that for several nights, he and his fellow villagers had to walk many miles to Chengdu to join the march.

> I remember the time that I went to Chengdu to join the march celebrating the liberation of Jinmen [Quemoy] island. My foot was hurting really badly, and it became incredibly painful. I had to wrap it up in some white cloth.
>
> It was the government order that all peasants had to go to the city that evening to join in the mass march. So we cut some bamboo and filled up its hollow part with kerosene. Then we lit it with rough straw paper. That's how we marched to Chengdu. We went to Chengdu to celebrate the liberation of Jinmen. The place was occupied by the Nationalists in Taiwan. We had to join in the march every night. It lasted for days. It was the government order. At the time we ate at the collective canteen. Once we had finished our supper, we had to prepare to join the march. During the march we shouted slogans like "Liberate Jinmen! Jinmen must be liberated." [Laughs] Oh, dear me!

Political Indoctrination

Ideological indoctrination was an integral part of the Chinese Communist political campaigns. Pan Zhenghui from Peng county in Sichuan, the former Great Leap Forward worker who lost her Party membership after she had taken a long leave to visit her terminally ill mother, remembers the ideological brainwashing she and her villagers received during the hard time of the famine.

> In those days there were political campaigns all the time, one campaign after another, until there was nothing left for them to take or to move. . . . At meetings we were told heroic stories like the one about how during the civil war the Communist soldier Huang Jiguang had used his chest to block machine gun fire, sacrificing his life for the Party and his country. Stories like this made a strong impression on me, and made me believe that the hardships we had to endure were really nothing.
>
> That's how the Communist Party educated us. The Party taught us how to overcome hardships. We were told that we must not let the hardships crush us, and we "must not fear the wolf in front of us and the tiger behind us," and that was the only way for us to go forward, the only way to fight hardship.

Another person I interviewed, Xian, comes from a very privileged background, unlike most of those I met. Both of her parents were high-ranking Communist officials, and she received her education in one of China's most prestigious institutions. She now lives in London with her British husband, but she too tells me political indoctrination and pressure were part of everyday life in China at the time of the Great Famine.

> People were under a lot of political pressure in those days. In times of crisis, the government tried to enforce

its control by putting more political pressure on ordinary people. I cannot say anti-revisionism was completely wrong, but I did not understand what revisionism was or what Communism was. None of us really knew what was going on between China and the Soviet Union in those days, nor did I understand how politically to protect our Motherland. I suspect the issues between the Soviet Union and China, between Chairman Mao and Stalin, were very complicated. But we were not told what was going on. We were not told how much of the famine was due to natural disaster, how much of it was man-made. . . . Many people were aware of the problem of exaggeration, no one dared to question. We did not think the so-called natural disaster was the result of the "Wind of Exaggeration." . . . Although the cadres knew what was going on, yet they were part of it. They were the ones who told lies. People like us who lived in the cities believed whatever the newspaper told us. We were not encouraged to think differently. We were brainwashed into believing the problem was caused by the Soviet Union, which tried to humiliate and damage China. The Party used such propaganda as a weapon to get ordinary Chinese people to unite behind it and to explain the problem of severe food shortages.

3

Unnatural Disasters

> In the past, many people felt that developing industry was too high a goal and very mysterious. They said: "It is not easy to achieve industrialization!" In general, there was great superstition in regard to industry.
>
> I do not understand industry either. I know nothing about it, yet I do not believe that it is unattainable. . . . I think that in ten years or so our country will become an industrial nation. We must not consider industrialization as something so serious. We must first hold it in contempt and then give it serious attention.
>
> "Make the high mountain bow its head; make the river yield the way." That is an excellent proverb. When we ask the high mountain to bow its head, it has to do so! When we ask the river to yield the way, it must yield!
>
> —*Mao Zedong, "Speeches at the Second Session of the Eighth Party Congress," May* 8, 1958

From 1958 onward the entire rural population in China was mobilized to transform the country into an industrial powerhouse. An industrial superpower needed a lot of steel. In August 1958, at the same Politburo meeting at which the People's Commune was inaugurated, it was also decided that the country's steel production would double within the year. The Chinese countryside was transformed overnight and became packed with backyard furnaces. Pots, pans, and tools were confiscated from people's homes and turned into useless slag. Meanwhile, agricultural fields were abandoned and turned to wasteland. Animals were left untended. Crops failed, and a food crisis spread across the country. Many of China's major agricultural provinces were hit the worst.

Sichuan is a good example. Situated in the southwest of China on the border with Tibet, it is China's biggest agricultural province, famously known as "the land of abundance." But industry has always been Sichuan's weak point, and its steel production had been relatively poor. After August 1958, the provincial Party secretary Li Jingquan promised that Sichuan's steel production would double or even triple by the end of the year. Within a few days, an estimated 800,000 farmers were sent up into the mountains to fell trees and to smelt iron and steel. When backyard furnaces turned out worthless lumps containing very little iron, Li came up with the method of "double cooking." This far-fetched idea came from the famous Sichuan dish "double-cooked pork." According to Li, iron lumps could be returned to the furnace and smelted again, just like returning the parboiled pork to the wok and cooking it again in sizzling hot oil. Although the double-cooked pork turned out delicious, trying to double cook slag did not work. This wasted a lot of time, effort, and precious fuel. By September 29, 1958, two days before the October 1 National Day, Sichuan boasted that its steel output had reached 10,000 tons per day! But every Sichuanese person knew that this was nothing more than a fairy tale. Worse still: autumn then, as it is now, was the harvest season. In the autumn of 1958, however, Sichuan's major farming force was tied up in steel production, leaving only women and elderly people to tend the fields. "The People's Commune has turned into a mothers' commune," people mocked. Acres upon acres of crops were left to rot in the fields, and at least 4 million pigs died because there were not enough hands to take care of them.[1]

The drop in grain production was also brought about by the mass movement of "deep plowing" and "close planting." The intention was to produce a higher yield per plot. The theory was that the deeper the planting, the stronger the roots and the taller the crops. Taller crops would yield more grain, and with more seeds in the fields, there would be more crops. Day and night, under the blazing sun and working by fire torches, farmers labored under the order to dig up perfectly good soil and transfer growing crops from various fields into the "sputnik plots," where they were planted in cramped lots. At the time this was called "revolutionary innovation," but it did not work, and the crops soon died. Grain production plummeted, and starvation in the countryside became commonplace.

Not only did agriculture suffer terribly, China's rich forests were also destroyed, as trees were cut down to be fed into the backyard furnaces, and tree bark was consumed by hungry villagers. Deforestation was carried out in many mountainous regions throughout China. In some areas the idea was to convert the land into rice fields, or to make way for irrigation canals. This turned out to be counterproductive. Deforestation had devastating consequences, such as soil erosion and sandstorms. It turned paddy fields into sandy beaches and farmland into swamps. The destruction was particularly bad in China's northwest, where about one-third of the forests disappeared. Today, traveling through Gansu and Shaanxi on the famous ancient Silk Road, one is overwhelmed by the boundless yellow earth, bleak and immense. Sandstorms are a common feature of the region. It is hard to imagine that this was once fertile land with an advanced irrigation system, a land where traces of China's earliest agricultural civilization can still be found.

To generate more power, gigantic dams were built throughout the country, as a result of which millions of villagers were uprooted from their homes. While most of these half-baked projects turned out to be an enormous waste of time and resources, the ecological consequences of the schemes continue to affect people's lives and the environment today. In the agricultural heartland of Henan, China's most populous province, more than 1.3 million peasants were drafted into water conservation projects or to make fertilizer under the radical provincial Party head Wu Zhipu. By the autumn of 1958, it was reported that the entire countryside in Henan had been fully irrigated, but this apparent achievement was in fact a complete disaster for the province. As we have seen, Banqiao Reservoir Dam in Henan's Suiping county, a major Great Leap Forward project built against the warning of hydrology experts, collapsed in the 1970s, killing more than 85,000 people and flooding twenty-nine counties. Not only so, but massive water conservation work, without a scientific foundation, caused terrible alkalization and waterlogging. These two problems devastated Henan. There was a local saying at the time: "Drought happens just once in a season, but alkalization lasts a lifetime." For many years alkalization did indeed prove to be extremely destructive for the region. Not only did it destroy crops, but it also damaged houses to the extent that many homes eventually collapsed. In December 1961, in his letter to the premier Zhou Enlai, the distressed newly appointed provincial Party secretary, Liu Jianxun, noted that "the vast plain along the Yellow River is turning into a total wasteland!"[2]

East of Henan is China's fruit and vegetable garden, Shandong province. Shandong is situated on the lower reaches of the Yellow River and extends out to the East China Sea. From 1954 until October 1960, Shandong was under the leadership of Shu Tong, another fervent supporter of the Great Leap Forward. Shandong was one of the first provinces to "shoot sputnik" from agricultural fields. It was also one of the first provinces to experience the famine. As early as April 1958, the food crisis in parts of Shandong had become so severe that the central government in Beijing had been alerted, but this did not stop Shu Tong in his determination to please Mao. In September 1959, against the backdrop of the Lushan plenum, Shu Tong launched vicious attacks on his opposition. More than 110,000 local cadres were denounced for "right deviationism," and some 40 members were expelled from the Party. Shu also rallied nearly a million farmers, most of whom were starving at this point, to support his massive water conservation and reforestation projects. Even Mao was astonished by Shu's charisma and organizing ability. Soon afterward, however, disaster struck Shandong too. The irrigation had not only allowed alkalization and waterlogging to become widespread, it had also prevented water from flowing downstream. The worst flooding in Shandong's history hit the region in 1960 and then again in 1961, leaving many villages drowned "like small islands in the ocean," said Hu Yaobang, then head of the Communist Youth League, during his twenty-five-day official tour around the region.[3] As no one wanted to be held responsible, the local cadres blamed the heavens and called the flooding "a natural disaster." This was the official phrase used to describe all the man-made catastrophes that occurred between 1958 and 1961.

Throughout the country the ordinary people knew these disasters were *unnatural*. China was such a big country, "how come natural disasters happened everywhere all at once?" an illiterate housewife with bound feet in Beijing asked. She was not convinced then, and more than fifty years later, the question still troubles her.

"Overtake Britain in Iron and Steel"

After he had managed to suppress the voices of opposition by launching the Anti-Rightist Campaign in autumn 1957, in early 1958 Mao Zedong called for Party unity, by which he persuaded the Politburo, as well as the rest of the country, to follow his slogan: "Overtake Britain and other major industrial countries in iron and steel production in fifteen years or slightly more." By the end of that year, Mao had reduced the fifteen years to five years. He wanted China's annual steel production to reach 50 or 60 million tons in 1962. "By that time," he says, "it will be said that we have basically transformed the entire country." No one dared to challenge the chairman's target, even though people knew much of what had been produced was useless.

At the provincial level, Party secretaries, fearful of getting into trouble, tried to outdo one another. In Hebei province alone, more than half a million backyard steel and iron foundries were set up. All metal objects were fed into the furnaces. At the time Sun Po, a housewife from Xushui, was in her forties. She remembers that she and other villagers were forced to contribute all their cooking tools in order to turn China into an industrial giant.

> The cadres told us that the nation needed to make machines, and that everyone had to work to produce steel after a whole day of working in the fields. We were not left with any time to prepare food at home. Also, steel production required every household to contribute a lot of metal. Knives, pots, hammers, door locks and keys, even pegs for holding pictures on the wall—they were all taken away by the Communes. We had no knife left to slaughter poultry with, and we had no pot to cook it in at home.

In the southwest of China, in Sichuan's Fushun county, Lao Yu, the retired man I met through Hushu in the deep mountains of Liangshan, recalls what happened in his home village.

> To make iron and steel anything containing wood was taken away. People even fed coffins into the furnaces. You weren't given any warning in those days—the cadres would just suddenly appear at people's doors and then take everything away. In the beginning they also demolished people's houses. Not just the landlords' houses—they also demolished the houses of middle-income and well-off peasants. The demolition was often carried out at night. When it was someone's turn to have their house demolished, the cadres would just call the family out and carry out the job straight away. Anything made of wood would be fed into the furnaces and burned in those days.

Just northeast of Fushun in Bishan county, near Chongqing in eastern Sichuan, Xu Yongling, a young wife at the time, and many of her fellow villagers were sent to work in the collective iron factory down in the south of the county.

> In 1958 we were sent to the iron factory. In our area everyone was requested to take part in the mass production of iron. Our factory was in Ding Jiagou. Every day we hammered at stones. We were told that it was the way to make iron. I don't understand why we had to do it. I don't understand why we had to make iron. [Giggles] What was it for? We were told it was the Party policy. I remember one night everyone was called out to leave. We were told to go to make iron.

> Blocks of carbon, steel sheets, and tree branches were all fed into the furnaces. All the trees in our area were cut down. Even the tools we used for sewing and household furniture were fed to the furnaces. The perfectly good weaving machines, as well as the tables and chairs, were all smashed into pieces before being fed into the furnace.

Back in Xushui county in Hebei province, north-central China, backyard furnaces could be seen everywhere. Under Zhang Guozhong's Party leadership, Xushui took the lead in the race and became China's model for the Great Leap Forward. In autumn 1958, in anticipation of Chairman Mao's visit, "free" food was put on display and the streets were lit with electricity. It seemed that Communism had truly arrived, and Xushui was ready to launch another sputnik in iron and steel production. Liu Xiansheng was a schoolboy at the time. He tells me there was more than what appeared in the official story.

> I was twelve years old in 1958. There were no classes on at the school! We were sent to do hard labor day and night. [To build furnaces] we were told to carry bricks from one place to another. The cadres were not very smart and had no plan whatsoever. After we had sweated like pigs to move all the bricks to the place they told us to, they would then decide that they wanted us to move them elsewhere. I quickly figured out that they had no idea what they were doing, and even if I moved the bricks somewhere else, they wouldn't notice. . . . So I took quite a few bricks, and gave them to people in my village. The villagers appreciated what I did, and they nominated me to join the reception team to welcome Chairman Mao, who was scheduled to visit Xushui.

> [On the day of Mao's visit] we stood on the main road for a whole day, but the chairman didn't show up. It was an exciting experience though, as we got to see the new multi-story building in the county town. Although it only had two floors, we had never seen a multilayer building before. We also saw electric lamps for the first time in our lives. To us this was modern stuff.
>
> At the school our teachers were pretty stupid. They ordered us to make steel out of a bucket of iron balls without providing us with any guidelines. We had to rely on our own intuition to make the steel. So we hammered the iron balls day and night. We managed get them into square shapes. We then presented them as our "handmade" steel.

South of Hebei is Henan province. Here almost 600,000 backyard furnaces had been put into operation by the end of October 1958. Pingdingshan, in central south Henan, today is essentially an industrial city. It originated as a product of the Great Leap Forward: in 1957 two agricultural counties in central Henan, Ye and Baofeng, were merged to form the Pingdingshan city. Together with nearby Lushan county, Pingdingshan was the champion in Henan province's iron and steel production. Here more than forty thousand agriculture laborers had been diverted to make iron and steel. According to local news reports, in August 1958 the steel production in this region had reached more than ten thousand tons per day. Guangzhong from Dinglou village was eighteen years old at the time. He tells me how such a large figure was "achieved."

> At the time everyone was mobilized to make iron and steel. Men, women, the young and the old—they were all

> sent to the river near Song village to dig up sand. People jumped into the river and used rattan buckets and iron tools to dig sand. We were told that the sand contained iron. Every day there was pressure from above asking us to report the amount being collected. People got desperate, so they stole sand from one another. In order to fool the cadres, the villagers cheated. When the cadres came to weigh the sand, the villagers would put everything they had collected into one big pile. As soon as the cadres made a move to the next place, the villagers would move the same pile of sand quickly to the next place, ready for inspection. In the end the figures the cadres collected were completely false.

Close to Taiwan, in the southern coastal province of Fujian, 250,000 backyard furnaces were constructed. Chan Daoching, the schoolboy from Fuqing county who had overseas connections and dared to argue with his teacher, tells me that he and the whole school were mobilized into iron production at the time.

> In my class, we were divided into six groups. One group went into the mountains to fell trees and to collect firewood. Another group made charcoal out of the firewood that was collected. A third group transported the charcoal to our school. A fourth was in charge of building the furnace. The fifth and sixth groups were responsible for smelting iron. I was in the last group. My task was to keep the fire burning. I did it manually with a fan. Each shift lasted two days, and we were not allowed to sleep while we were on duty. We never managed to make any iron in the end. All we got was a few drops of hot liquid that had seeped out of the furnace.

> There was not enough to solidify into iron. Our attempts at building furnaces and making iron and steel were rather like children playing games.

West of Fujian is Guangdong province. Deng Xiansheng, the Cantonese man who was forbidden to speak his native dialect and had no meat to eat at the time, remembers the destruction in his home village in Dongguan during the mass campaign to produce iron and steel.

> We were told to make iron and steel. It was Mao's order that we had to catch up with the Americans and the British. . . . So the entire labor force was sent into the mountains to make iron and steel. There was no one left to do the agricultural work. . . . Backyard furnaces could be seen everywhere. Trees were cut down; anything that was made of metal was taken away. People's homes had no windows, because they had been made of iron. We tried to make iron and steel day and night, and in the end all we got was useless slag. We had to abandon the project. In our area there were hardly any trees left—they had all been fed to the furnaces.

Xu Xiansheng is a university lecturer in Jinan, Shandong province. He had come from Heze in southwest Shandong. Heze is famous for its peonies, and is rightly known as the "Home of Peony." April is the season when the flower is in full blossom, and Heze is usually bathed in bright colors of red, pink, and white at this time. But Xu Xiansheng tells me that in April 1958 there were no peonies to be seen in Heze, as every backyard was filled with scrap metal and rudimentary furnaces. He was a student at school at the time. Like everyone in Heze, he joined in the mass production of iron and steel.

> In order to make iron and steel, [the cadres] took away every family's iron wok. No one was allowed to do any cooking. They smashed all the iron woks into pieces. They even took away the iron rings on doors, and on the furniture. Anything with metal in it was taken away, including the copper bowls we used for washing our faces. I also took part in iron and steel production. At school we dug quite a few holes in the ground and lit fires with logs. Then we would throw the broken pieces of metal into the fire. We thought that we would be able to smelt iron that way. In the end all we managed to get were blocks of slag. This was useless rubbish that looked a bit like bean curd residue—we had to throw it away. What a waste! Perfectly good woks and pans were smashed to make slag.

Agriculture

While backyard furnaces produced lumps of rubbish, "sputnik fields" grew mostly weeds. Reading through official newspapers and literature of the time, one is overwhelmed by the image of "bumper harvests" all over the Chinese countryside in 1958. The reality, however, was very different. Since the majority of the agricultural labor force was diverted for the purpose of building irrigation projects or for mass production of iron and steel, hardly anyone was left to tend the fields. Weeds grew wild, and crops were left in the fields to rot. In addition, the "deep plowing" and "close planting" methods, which were intended to produce high yields, ended up actually killing the crops. Agricultural productivity plummeted. By the end of the year hardly anything had been harvested. As China's biggest agricultural province, Sichuan suffered the worst.

At Xu Yongling's village in Bishan county, eastern Sichuan, as most agricultural laborers were engaged in iron work, local farming suffered badly. To this day Yongling speaks with great exasperation about what happened.

> In 1958 we were sent to the iron factory to join in the mass production of iron. . . . There was hardly anyone left to do the farming. At home there were only a few elderly people left—all the young and strong ones had gone to work in the iron factories. The old people had to tend the fields. Sometimes they had to work through the night to tend the fields. . . .
>
> Although one could see the fields full of rice plants, yet the plants had no grain in them—they only had slender leaves with no grain. There were also a lot of weeds growing in the fields. In the end nothing was harvested. Of course there was a famine. We had no food to eat. Thinking about what happened then saddens me. It was very depressing. There was not even any salt in those days. . . . What a terrible time.

Northwest of Bishan is Anyue county, a major agricultural base in Sichuan. It is now famous for its locally produced pork and citrus fruits. But during the Great Leap Forward, Anyue's agricultural productivity suffered badly as a result of unrealistically high government procurement quotas, the "Wind of Exaggeration," as well as many arbitrary and impractical directions given by the local cadres. Mrs. Zhou, now in her seventies, remembers what happened in those days:

> After the People's Commune was established, . . . farmers were sent away to make iron and steel. Hardly anyone was left to do the farming. Production plummeted. The cadres then ordered us to carry out "deep plowing." We had to dig more than one meter deep. In the end nothing grew. So much land was wasted that way. When production failed, the cadres came up with another method—"close planting." They told us that the more seeds were planted, the more grain would be harvested. . . . But as soon as the crops started to grow a bit tall they would start to wither straight away after evening dew. So nothing was harvested. All the crops perished because they were packed too tightly together. Try to imagine that the whole field was covered with a thick layer of seeds: there was no space for the growing crops to breathe; how on earth could they grow?

Down in southern Sichuan's Fushun county, Lao Yu paints much the same picture.

> In those days there was no one in the countryside to do the agricultural work. The fields were covered in weeds and they grew taller and taller. . . . All strong and young laborers were sent to make iron and steel, leaving only a few women, elderly people, and children at home. . . .
>
> Besides "deep plowing," we also had to collect fertilizer in those days. Through the course of one night we had to collect more than ten thousand kilograms of fertilizer. How is that possible? Cadres lied all the time. They forged the production figures: someone boasted that one mu of land had produced ten thousand catties of grain. Others had to

> catch up since no one wanted to be left behind. There used to be a saying: "ten thousand catties per mu is not bad, but we can easily produce twenty thousand catties. After we have achieved twenty thousand catties, we will call on Chairman Mao." What nonsense! Because of the unrealistic exaggeration, Sichuan ended up having to send food to support the rest of the country, even though there was hardly anything being produced locally. I was still in my home village then, and I watched food being transported away. If we produced anything at all, it was sent away immediately. So many people died of starvation as result.

Farther north from Fushun in Ziyang county, Chef Yan remembers that hardly anything grew in his home village.

> During the Great Leap Forward I was still young, but my elder sister and my father were forced to work in an iron factory. . . . There was no one left to do the farming. The weeds grew to human height in the fields. There was no rice growing, not even any sweet potato growing. Once, the canteen manager tried to collect some sweet potato from the field, but after digging for half a day he could barely fill half a bucket.
>
> The iron factory didn't last long. After its closure, people were sent back to the villages. They looked so thin, just like beggars. I watched some of them carrying their bags, looking so desperate.

Renshou county was close to Ziyang. Hushu tells me he could never forget what happened in his home village at the time.

> Villagers were first ordered to make iron and steel. They were then told to deep-plow the rice fields. The cadres told villagers to dig almost a meter deep. As a result, the soil was tilled upside down—the rich soil got buried underneath, and the poor soil sat on the surface. The crops suffered as a result, and so did the farmers. The official orders were completely impractical in those days. When the amount of food being produced fell short of the government target, the cadres would forge the figures. . . . When the government inspection teams came, the cadres would move the crops from various fields into one plot and boast: "Oh, come and look, the field is packed with rice crops. There is hardly any gap between the crops and you can even drop a small child on top of them." What they were insinuating was that a lot of food had been produced. But in reality there was no food. It was only false claims.

All the way down in southern China, next to Hong Kong in Guangdong province's Dongguan, no agricultural fields can be seen today. This is China's factory: most things "Made in China," including a large amount of fake goods, are produced here. A majority of residents in Dongguan are factory girls from all over China along with overseas businessmen, but Deng Xiansheng is one of the very few people still alive who was born and grew up there. Now living in Hong Kong, Deng cannot forget the days of "close planting" and "deep plowing" in Dongguan.

> The order to start close planting came from the central government. I don't understand why we had to do it. All the old farmers had warned the officials that the crops needed

> space to grow. They didn't listen, and insisted that we must plant the crops as tightly as possible. In the end hardly anything grew. . . . The "deep plowing" was even worse. We were told that the deeper the land was tilled, the better the crops would grow. We dug nearly one meter deep, so deep that once an ox fell in and couldn't get out.

In eastern China, Xu Xiansheng, the university teacher I met in Shandong's provincial capital, Jinan, remembers the consequences of "deep plowing" in his home village in Heze in southwest Shandong.

> In order to get a high yield, [the cadres] completely ignored science. . . . At the time everyone everywhere had to apply the "deep plowing" method. Besides farmers, students and cadres also had to go to the countryside to plow the fields. I had to go too. We were made to work all night long, so we just rested in the fields. In those days the general Party line was "Go all out, aim high, and build socialism in a greater, faster, better and more economic way." There was no schooling for us students—we all had to go to the countryside to do our bit for "deep plowing." When we got tired, we would just take a little nap by the field. Normally one would plant 20 kilos of seeds per mu of land, but our headmaster thought that the more seeds you planted, the more crops would grow. So we were told to plant 230 kilos of wheat seeds in one mu of land. In the end less than 50 kilos of wheat were harvested. What an enormous waste!
>
> . . .
>
> This is how to describe 1958: although we were told there were "bumper harvests" everywhere, in fact nothing was

harvested at all. Because everybody's energy was invested in "deep plowing" and the mass production of iron and steel, in the end there was no one left to harvest the crops. . . . Almost 80 percent of the radishes and potatoes grown were left to rot in the fields. It was the same with soybean and sorghum.

From 1958 local agricultural productivity was badly damaged. That left a very deep impression on me. Before that time people used to keep a lot of oxen and sheep in our area. [After 1958], there was no food to feed the animals. Even straw had become scarce. In the beginning, the oxen were fed on stalks, but after a while as all the stalks were burned as fuel, the oxen began to die of starvation. Gradually there were fewer and fewer oxen left. Each production brigade had only a few oxen remaining. I remember more than five or six oxen dying of starvation in one village. In the end there were only two left. In those days, never mind the animals, even human beings like us didn't have anything to eat. Without animals, productivity decreased. Human labor had to replace the animals, from plowing the fields to transporting the fertilizer. It was very labor-intensive. Several people would be required to carry out one job that before would have been done by one animal. Humans were also much slower than animals. This situation lasted until the late 1970s.

Deforestation

While fields were covered in weeds and animals died of starvation, the furnaces were kept going all day and all night in order to reach Mao's target for 60 million tons of iron. This required a huge amount of fuel. To meet the need, trees were cut down and lush forests were destroyed overnight. In southern China's Fujian province, close to Taiwan, forests had always been a precious resource. Fuqing county in southern Fujian is famous for bird watching, as the bay area in Fuqing, a protected wetland nature reserve, attracts thousands of different bird species each year. Many years ago Fuqing also boasted of its beautiful forests, but this was to change. Chan Daoching, who was born and grew up in Fuqing, recalls the damage to its forest caused by the Great Leap Forward.

> To make iron and steel, one group of students was sent into the mountains to fell trees. Another group followed them and burned the trees to make charcoal. The charcoal was transported back to the school to feed furnaces. But there was not enough. . . . There were quite a few furnaces in the school at the time. All of them were built by students from various classes. They sat inside the school hall. Since there was not enough fuel, red bayberry trees were cut down and used to feed the furnaces. Red bayberry trees were the most highly praised fruit trees in Fuqing. All of the red bayberry trees were chopped down and fed to the furnaces. The school authorities even chopped up the wooden frames from the school windows to use as fuel. It was a stupid thing to cut down trees in Fuqing. Without forests there was a lack of firewood. Since there was no firewood, villagers had to use cow dung as fuel.

Similarly, in neighboring Guangdong province vast forests were destroyed for the sake of the Great Leap Forward. Liang Xiansheng was nine at the time, and his home village was in the Zhongshan region, close to Macau. Zhongshan was once famous for its vast forest, which contained many rare subtropical plants. Most of these have gone now.

> Our village was in the mountains. It used to be covered with trees, but all of them were cut down in order to make iron and steel. . . . The trees were planted to protect the village from strong winds—every village was like that. But during the Great Leap Forward, no trees were left, so when the wind picked up it was brutal.
>
> I was in school in the fourth grade at the time, but instead of studying we were forced to go out to collect fuel. Every week each student was required to collect fifty kilograms of fuel. After all the trees had been felled, we even dug up the roots and used those as fuel.

The same calamity occurred elsewhere in China. In the southwest of China, Sichuan province's Ya'an region, close to the Tibetan border, had one of the most impressive virgin forests in the country. Fr. Armand David (1826–1900), the Catholic priest, zoologist, and botanist who was the first to witness the giant panda in Ya'an, was deeply impressed by the rich forest and many rare plants in the region. He would have been pained to learn that during the Great Leap Forward massive deforestation was being carried out systematically under the order of the central government in Beijing. Pan Zhenghui from Peng county was one of many peasants in Sichuan to be drafted into the government deforestation project.

> Our Party secretary Zhang Zhijin took a team of us out to chop down trees in the forest in [Ya'an region's] Tianquan county, but after we arrived he left us out there by ourselves.

> I was put in charge of the team. I worked so hard in those days. . . . In Tianquan we felled trees with electric saws. Logs were used as fuel to replace coal. The central government in Beijing was directly in charge of the logging in Tianquan.

Besides the mass production of iron and steel, there were many other national construction projects prior to, and during, the Great Leap Forward that also required large amounts of wood. Jiang Jiujiu was a first-generation CCP-trained Communist cadre. After graduating from the Party school, he was seconded by the government to work in the Ganzi Tibetan Autonomous Region, west of Sichuan. He recalls the destruction of ancient forest in the region.

> Large parts of Ganzi Region used to be virgin forest. In 1951 to 1953 I was working in Ganzi's Yajiang county, and I could see virgin forest everywhere. . . . Before 1958 there were already many forest bureaus in Ganzi—almost every county had one. They were in charge of logging. The trees were felled to support various national construction projects, to build houses and railways. Deforestation had already begun before the Great Leap Forward. Logs were being sent to different parts of the country by truck and by boat. By the time of the Great Leap Forward, deforestation continued and expanded across wider areas. I cannot remember the exact figure. In a number of places, in order to make iron and steel, all of the trees were chopped down. There was hardly anything left. . . . Soil erosion became a serious problem in the region.

Across from northern Sichuan, Hui county in southern Gansu province, northwest China, is also known for its rich forest. It is home to nearly 260 rare animal species, including the giant panda and the golden monkey. But during the Great Leap Forward more than half of the forest was destroyed. Chen Apo and Chen Gonggong used to live high up in the forested mountains in an area covered with giant trees, but during the Great Leap Forward they were forced to move down from the mountain as the trees were felled to feed to the furnaces and to make way for a local irrigation project. They are in their late seventies now. I was introduced to them by their grandson, who was studying at Sichuan University. Living at the bottom of a high mountain, and far away from anywhere, the Chens rarely have any visitors. They were rather thrilled by my visit. When I told them my intention, they sighed. Chen Apo pointed to the mountain above and told me what had happened.

> Our house used to be right in this mountain and the mountain was covered with huge trees. In 1958 and '59 all the trees disappeared around here. They were chopped down to make iron and steel to begin with. Shitou ping was the site for producing iron and steel. It wasn't far from here. Many people were sent there, and on the first day they were lined up to salute [the Great Leap Forward]. The work was exhausting, so exhausting that many people almost died. Some entire families were sent out to make iron and steel. In my family eight members were sent to the job. I stayed at home. I was in charge of cooking in the canteen. I cooked for those who were left behind. Only a hundred-odd people stayed back. These were mostly children. All those who could work were sent away, including women as well as men.
>
> The worst destruction of the forest took place during the construction of the Snow River irrigation project. Trees were

chopped down to make way for irrigation pipes and canals. The idea was to divert the snow water from the mountain and use it to irrigate the land. More than ninety strong laborers [from the village] were sent to build the Snow River project, at least two or three people from each family.

Every day, people went out to dig the canals until seven or eight o'clock in the evening, after the sky had turned dark. We ate at the construction site—there was a canteen there. The construction site was huge, covering an area of nearly a hundred kilometers. We had to walk from one side to the other. We also lived on the construction site. We were divided into teams, and each team lived in one big room or tent. We chopped down trees so that we could dig canals on the ground where the trees had been growing. The mountain was covered with trees in those days. They were all chopped down to make way for the irrigation canals that were dug across the entire mountain. The project lasted over a year and was never completed—the money ran out. The commune asked [the government] for some more money, but the government gave nothing. In the end the project was abandoned.

The situation was no better in the east of China. Xu Xiansheng, from Heze in Shandong province, recalls the destruction there.

In the olden days, straw stalks were the main fuel in the countryside. But in 1958 [at the time of harvest] no one was left to gather straw stalks. There was no fuel. The collective canteen had to cook for so many people, so they started to chop down trees after the fuel ran out. Almost every village in the Heze region started to burn logs and tree branches. So many trees were chopped down.

It was even worse during the mass production of iron and steel. I still remember it clearly. . . . To make iron and steel, almost all of the trees in our area were chopped down. The environmental damage was enormous. Before that our village used to be full of trees, very big and old trees, including lots of poplar and jujube trees. Gazing into the distance you could see miles and miles of trees. These were all destroyed.

It was like this in the surrounding countryside too. The east of Heze county used to be covered with ebenacea [persimmon] trees. Dried persimmon fruits from the area were famous throughout China. But all the ebenacea trees were chopped down during that time—more than ten thousand of them. Our village also had hundreds of jujube trees. They were huge. In the summer we used hide beneath them to keep cool, but all that went too. From winter 1958 into early 1959, tree logging was endemic—almost all the trees were chopped down.

North of Shandong, in Hebei province, although there was not a huge forest, a strange phenomenon happened during the time of the famine. As starvation became widespread, trees suffered as a result. Hui Xiansheng, a university student in Tianjin at the time, was sent to the countryside by the government to study the situation. He was astounded by what he saw in the countryside.

Between 1958 and 1962 I lived in Tianjin. I was a student at university there; 1960 was my final year at the university.

> We heard there was no food to eat in the countryside. The government said that this had been caused by problems in some of the People's Communes. So they sent us students to the countryside to sort out the problems at the People's Communes. I was sent to a village in Hebei. I stayed there for over six months. The countryside was very poor. There were no trains, so I traveled to the village with my fellow students on a lorry carrying goods. When I got off the lorry, I was stunned by what I saw. All of my fellow students were stunned by what we saw! The trees in the nearby countryside looked completely white! All of the trees were white! What really was going on? It turned out that the trees had been stripped of all their bark—the bark had all been eaten by the villagers. In that village the people had nothing to eat but tree bark. Soon I became one of them, and found myself eating tree bark too. If I hadn't, I wouldn't have had anything to eat. Rice, what rice? The government ration was one hundred grams of corn per day. We had to fill our stomachs with tree bark.

As food shortages continued for many years even after the famine, in Hebei trees continued to stand bare well into the 1970s. Frances Wood, the curator of the Chinese Department at the British Library, was a student in Beijing in the '70s. She tells me that one thing that struck her the most was that the trees she saw in Hebei were utterly bereft of low branches—they were long tall sticks with little tufts of branches and greenery at the very top because they were stripped of all lower foliage and branches by hungry people and animals. The damage caused by the Great Leap Forward was not only to trees, but to China's environment as a whole.

Environment

The mass production of iron and steel, the deep plowing, the deforestation and the countless half-baked Great Leap irrigation projects were not only an enormous waste of natural, economic, and human resources, but also left large parts of the Chinese countryside scarred forever. Man-made environmental disasters soon followed. The collapse of Banqiao Reservoir Dam in 1975 is but one example. Even today, the ecological consequences of the Great Leap Forward continue to affect people's lives and the environment in China.

Xu Xiansheng from Heze in Shandong, the home of the peony, recounts the consequences of unrestricted logging and irrigation projects in China's agricultural heartland in the north and central China plains.

> Chopping down so many trees was very damaging to the local environment. One began to see alkalization at that time. Almost all of the farming fields were damaged by alkalization. In the winter everything looked white. This was because of the high salt content in the soil.
>
> Before 1958, the soil in our area was relatively rich. But after 1959 and 1960, alkalization became a serious problem. Winter was the worst, as all the salt rose up to the earth's surface. In those days, no matter where you turned, all you saw was white-colored earth, whether inside the village or outside. Because peasants were very poor at the time and they had no money to buy salt, they would scratch off some soil and gather it together to make salt. They would put the soil into a basket, and put a layer of straw underneath it. After that they poured water on top of the basket so that the

straw became soaked in the salty water. Then they would dry the straw out in the sun. That's how people made salt. We called it "small salt" since sea salt is called "big salt" over here. You can just imagine how bad the alkalization was in those days.

The other thing was the irrigation projects. These started over here in 1958. Water conservation was meant to benefit agriculture, but in those days [the cadres] completely ignored science. We were instructed to build a labyrinth of canals and water channels, but in the end these all lay to waste. They couldn't get the water into the canals. I don't know whether alkalization had anything to do with it, but there is no doubt that those massive irrigation projects caused harm to the local environment. For the next ten years, alkalization was a huge problem in the regions around here, from Kaifeng and Shangqiu in the east of Henan all the way to northern Anhui and northern Jiangsu.

Alkalization badly damaged local agriculture. Production plummeted. Every year these regions suffered from food shortages. In 1963, after the famine had ended in the rest of China, and the problem of starvation was no longer a pressing issue for a majority of the population, over here and in the surrounding areas agricultural productivity remained low because of the problem of alkalization. Peasants continued to starve. . . . This went on until 1978.

Apart from alkalization, local people also suffered the devastation of floods. Qiaoer's home was in a mountain village in Huang county, Shandong province. She remembers what the locals had to endure in 1960 and 1961.

Our house was very close to the river. Flooding was a problem. After the river was flooded, water came into our courtyard. I remember my mother running out into the courtyard a few times with a chopper in her hand and shouting, "Dragon god, please divert the flood away." I don't understand fully why she used a chopper. It was the local custom. When there was a flood, people would bring out their choppers and plead to the gods to stop the rain. . . . I remember that quite a few times the water nearly entered our house. My parents were desperate. If our house had been flooded and damaged, we would have had to leave. We would have had to escape into the mountains with all our possessions. There were a few times like that when the rain didn't stop for two or more days. It rained savagely. . . . There was thunder and lightning—it was very frightening. I was so scared that I couldn't sleep, so I sat up all night watching the rain. I was afraid the water might come in and destroy our house and we'd lose all our possessions. . . .

[In our area] some houses did collapse, and people had to move up into the mountains or go to live with their relatives. The government only helped these families rebuild their houses, but that's all, nothing else.

In the east of our village there was a temple dedicated to the dragon god. Sometimes we would go there to pay our respects. When there was a flood, villagers flocked to the temple to ask for help. . . . Even after we joined the People's Commune, people continued to go to the temple. Many were still quite superstitious in those days. The government really didn't help people much. They helped with small

> things, but nothing very useful. So a lot of people, especially the older ones, would go to the temple to seek the help of the dragon god instead. My parents did not believe in gods, but they went to the temple anyway.

While floods and alkalization devastated north and central China, in the northwest, as a consequence of deforestation, sandstorms hit the region regularly, seriously damaging local life and agriculture. At the time Xiao Bai was a teenage orphan living in Gansu province's Dunhuang county. Dunhuang is famous for its ancient cave paintings, and it attracts a huge number of visitors each year. But in Xiao Bai's memory, this is a miserable place with extreme weather all year round, and sandstorms were a regular feature when she lived there. She remembers how she used to toil all day long to no avail.

> On many occasions I spent all day watering the fields, and in the evening they would be covered in sand again. The harsh wind often swept across the Gobi desert and covered the land with a thick layer of sand. So the next day I would have to repeat my work all over again. . . . Life was very bitter for us at the time. Apart from the hunger, the weather was also very severe in Gansu. It was terrible. We were regularly hit by fierce wind storms. There were sandstorms all the time. . . . Because there was a lot of sand around, younger people would make sand balls. My younger sister was hit by sand balls many times. Her eyes were covered with sand, and she cried and cried. I could never forget how miserable it was for us.

"Natural Disasters"?

On October 1, National Day, 1960, an editorial in the *People's Daily*—the official voice of the Chinese Communist Party—lamented that in the previous two years the country had witnessed unprecedented "natural disasters." This became the official line for explaining the devastating famine. Ordinary people did not dare to challenge the authorities, but they knew there had been no "natural disasters."

Wu Laotai is an illiterate housewife from Beijing. Born in the beginning of the twentieth century, she has lived under four different regimes—the Manchu empire, the Nationalist government, the Japanese occupation, and Communist rule. She was sold to be married when she was only ten years old. For the following eighty years she has lived in the same area of south Beijing, and has never been anywhere else. She is now in her nineties, and bed-bound because of ill health. Being poor and old, she is left out of the government's social health insurance reform. She has been living in a small dark room for nearly sixty years. There is no running water, kitchen, or toilet. I am told that she might be forced to leave her home because Beijing is undergoing massive reconstruction, and the area where she is living is in danger of being demolished. Lying on the bed, she shares her fear of the uncertain future. When I asked her how life was for her at the time of the Great Famine, she tells me that until this day she has not understood what really happened in the late 1950s and early '60s.

> In 1960 there were severe food shortages everywhere. It was a very difficult time—even with money we had no way of buying any food. . . . I couldn't understand why there was no food. All over the country, from Shanxi to Hebei and

Henan, people could not get enough to eat. It was called a "natural disaster," but how could it have been "natural"? Such a big country—how come natural disasters happened everywhere all at once? I didn't understand. I didn't even know what a "natural disaster" was. Was it really that there was no rain and no food growing? Three years of "natural disaster"! Everyone suffered from starvation. My husband and I thought that as we had finally been freed from the tyranny of my mother-in-law, and my husband had a secure income, life would improve for us. But we could not get any food to eat. We were told that we had to eat at the collective canteen, so there it was, we lost our freedom all over again. We handed over our food rations in order to join the canteen. At the canteen, we ate whatever we were given. . . .

I was pregnant with my youngest son and I was craving some sour plums. But all the grocery shops in Beijing were empty, and we couldn't even buy any soybean paste. What kind of "natural disaster" could be this severe? How come all the shops were empty? How come I couldn't even get my hands on any sour plums?

Liushu, the man from Wengong district in Sichuan's Renshou county who told me that he has supported the Communist Party most of his adult life, however disagreed with the Party on the issue of "natural disasters." He reflects on what happened in his village during those years.

As part of the Great Leap Forward, people were ordered to produce large amounts of iron and steel. Many farmers were sent away to make iron and steel, and some were sent to work in coal mines as well. There were hardly any laborers left in the countryside. Some people escaped and returned home, but they were punished by being deprived of food. After that no one dared to run away, otherwise they would have had nothing to eat and they would have starved. . . .

The reservoir construction in Wengong started during the time of the Great Leap Forward. It was a failed Great Leap Forward project. It was abandoned after only one year. . . . All over the county, more than ten thousand people were sent to build the reservoir every day. This lasted for a year. After a year, the project was stopped. It turned out that they had got the measurements wrong for the geology of the area. At the time they didn't tell us anything—not even whether the project was going to go ahead or not. This went on for a year. In the second year, they stopped building the reservoir, so it was just left like that. They did not explain their reasons, and no one dared to ask.

The government also misled us over agricultural production. The "Wind of Exaggeration" blew across the country. We were told that the more we grew, the more we would harvest. They told us that if one crop could produce so much grain, then three crops would produce three times more, and four crops would produce four times more, and a hundred crops would produce a hundred times more. That was the way that they calculated. We were told that for each mu of land we should grow eighty to one hundred catties of seed. According to their calculations, the more we planted the more we would harvest. In the end hardly any food was produced. This was the result of the "Wind of Exaggeration." It was the blind leading the blind. The upshot was a decrease in agricultural productivity. Hardly anything was produced. Imagine seventy to a hundred catties of seed for each mu of land—how could anything grow? In the end nothing was produced at all.

At the time we also had to deal with having to work in one place on one day, and another on the next. Sometimes we even had to work in different places on the same day. Occasionally, the government inspection teams would turn up, and we had to be prepared. Before they appeared, we were hurried around from one place to another, and then again and again. We would have to race to any number of places to work. We ran around all day long and then when it came to mealtimes we couldn't eat because the inspection teams still hadn't left, so we got desperately hungry.

Even on New Year's Eve, we still had to do a half-day's work. On one New Year's Eve, we were told to make fertilizer. In those days, to make fertilizer meant to shovel soil and grass. There were no chemical fertilizers at that time. When the "Wind of Exaggeration" was blowing there was one day when the cadres told us to transport the soil up onto the hill, and to pile it up neatly. After we did all that, on another day they told us to move the soil back into the farming field. . . . In order to pass the inspections, people would cheat. We would point at the grave mounds farther away and tell the inspection teams what they could see in the distance were the piles of fertilizer that we had gathered. That's why productivity decreased so dramatically during those years. I remember that one year our production brigade produced only a little over ten catties of cotton per mu. How hopeless!

> At the time, the government called it a "natural disaster." How could the whole country suffer from the same "natural disaster"? It was the same all over the country. . . . This was the Great Leap Forward. Instead it actually reduced productivity. . . . In many respects, the damage was enormous.

Not far from Liushu's village, at Hushu's home village in Renshou county's Wangyang district, the local villagers understood clearly at the time what the problem was.

> My home village was in Wangyang. The local people used to say that the famine was not a natural disaster. They said that the weather we were having was perfect for the crops. So what actually happened? It started with the Great Leap Forward, making iron and steel. In 1958 all the young and strong laborers were sent to make iron and steel. Even the women in our village were sent out to Leshan to build the railway. Only the elderly and the sick were left at home, so no one was there to harvest the crops when they became ready, and the crops were left to rot in the fields. How can you say that this was a "natural disaster"? It was clearly a man-made disaster!

4
Starvation and Death

As the year 1959 continued, so the famine worsened. It was exacerbated by intense violence in the communes, endless political campaigns, and a redoubled effort to push the Great Leap Forward after the August 1959 Lushan plenum. By the time winter arrived, famine had taken hold in most parts of China.

The government failed to provide adequate health care or famine relief strategies. Illnesses such as edema, caused by malnutrition or eating poisonous food substitutes or rotten food, became endemic. Amenorrhea, the cessation of menstrual periods, was widespread among women, and birth rates dropped dramatically.

At the forefront of the Great Leap Forward were the four largest agricultural provinces—Sichuan in the southwest, Anhui and Henan in central China, and Shandong in the east. Between 1959 and 1961 these four provinces had also clocked some of the highest death rates in China. To this day it has never been clarified exactly how many people died in this largest famine in history, but a government agent's investigation compiled in the autumn of 1962 indicates that at least 12 million people were wiped out in Sichuan alone.[1] In parts of eastern Sichuan and in the province's western frontier close to Tibet, death rates exceeded 50 percent in 1961. Anhui may have lost fewer people than Sichuan, but its overall death rate was the highest in the country, accounting for almost 20 percent of its population. In the province's agricultural heartland, more than 2.4 million people perished in the famine between 1959 and 1961 in the Fuyang region alone.[2] At the time, Anhui's provincial Party secretary was Zeng Xisheng, a devotee of Mao and an ardent supporter of the Great Leap Forward. Often referred to as a tyrant, Zeng launched endless water conservation projects in Anhui, which used up agricultural fields. These costly projects not only killed crops but led to mass starvation in Anhui. Millions died. Local cadres were terrified of Zeng, and they tried to cover up the numbers of deaths. In the Fuyang region, in preparation for Zeng's inspection, a severe edema sufferer was forced to hide underneath a stone mill: she died the next day. In Taihe county, at least 85,628 people died in 1960, but only 68,000 deaths were reported. Any cadres who dared to speak the truth about the damage caused by the Great Leap Forward were purged and expelled from the Party.[3]

In northeastern China, another grain surplus area, the death toll was comparatively lower, and the impact of the famine seemed less severe. This was largely linked to the region's low population density, since Party documents show grain shortage was also a problem in the region.[4]

With such a large number of people dying every day, bodies were often left exposed. In the majority of villages there was hardly anyone left to deal with the dead. The smell of rotting flesh filled the air. Many corpses were devoured by hungry rats; some mummified. Inured to the death around them, people were forced to struggle on with their daily tasks, passing by dead and decaying bodies as if nothing had happened. Eventually, many of the living resorted to eating the flesh of the deceased. While cannibalism remains a disturbing and usually rare event in human societies, for those who were surrounded by raging violence, horror, and death, eating dead human flesh did not seem so extraordinary.[5]

When the scale of the famine could no longer be contained, the government at first tried to blame the local cadres. It was only after the second half of 1961 that the leadership, directed by the state president, Liu Shaoqi, began to introduce changes to limit the damage. By then millions of people had already died, and famine-related deaths continued well into 1962. As I was interviewing for this book, I was often told that at the time many people had believed that if the devastation was to continue for much longer, no one would get out alive.

Dingyuan county in eastern Anhui is not far from the Fuyang region. Being the biggest and the most populated county, Dingyuan is now Anhui's granary. "Dingyuan pork," "Dingyuan duck," and peanuts from Dingyuan are delicacies much sought after by people from all over China. More than fifty years ago, however, Dingyuan was a very different place. Although it boasted huge numbers of "sputnik fields," in reality very little food was produced. A huge number of villagers starved to death, and in some villages the death toll was as high as 60 percent. Huang Manyi, the woman who earlier recalled that life in the People's Commune was terrifying, at the time of the famine was around nineteen or twenty. Her story of the famine in her village horrified me.

> In 1959 we survived like animals, grazing [eating straight from the ground] on raw beans, wheat, and rice. By the end of the year—just before the western New Year in 1960—the death toll had become very high. There were so many dead bodies lying around, and the government officials didn't seem to notice. Toward 1961, people were dying on a daily basis. I don't want to continue anymore. I cannot bear to go on. [Pause]

In my village, more than half of the people died of starvation. Originally there were seventy families with a few hundred people. [During the time of the famine] some entire families died out. There were four people in my aunt's family: two adults and two children. All of them starved to death. In my eldest sister's and second sister's families, six people died of starvation. My big sister's two boys starved to death too. My fourth uncle lost a son and a daughter plus one grandson. No one was left in my mother's brother's family—they all died. My grandmother and grandfather also died. So many people died in those days that there were not enough coffins for the dead bodies.

From this area, as well as a great number of children and old people, many people in their forties also died in the famine. Most of them had been sent off to build dams and canals. A few managed to escape. They ran to faraway places in southern China and survived the famine.

Our village used to be quite big, with a few hundred people. But in those days hardly anyone was left in our village. More than half of the villagers died during the famine, including quite a few entire families. But there were no official [death] statistics. Even now it's still forbidden to talk about what happened.

South of Dingyuan, in a small village in the Chaohu region, I met with Zhang Wuhan, a man in his sixties who used to keep the fire burning at the collective canteen. Zhang's village is surrounded by the beautiful Lake Chao and fertile agricultural land. It has earned a reputation as the "land of fish and rice," but during the famine period, as elsewhere in Anhui, starvation, violence, and death haunted the farming population in Zhang's village and the whole region. To survive, Zhang tried to run away, but many villagers were not as lucky, he tells me.

> In our village too many people starved to death. Zhang Wukui's entire family died of starvation, including his wife, mother, and daughter. They used to be "middle peasants," but [during radical collectivization] everything they owned was taken away by the People's Commune. The cadres went to their house several times to search for stored food. Not a single item was left in the end. Zhang Wukui didn't have the guts to steal—he was too timid. In our village anyone caught stealing was beaten to death. One woman in the village was caught stealing a mosquito net. She was taken to the big brigade and was badly beaten. Afterward she committed suicide. As a result her husband went crazy, and he died soon after. . . . My uncle had one son and two daughters; both daughters died of starvation. . . . My father died in 1962 because of liver problems.
>
> . . .
>
> Xiao Wuzi [is from the same village]. His father was in his forties at the time. Being a strong and good worker he was dispatched to a canal and dam construction site to transport sand. The work was too tough, and there was nothing to eat. Not long afterward his health deteriorated. [The official in charge of the construction] dismissed him and sent him back to the village. He died as soon as he got home. Xiao Wuzi survived only by stealing food.
>
> . . .
>
> I ran away with the person in charge of security in our village. If I had not run away, I'd have starved to death too.

Being another important agricultural province like Anhui, Sichuan was also badly hit by the famine. My father used to tell me about the devastation of the famine in Renshou, where he was sent briefly to conduct medical research at the time, but it was not until I heard Liushu's story that I began to understand the scale of the famine in the area.

> For the first few months at the collective canteen conditions were not too bad: we could at least fill our stomachs with either sweet potatoes or radishes. Later on, agricultural productivity decreased. This was due to leadership errors. After the harvest, much of the grain was taken away to meet the government quota. In those days, the government imposed a procurement quota on each commune, and this had to be met first. What was left over was given to us. There was hardly any food left for us to eat. There were no government food supplements at the time, so we just had to eat whatever we got. Many people died of starvation.
>
> The worst year was 1960. Since there was not enough food, the canteen had to boil a big pot of water. They added the boiled water to the food, so people filled their stomachs with large quantities of liquid. People were desperately hungry. They grazed on raw peas, broad beans, and wheat grain. Grazing was extremely common in those days. As soon as the young pea pods began to appear, people would pick them and eat them raw. People were so desperately hungry that they would eat anything raw. . . . Over here many people suffered from edema, and their legs became swollen. Some people's legs swelled up so badly that they could no longer walk.

I remember that it was also in 1960 when the county introduced "crossing village farming." In Fangjia, the area where the "Wind of Exaggeration" blew most vigorously, after the government quota had been met there was hardly any food left for the villagers to eat. There was just one hundred grams of maize per person per day. Can you imagine eating just a hundred grams of maize a day? So little food! After a week, people began to die. I remember we were sent to Fangjia to do farming because so few villagers were left there. The village used to have three hundred people, but after half a month there were only a little over a hundred people left. Some died of starvation, and others, mostly women and children, had run away. The local population decreased dramatically. Dead bodies could be seen everywhere.

High up in the mountains of northwest Sichuan, in Mrs. Luo's village, very few people managed to survive the famine. Fifty years later, in May 2008, the village was buried by the Sichuan earthquake. Once again, Mrs. Luo was one of the few lucky survivors. Although Mrs. Luo managed to survive both the famine and the earthquake, being lucky did not bring her any luck. In 2011, disaster struck her village once more, and soil erosion destroyed the plot of land she had tilled. Suffering unbearable rheumatic pain, Mrs. Luo could not afford any treatment. But the bodily pain she is suffering now cannot compare with the pain of watching her loved ones die of famine, as Mrs. Luo tells me.

Life was very harsh at the time. In the collective canteen [each day] each adult only managed to eat one hundred grams of rice. The rice was often mixed with soybean residue.

The amount children could eat was even less—only half of what the adults got. We got hungry very quickly, but we had to keep on plowing the fields. Many people collapsed. Their bodies were laid out in a line. No one dared to go home for fear of being scolded by the cadres. But since no one had any strength left, we could do nothing but lie around. So many children died at the time. Some families had no one left. I remember going to visit one family. I called out to them, but I got no answer. They had all died. I often saw people collapse on the ground and never get up again. If I was not sent to work on the Yuzui [hydropower] construction project, I would never have survived the famine.

In my family I was the only one who survived. Both my sister and my mother starved to death. My sister was very frail at the time. She was so thin that she looked like a spring onion stalk. We received a ration of only one hundred grams of food at each meal, two hundred grams in total each day. She didn't last long. A huge skin ulcer developed on her body, and she could hardly walk. She sent her child to fetch food [from the collective canteen], but the child ate all the food in one go. That was all the food there was, and only two meals per day—how could one survive like that? The child died first, and my sister soon followed. After my sister went, my mother also died.

When my mother passed away, I did not go to pay my respect to her body. My husband went over. When we heard the news, my husband rushed over to help bury her. I wanted to go but I had to take care of my child. My mother-in-law urged me: "Don't go anywhere with your child on your back." . . . Cry? Yes, I cried. I carried my child on my back and I mourned for my mother. What did I think? My mother had died and I had to let it go. Even crying my heart out wasn't going to bring her back. Of course I felt sad—she was my mother. I didn't even know how old she was when she died.

My first child also died because there wasn't enough food to eat. The child was already two at the time. He was so hungry. He saw other people chewing maize cobs, so he picked one up too. But he couldn't digest it because it was so hard. Bits of the cob got stuck in his throat and he couldn't breathe. There was no hospital here. If he had been able to go to a hospital, he might not have died. If we had asked for time off to take the child to a hospital farther away, the cadres would have deprived us of our food rations. In the end we could do nothing but watch the child lying on the ground with saliva dripping from his mouth.

Of course I was sad. He could already call me "mother." He could also say "grandmother." When he saw my mother-in-law walking through the door, he would say: "Grandmother is back." And she would answer: "My grandson, are you waiting for me?" The boy spoke with a real charm. When he died it broke his grandmother's heart. She cried. She used her food rations to [hire some villagers to] bury the child. It's a custom over here not to bury our own deceased children.

Hushu's home village in Sichuan's Renshou county was topographically much better situated than Mrs. Luo's, surrounded as it was by fertile green hills. And yet, as in Mrs. Luo's village, very few people managed to survive the famine. Like Mrs. Luo, Hushu was one of the very few who was lucky enough to escape. Although moving deep into the mountains of Liangshan saved Hushu's life, in Liangshan there has not been that much of an improvement. After being forced by the local government to undergo a vasectomy three times because of the compulsory family planning program, Hushu now suffers from bad health. With no medical insurance or pension, he supports himself and his wife by running a small corner shop. He first mistook me for a journalist, and he wanted me to write about the injustice in his life. When I told him that I was collecting interviews to write a book about the Great Famine, he was more than eager to help. He told me straight away what happened in his village and family at the time.

> After 1958 there was practically nothing left to eat at the collective canteen. Almost all the food that had been kept in reserve had been consumed by that time. Each villager was only receiving one hundred grams of food rations per day, which consisted mostly of sweet potatoes. Ninety-five percent of the people in our village suffered from edema. Many villagers collapsed while out on the road. One day a group of people attempted to walk to the market, but they all collapsed and died halfway.
>
> In those days if anyone was caught stealing food they would be beaten to death by the local cadres.
>
> My oldest sister died in 1960. Except for one daughter, her entire family died of starvation. The daughter survived only because she was given away to another family. The rest of her family, including two sons, a daughter, and my sister herself all starved to death. The local cadres wrote me a letter announcing the news of my sister and her family's death. It

> didn't say how or why they died. I wanted to find out more about what had happened . . . but my older brother told me that I was looking for trouble. In the end I gave up.

To help me with my project, Hushu introduced me to his wife, Luo Guihua. Now in her seventies, Guihua was born and grew up in Sichuan's Jingyan county, not far from Hushu's village. In 1958 she was recruited to work on a railway construction site some forty-six kilometers away from her home village, and she was terrified by what she witnessed there.

> In 1958 I was sent to Leshan to build the railroad. I was only eighteen at the time. . . . Our group was assigned to transport coal. We had to pull the coal up from a ditch, and then bring it onto the main road. . . . My main duty was to load the coal onto the truck. Every morning I would get up at three o'clock to deliver and load the coal. I worked until eight before I could take a break. At three in the morning, the sky was still dark. One morning three of us were pulling the cart, and I was on the right-hand side. Suddenly I found myself stepping over a dead body. I immediately dropped my digger. But still I had to walk over the dead body—there was no way around it. The body felt very soft. I ran as quickly as I could. I was so frightened. While running back to our sleeping quarters, I looked underneath the bridge and saw a lot of dead bodies lying by the side of the river. They had come down from the upper reaches of the river. . . . Many people starved to death, and their bodies were washed down the river by floods. There were piles and piles of dead bodies. Sometimes a few families came to take the bodies away. For

the unwanted bodies, local people just dug a hole by the river bank and dropped the bodies into the hole. When the river flooded again, the bodies were buried beneath the water.

I was terrified at seeing so many dead bodies, so I decided to walk on the far side of the road away from the river. But to my surprise I found myself walking over a dead body once again. When I walked down to the river, I stepped over yet another dead body. It was a small child's body. I was really, really frightened. . . . I cried and asked for permission to return home. . . .

Back in my home village, life was terrible. . . . There was no food to eat. Not even rotten sweet potatoes. . . . How could we fill our stomachs? Sometimes we had to resort to eating earth. It was called "immortal grain" [*guanyin tu*]. Many people dug it up from underneath the walls and pressed it into cakes. To get some "immortal grain" people had to queue up. . . . We ate anything we could find, and some of the things we ate were really crude and rough. People often suffered from constipation. My grandparents, for example, became constipated after eating [immortal grain], and they had to use their fingers to scoop out the hard stool. At the time, we also had no money to buy medicine, and eventually my grandparents died of hunger. Well, one might say that they died as a direct result of eating soil. They died of dysentery . . . but ultimately their death was caused by starvation. There was nothing to eat, and neither was there anything to wear. When my grandparents died, we could not even afford a coffin, so we had to wrap their bodies up with dried straw. Life was that miserable. . . .

I made offerings when my grandparents died. There was nothing else I could do. I had seven brothers and sisters. I blamed it on—who was it?—one of my uncles. After one of my grand-uncles died, this uncle brought his dead body to our house, and afterward people kept on dying in our family. For example, four of my brothers and sisters died after that. They all starved to death. Seven people died in my family all together. In my area a lot of people died at that time.

From a small village in Sichuan's Ziyang county, Yan, the chef, still a child at the time, witnessed the famine taking three lives in his family.

Life was very harsh at the time and there was hardly any food to eat. In our village the majority of people suffered from edema, and more than one hundred of them died as result.

The number of deaths was horrifying. There were no such things as coffins. Dead bodies were simply shoveled into an empty cellar. Some surviving family members might go to pick up the dead bodies of their relatives, but if no one was left in the family, the edema clinic would just shovel the body into an empty cellar used for storing sweet potatoes. They would just put some earth on top to cover up the bodies. [Laughs]

When the government officials came [to inspect], they were told that life was very good. All the edema patients from the clinic were dragged away from view into the sugar-cane fields so that no government official could see them. Only after the officials left were these patients allowed to return to the clinic.

My younger sister, my father, and my second elder sister all starved to death. My younger sister was only a few months

> old when she died. There was no one at home to look after her. You see, in 1958 people worked collectively. From early in the morning adults had to leave home to go to work. In the evening they had to work extra hours. Even as a child I had to work extra hours at night time. We children had to pick grass in those days.

Zhu Erge was also a boy when the famine broke out in Sichuan. He lost two grandmothers and a little brother. In his village 70 percent of children born at the time suffered from Kashin-Beck disease—a chronic degenerative ailment that destroys the growth cartilage and joint cartilage in childhood.[6] Known locally as "big bone disease," the victims were unable to stretch their knees or to walk. Because of this others in the area called the village "dwarfs' village." On my last visit there in October 2010, a number of villagers suffering from the disease told me that they continue to experience chronic pains. Discussing the problem with Zhu Erge brought him back to those terrible years during the Great Famine.

> In our village most of the children born in 1958, '59, '60 and '61 suffered from "big bone disease." Before that there were only two or three such cases in the area. . . . But during the period of collectivization, big bone disease became endemic in our village. . . . Many people born in those years lost the ability to walk. Even now, many of them still cannot walk. . . .
>
> An entire community of dwarves like ours is quite rare. . . . From 1958 our area faced severe food shortages. Our village had a collective canteen, but the standard was very low. . . . In the canteen each person received only one hundred grams

of rice per day. On a better day, we might get to eat two hundred grams of rice, but most of the time we only got a hundred. . . . The food was divided up according to the number of villagers. The amount of food each family got depended on the number of people in the family. Sometimes we only managed to take home one spoonful of food. . . . The amount was not enough for each person to have one mouthful, so we had to dilute what we had with water. We had to find a way to fill our stomachs. Even if it was just liquid, it could keep us going for a short while. After a while many villagers suffered from edema. The disease was widespread here. Some people had huge swelling spots growing on their skin. Many became severely ill, and eventually died. . . .

A lot of people died in those days. Some entire families were wiped out. . . . In our area, almost every farming brigade lost several families. . . . In our village, a number of families ceased to exist. They all starved to death. So many people died of starvation, including many entire families. Let me think, at least thirty or forty people died here. There used to be more than a hundred people in our village. By the end of the famine very few people had managed to survive. . . .

The situation in my family was comparatively better than that of others, but still three of my family members died. They all starved to death. . . . Both my grandmothers, from my father's side and my mother's side, died of starvation. There was nothing we could do. My father was a cadre at the time, but even he nearly starved. . . . It was pretty hopeless. One of my younger brothers, a lovely boy, also starved to death. He was always hungry, so hungry that he would even gobble down a whole green chili. Never mind green

> chili, in those years we ate almost anything—from sweet potato leaves and stalks to leather chairs. We soaked the leather chair in water until it turned soft. Afterward we cut the leather into pieces and cooked it. Then we ate the cooked leather piece by piece. Each leather chair was sold for half a yuan or one yuan. Even worse, we also filled our stomach up on the chaff used to stuff pillows. Yes, we ate pillow chaff. The situation was as bad as that.
>
> I remember there was one young boy who died after he swallowed some unshelled raw broad beans he had just picked from the field. He choked on them and died there and then. People wrapped his body in some sweet potato leaves and stalks. He was left like that for several days before being buried. After he was buried, we even ate up the sweet potato leaves and stalks [used to wrap his body]. How terrible things were!
>
> When somebody died, there was no such thing as people coming to pay them respect. No such thing. Dead bodies were left out for many days before the farming brigade could find people to bury them. The dead bodies were pulled out, or carried to a ditch on a ladder, and then thrown down. The bodies were covered up with a bit of earth. . . . When there was hardly anyone left to transport the dead bodies to the ditch . . . the corpses were simply wrapped up in pieces of badly torn bamboo mats. That is if there were any bamboo mats left. . . . Otherwise people might shovel on some earth to cover up the body. Often the feet were left exposed. It was terrible to watch.

Health problems among children due to severe malnutrition were not unique to Zhu's village. Birth rates also dropped sharply. In villages such as Luo Guozhen's, in Hongya county, I was told that hardly any children were born between 1959 and 1961. The village, in southwest Sichuan close to the border with Tibet, is very picturesque, surrounded by high mountains blanketed with evergreen trees. The vast, lush forest not only sustains more than four hundred species of wildlife, it also provides the surrounding area with rich natural resources. Today the area is also famous for its high-quality dairy products, and a large part of the land has been converted into organic farms. But back in 1959, the Year of the Pig, which is usually regarded as a year of fertility and prosperity, hardly anything grew here. Most women were barren, and almost no children were born. At the time, Luo was working elsewhere, and during one of his visits home, he was greatly pained by what he saw:

> In 1959 when I went home for a visit, I saw a bowl of food in the cupboard. I thought my mother had made a special treat to welcome me home, but when I tasted it, it turned out to be unbearably bitter. Too bitter to swallow! I learned that my mother had to eat this stuff every meal. She gave all her food rations to my three younger sisters. The oldest of my younger sisters was eleven or twelve at the time, and my second younger sister was eight or nine. My youngest sister was only three or four. There was hardly anything to eat in those days. Every time my mother brought food back from the canteen she would let my sisters eat first, while she would go and find wild grass or bitter buckwheat for herself. She mixed these with chaff, which she had to hide under the roof. She even ate mud. She didn't eat these things for nutrition—she only ate them to fill her stomach.
>
> Many people suffered from edema. It was caused by malnutrition, lack of food and starvation. Their bodies

swelled up, and their skin became very tight, smooth, almost shining and transparent. If one pushed a needle into the skin, liquid would burst out. . . . My father was in his fifties then, and he was a strong worker. But because there was no food, he starved to death.

. . .

At the time, there was only one traditional medicine doctor working at a clinic at the nearby market town. When people went to him for treatment, he simply told them: "If you can find some squash or pumpkin, cook them up together with some maize flour. Get that down and you might be able to live." That's all. There was nothing at the time, no medical care. People were at the mercy of the cadres. A cadre's words were worth gold. It was considered amazing luck if they happened to let you have some food. Most of the time people ended up with nothing.

There were seven big production brigades in our area. During that year, not one woman gave birth to a child. Why? Because people had nothing to eat. Most people were so poor and hungry, and their health was in a terrible state. It is no wonder that women could not bear children. Many women suffered from amenorrhea, and infertility was widespread. Infertility was linked to amenorrhea. It was caused by malnutrition. Men also had a very low sperm count. Only the wife of a local village Party boss managed to give birth to a baby. There were no other children of the same age in the whole region. There was a local saying: "Cadres are always full, but peasants are always starving." Privilege came from power. Cadres took food for themselves, so no wonder they were able to have children. But ordinary villagers looked

> sallow and emaciated. They could barely walk steadily, and most of them were having a hard time keeping themselves alive. How could they bear any children? Never mind raising children, people weren't even able to carry any children. That's how it was.
>
> . . .
>
> So many people starved to death at the time—it's horrifying. It was so painful. Even now, when I think of that time, I still feel a great pain.

Zhang Dabai, another person I met through Hushu, also lives in Zhaojue in Liangshan Yi Autonomous Region in the southwest of China. He was one of the first Chinese to migrate there in 1957, soon after the Chinese Communist army had conquered the region. To consolidate its rule, the government sent many ethnic Chinese to help in "developing" Liangshan. Zhang was among them. During the time of the famine, Zhang worked as a driver for a government-run transport company. On his many journeys, dead bodies were the most common sight he came across.

> At the time of the famine, my salary was only fifteen yuan per month. For fifteen yuan, I had to drive day and night. I worked double shifts, and I did not get any breaks for sleep. There were two drivers allocated to each vehicle, so when I felt really sleepy and couldn't go on any longer, I'd put two wooden boards on the back of the truck and sleep on that.
>
> What was Zhaojue like in those days? At the time, nothing grew here. Even a box of matches had to be ferried in from Chengdu. With my fifteen-yuan salary I couldn't even afford to buy a pumpkin. . . . Over here there was a saying that

"three people share one pair of trousers." It's true that in those days one pair of trousers would cost the equivalent of three persons' cotton ration coupons.

Over here the local population was from the Yi ethnic group. We lived with them, and slept above their stables. In order to build the road [from Sichuan] to Yunnan, we had to go up into the mountains to work. We camped in tents: twenty-four people in one tent. . . . The weather was much colder in those days. . . . In the winter everything was covered in snow. Rivers were frozen, so there was no water. We didn't have anything warm to wear, and there wasn't anything to eat. It was very tough.

. . . In those days when you walked in the streets you would always hear people saying: "I'll give you money if you give me your rice coupon." Another common saying at the time was: "Let's fill our stomachs today so that we may die content. It's better to die as a satiated ghost than as a hungry ghost." At the time half-kilo national rice coupons were sold for three yuan each. My monthly salary was only fifteen yuan! Sichuan also had its own ration coupon system, and the provincial rice coupon could only be used in Sichuan. But in the Ya'an region, not far from here, the rice coupons were useless because there wasn't any food in Ya'an.

There used to be a saying that "people were bloated to death." What did we mean by that? We meant the dead people were all puffed up. How come? Because many people in those days died of edema. Their bodies were very swollen. There were also a few people who died because they had eaten too much. They were so hungry that having managed to get their hands on some food they just couldn't stop

> eating. Because their stomachs were completely empty, they couldn't digest that much food all at once. . . . I knew one family in which every single person died.
>
> When I was out driving on the roads, I often left [Zhaojue] and saw people lying around all over the road. Many of them could still move. But on my return from Chengdu at night all I saw was dead bodies along the road. Some bodies had their eyes missing—these had been pecked out by the hawks. . . . I was lucky to have managed to defy death and to survive, but many people did not make it.

Far from Sichuan, Henan in central China is another major agricultural province. Also densely populated, Henan matched Anhui and Sichuan in its death toll. Yeshu's village is located in Zhangliang, a small historical township under the administration of Lushan county—Henan's Great Leap Forward model county, which boasted of its high steel production. One crucial fact the official propaganda left out was that during the time of the famine Lushan county also achieved some of the highest death rates in southern Henan. Yeshu is one of the very few still alive who witnessed the massive deaths at the time.

> From the second half of 1958, food had become scarce, but the cadres lied about the actual situation. Different communes exaggerated about the amount of food they were producing. They were encouraged to launch agricultural "sputniks." Whoever boasted of the highest production figure was given the greatest praise. Some of the figures were very high, but in reality hardly any food was being produced. There was nothing to eat, and many people starved to death over here. . . .

I don't remember exactly how many people died. . . . I only remember that after people died the commune sent a cart to take the dead bodies away. In those days our farming brigade kept donkeys, and they used the donkeys to pull the carts carrying the dead bodies. Since so many people had died, the commune could not keep up with the rate at which people were dying. They failed to remove all of the dead bodies from people's homes. Many corpses were left lying around until they began to stink. Some bodies eventually mummified. Families had to carry on their daily activities as normal with the dead bodies lying around in the house. It was as if nothing had happened. People had to continue doing whatever they had to do.

In my brigade there was a man who was just a little older than me. After he died, I was given the task of burying him. [There was no coffin,] so our village cadre told me to cover his body with two earthenware jars. These jars were made by the villagers. In those days I hardly had any strength left myself—how was I going to manage pulling a dead body as well as two jars? I was exhausted. I dropped the body into a dried-up well first, and then I dropped the two jars into the well. The jars sealed up the well completely. That's how I buried him! That's the way he was buried!

. . .

This person's mother also starved to death. Actually his father died first. They threw his father's body into a ditch and covered it up with two earthenware jars as well. When his mother died, they threw her body into the same ditch, and once again covered it up with two more jars. Later they sealed up the ditch with some earth. Eventually this man's brother also died. The brother was about three or four years older than me. . . . When the brother died, they put his body into a used food sack and tied up the top end of the sack. Afterward I threw his body [into the same ditch with his parents]. At least the three of them were buried in the same ditch. Three bodies! Four people in total died in that one family. There was only one brother who managed to survive in the end. He was desperately hungry and fled to Xinjiang.

I also wanted to escape to Xinjiang, but I was not on my own then. If I was on my own, I would have run away. . . . For the majority of people here there was no escape at that time. To where? Where could one escape to? We belonged to one commune, one brigade, so where could we go? Only a few managed to run away, and they survived. The ones who managed to run away escaped death. They were all very capable people, but there were very few of them. The majority of villagers were very obedient and meek. Most people did not dare to move. In those days people were allocated to collective canteens depending on where they lived. Everyone ate at the canteen. We were tied to the canteen—there was no escape.

After people had been starving for a long time, their bodies started to look extremely thin. When their condition deteriorated, their bodies started to puff up and they looked as if they were really fat. Many of them looked awful and they developed terrible shakes. Their hands and feet became so swollen that they could barely walk. You could see people like that everywhere. In our village there were people lying around in the fields at every turn.

. . .

When things got really bad, the district government set up a clinic. . . . Those who suffered from edema were sent to this clinic. People were told not to smoke—they were told that smoking would make their edema worse. But these people could not resist their craving for tobacco.[7] They would hide tobacco in their pockets. The more they smoked, the more swollen their bodies became, but the more they were told not to smoke, they more they just craved for tobacco. Many people died in the clinic. I think that the reason people were sent to the clinic in the first place was that they were already dying.

. . .

In those days even the pigs had hardly anything to eat. They were given whatever we were eating. In their desperation, hungry pigs started eating other pigs. Big pigs attacked and killed small pigs, and ate their flesh. . . .

In our area, although people were desperately hungry, we did not hear of any incident of humans eating humans. I did however hear about people eating cow dung. When people were desperately hungry, they would slice the cow dung into small squares, and then eat it just like one would eat sliced cake. Besides cow dung, people also ate the straw used to feed animals. Some villagers used to chew straw with their teeth.

Eh [long sigh], thinking back now, how desperately hungry we were in those days! The reason I didn't die was because I had two sisters. They went everywhere looking for food. We survived on what they brought home. Because of their resourcefulness the three of us did not starve. Those who had no means of finding food did not survive the famine. Many people over here starved to death.

Liu Moumou's village in Fangcheng county, Nanyang region, is only about fifty kilometers south of Yeshu's village in Lushan. Liu was only four or five years old when the famine broke out, but the howling sound of those mourning for the dead made a deep impression on him.

> Many people died in the village next to ours. It's the local custom to mourn when someone dies. Our village and that village are separated by a river. In those days every time we heard someone crying, adults would tell us that someone had just died of starvation. We could hear people crying almost every day, and we knew that someone had just starved to death. We could tell how many people had died by listening to the sound of people howling.

East of Henan is Shandong, one of China's most important agricultural provinces, and widely known as China's "fruit and vegetable garden." Jimo county is situated in the prosperous eastern part of the province, close to the wealthy cities of Qingdao and Yantai.[8] During the time of the Great Leap Forward, however, the region was devastated by poverty and starvation. Li Dabai, the villager who told me how this was caused by the extreme left policies, was twenty-four years old at the time. The famine took the life of his father, and fifty years later he is still troubled by what happened then. As he speaks he bursts into tears.

> My father starved to death in 1961. It's really hard for me to talk about that time. [Crying] In those days there weren't even any coffins for those who died. The bodies were just covered up with some earth, and their feet were often left exposed outside.

In southern China, across the border from Hong Kong, the situation was no better in Deng Xiansheng's village in Dongguan. In 1962, the very few villagers like Deng who managed to survive the famine joined the mass exodus and escaped to Hong Kong. Today, living fairly comfortably in Hong Kong, Deng Xiansheng is still haunted by the horror that happened fifty years ago.

> Many people suffered from edema [in my home village]. It was caused by malnutrition. People's bodies became swollen. Some even had swollen eyes. In more severe cases people's skin turned semi-transparent. In our village people died almost on a daily basis. There were not enough coffins to bury all the dead, so people took down doors and covered the dead bodies with wooden doors. Watching people dying every day, and with nothing to eat, no one had any desire to do any farm work. The only thing people felt in those days was hunger.

All the way up in China's northwest frontier, Gansu province, surrounded by high mountains and the Gobi desert, is relatively poor. Under the extreme left leadership of Zhang Zhongliang, millions died in Gansu during the Great Famine. By comparison, Hui county in the southeast of the province is relatively wealthy, and rich in natural resources. But, as Chen Apo and her husband recall, many of their fellow villagers did not escape the famine. Death by starvation was commonplace at the time.

> At the collective canteen there wasn't much to eat. As time went on, food shortages became even worse. All the food we owned was handed over to [the commune]. In the

> beginning we were fed soybeans, but eventually these ran out. People were so hungry that they had no strength left to walk. Villagers went around looking for wild herbs to make soup. Many people died [of starvation] during the time of the collective canteen. . . . In one family all eleven members starved to death. I saw it with my own eyes. I went there to count the number of the deceased. In those days we all knew who had died. We ate in the same canteen, and we could see who had died. My second aunt and uncle died during that time. . . . I went to look after them. There was nothing to eat, and they died within a few days.

Compared with Hui county, conditions were far worse in other parts of Gansu. Dunhuang, one of the far western counties in Gansu famous for its ancient cave paintings, was also one of the poorest at the time. Xiao Bai, now in her late sixties, was born in a small village in Lushan county in Henan province, central China. In 1957 the family moved to Dunhuang under the government migration program, which was intended to consolidate the Communist government's rule in the frontier regions. In 1959 Dunhuang, like the rest of Gansu, was badly hit by the famine. It took the life of both her parents.

> From the second half of 1959 up until the first half of 1960, life became unbearable. For almost a year we literally had nothing to eat. Many people died in rural Gansu. . . . Among those villagers who had moved from Henan to Gansu with us, quite a few starved to death. . . . I don't remember the exact number—at the time I was still quite young. I only know that from one big village in Lushan over a hundred

families migrated to Gansu, and about thirty or forty of those people died. I did not go to see their dead bodies.

Both my parents were severely ill during this time. It may have been related to the famine, but I don't know for sure. No one could tell me what was wrong with them. At the time medical facilities were poor, and we had no money to pay for treatment. According to government policy migrant families like ours should have received help from the local government, but in reality we had no help whatsoever. My father died in 1959, and we didn't know what illness he had at the end. I remember that in his last days my father had hardly anything to eat. At the time we were so poor, and he was hungry all the time. My father was a big man, but he looked completely worn out.

The morning my father died, my sister and I went to the collective canteen as usual to collect our food. We were both very young at the time. We put a terracotta jar on a pole and we each carried one end. The canteen was very far away and it took us more than half an hour to walk there. After we returned home, I said to my mother, "I've heard that father is ill." She answered, "After you two left, he called for you. I told him you had left. He called for you again." . . . I went to see him. I called out to him, but he could no longer speak. It was about eight o'clock in the morning. He died later that evening. . . .

My mother was already very ill herself by then. After my father died she became really depressed. She wanted to take me and my sister back to Henan, but we had no money. To raise money, my mother started to sell our possessions. She sold things for whatever money she could get. . . . In the end she sold almost everything we owned. . . .

Gradually my mother became very thin and her skin turned yellow. When her condition became critical, she was admitted to the commune's health clinic. She stayed there for a week, but they couldn't find out what was wrong with her. So they told us there was nothing the matter and they discharged her. At the time she was already so weak that she could barely sit up or speak. Half of her face was swollen, so I told her to change her position a little. But soon after the other half of her face also swelled up.

We had planned to leave for Henan on January 6, during the [Chinese] New Year period. But on the fifth, at around three or five in the morning, my mother got up to urinate. I remember asking her, "Mother, why are you sitting up like that?" She answered, "I am going to pee." So I went back to sleep again. After a while I woke up and saw her still sitting there. Once again I called out to her, but she didn't answer me this time. The first time I spoke to her was at around five in the morning, and the second time was at around seven. I called out to her again and again, but she did not answer. She just sat there with her head drooping downward to one side. I didn't know what to do, so I helped her body to lie down. We had no relatives in Gansu and there were hardly any neighbors living close by. The one family next to us was local, and we had very little contact with them. In the end I had to run a long way to another Henan immigrant family for help. That family lived several kilometers away. I ran over there and told them what had happened. They followed me back to our place. But my mother didn't open her eyes, and neither did she speak. It was January 5, 1960, in the Chinese calendar when my mother died. She

> was only thirty-nine. She left me and my younger sister to look after each other.

While several million children like Xiao Bai lost their parents in the famine and became orphans, a huge number of parents also lost their children. Huang Mama, from a small village in the western Sichuan plain, just forty-seven kilometers southwest of Chengdu, tells me that she had to watch her own child succumbing to the famine.

> When government officials came to investigate they asked about how much food we had left. [The cadres] lied. They told the officials that there was plenty of food left. They filled a few storage rooms with sweet potatoes to fool the officials. When the officials uncovered the truth of the situation, they beat up the local cadres. But if the local cadres had been honest with them, they would have been beaten up anyway. The sweet potatoes ran out quickly, and there was no more food left. We were told the government was going to send us rice and that soon we'd be able to eat cooked rice, so on and so forth. What rice? On the contrary, we were left to starve. Many people starved to death. People collapsed on the road like sick cows.
>
> And still we had to carry on working in the fields. How could we not? We were told to plow the fields, dig the earth and till the soil. The government ordered us to make fertilizer. To do so we had to till the soil. We piled up some grassy earth into one big pile and used this to fertilize the fields. Sometimes we had to work till very late at night by the light of flame torches.

As time went by people had no strength left. They were called to go out to work, but all they could do was lie down next to the fields. All over the hills you could see people collapsing at every turn. They lay around looking like scarecrows. Many people died for the sake of collectivization. Too many people died in those days, and it wasn't possible to count how many. Dead bodies were just all over the place. I know that in our village many people died, but I can't remember the exact number. My own son starved to death—there was nothing for him to eat. Being a child, he couldn't digest very coarse things. Those rough vegetables, for instance. Day after day, he just got thinner and thinner. In the end he was nothing but bones—there wasn't a bit of flesh on him. His health deteriorated and eventually he died. Watching him dying, I couldn't feel anything. What was there to feel? There was nothing I could do but watch him die. Of course I was sad, but what could I do? In those days even lots of strong men died, so what hope was there for a weak child? Not long afterward, my husband also died. That all happened during the time of collectivization.

Li Anyuan, the villager from Langzhong county in northern Sichuan, also watched his own children die without being able to do anything.

I had nine children, and two starved to death during the time of the famine. In those days even adults couldn't get enough to eat, and it was even worse for children. Many people got ill and then died. People collapsed in the collective canteen. Cry? I am a man, I could bear it. But it's different

> for women. My wife wept. How did I feel? What could I do? These were my own children. Yes, I was sad, but what could I do? I had no other means. I was barely surviving myself, so what could I do to help my children? I had to leave it like that. Their little bodies were thrown away. The best we could do was to ask some people to help cover up their bodies with earth. Who cared what happened? No one cared in those days.

Southward, in central Sichuan's Jianyang county, Zhu Erge tells me that in his village—the "dwarves' village"—the situation was equally hopeless.

> People were dying at such a fast rate, . . . no one had the capacity or energy to care for anyone else. . . . Both of my grandmothers died of starvation. Of course my parents were sad about their deaths. But in those days, we had nothing, how could we care for the dead? . . . In those days every family lost a few people. By 1961 most families in our village had only two or three people left. If the situation had gone on for another two years, most people would have succumbed in the end. There would be no one left to care for anyone.

Close by in Mao Xiansheng's village in Renshou county, I was told that when the famine became really severe and a vast number of people died, the government did nothing to remedy the problem, save to hold a local cadre responsible for the disaster.

> Many people died in our area. A large number of deaths started occurring in 1960. On my way into town I often saw people collapsing and dying on the road. Dead bodies

could be seen all along the canals. Some of the families next door also died. In 1961 was the worst. Many people died of starvation. No one knows how many died. I only know lots of adults and children died of starvation. . . . One of my neighbors died at this time. The government did not send any food to help. They told us the famine was caused by "natural disasters." . . . Because so many people in Xianfeng commune died, the Party secretary Chen Kewu lost his position. He was held responsible and demoted to the position of a security guard. . . . It was only in 1962, at a meeting we were told the government would send some food to rescue us. If they'd waited a little longer, there would have been no one left.

5

Orphans of the Famine

Of the millions who died in the famine, about 20 percent were children. While too many parents watched their children vanish overnight, the famine also deprived several million Chinese children of parental love and care. Some children were abandoned simply because their parents had no food to feed them. Barely keeping alive themselves, many desperate mothers and fathers abandoned their children by the roadside or in outlying villages in the hope that some kind-hearted soul might take them in. For a bowl of grain, some mothers left their husbands and children to find a new husband elsewhere.[1] These "lost" children grew up not knowing where they had come from or who their parents were. An even greater number of children watched their parents starve to death.

Sichuan, one of the worst-hit famine regions, had the highest number of orphans. Between 1958 and 1962 more than 2 million children in the province lost their parents.[2] In China's relatively wealthy eastern region near Shanghai, the number of orphans was also shockingly high. One published report suggests that between January and March 1960, 5,277 orphans from the nearby countryside were admitted into orphanages in Shanghai.[3] One orphanage alone took in 109 homeless children on a single day. But even big and prosperous Shanghai offered no shelter for these vulnerable and starving children. When the food crisis finally hit the city toward the end of

1960, these children simply became a burden. More than 3,000 of them were transported from Shanghai to China's Inner Mongolia in the Gobi Desert. Those not lucky enough to reach Inner Mongolia were left to walk along the railway tracks. Some ended up in Shandong in eastern China, or in Henan and Hebei provinces in central China. Others got as far as Liaoning or Jilin in the northeast. Quite a number also wandered northwest to Shaanxi, Gansu, and Xinjiang. Anywhere there was a railroad, there were orphans to be seen. They became widely known as the "Shanghai orphans." No one knows how many Shanghai orphans there were in total, but one conservative estimate suggests there were at least 50,000.[4]

At orphanages and with their host families, a number of children suffered mental and physical abuse. Some eventually died of starvation, or from disease or constant beatings. In one orphanage in Sichuan, according to an official investigation at the time, half of the children suffered physical abuse and fourteen methods of torture were used regularly as means of punishment. Fourteen children died as a result.[5] Many of the orphanages were filthy; lice and disease were widespread. In some places orphans were not given anything to wear, and they were obliged to fill their stomachs with dead rats from the latrines.

In times of crisis, children are the most vulnerable, but they can also be the most resilient. Their ability to survive sometimes surpasses that of adults. Without a shoulder to lean on and with no home to return to, some of the orphans of the famine grew strong and resourceful. Many of them are now in their late fifties, married with children, but they continue to live with the nightmare of the famine. The deep mental scars inflicted by losing their parents, and by the brutality, hunger, and disease, will take more than one lifetime to heal.

I knew Wang Degao because his family had come from the same village as my grandfather. My grandfather was a poor peasant, but the Wang family was relatively wealthy in the village, with a business in the city. The Communist Liberation in 1949, however, changed the fate of the Wang family. His father died of starvation and illness in a Communist labor camp in the northwest of China. His "crime" was being a member of I-Kuan Tao, a religious cult banned by the Communists.[6] Not long afterward, Degao and his siblings also lost their mother. Wang Degao was in his teens when the famine broken out. He had a grandfather who was at very advanced age, and needed to be cared for. He tells me how he and his siblings struggled to survive in addition to caring for their grandfather.

> My father used to own a fabric shop in central Chengdu, but after the [Communist] Liberation he disappeared. We did not know why at the time. . . . As a child I had little contact with my father. My eldest brother was the only one who knew anything about him. He had gone to Chengdu when I was very young. My only memory of him was that he came home once a year over the New Year. Sometimes he wouldn't come home for a year and half, and sometimes he didn't come home at all. When business was busy, he would have to stay in Chengdu to look after the shop.
>
> After the Liberation, my father fled to Xi'an. . . . He was reported to the authorities. . . . They arrested him and sent him to a labor camp. The camp was in Shaanxi province. My father worked at a kiln there. This is where he became ill with edema, and later died. He was buried by the roadside close to the kiln. We received an official letter announcing his death. We also received a small amount of money.

At home, there were four of us, including my two younger sisters, I and my mother. Life was very difficult for us. I also had two brothers who had moved to Chengdu with my grandfather a little earlier. . . .

Earlier on my grandfather bought some land in Qingshui [just outside Chengdu], so that's why we moved here in the 1950s. Soon after we arrived my mother died and we were left to make do by ourselves. I was only thirteen years old when my mother passed away. To survive I had to go to work. I pulled carts, I did hard labor, I harvested grain and I did handiwork for people. I did many things. I had to find the money to support my two younger sisters. The government? What government? I was completely self-reliant. We hardly had anything. Life was totally desperate. It could barely be called living. We only just managed to survive. We were orphans! No one helped us. No one cared. We were born into the wrong political class. Because my grandfather had bought land, we were classified as landlords. We were also classified as industrialists, because my father owned a silk shop. No one would help people like us. We had to survive by ourselves.

We had no money to pay the rent, so we were forced to become squatters. The three of us first moved into a place about the size of a shoebox. We kept on moving from one place to another. From one small room in this courtyard we then moved to another room in the courtyard over the other side. Eventually we ended up squatting in a tiny room above someone's pigsty.

The responsibility of looking after our grandfather was shared between us three brothers. We took turns to provide food for him. Each of us would take care of him for ten days. . . . In those days, if we found some food, we would let him eat first. My grandfather had a good appetite. After he finished eating, we would eat what was left. He was our grandfather—we couldn't let him starve. He lived into his eighties. He was an elderly man, and we couldn't let him go hungry.

At the People's Commune, I was given the task of collecting human waste. I did that for several years. Each morning I had to get up at four o'clock to go to work. I could rest a little between my morning and afternoon shifts. In those days we had to do whatever we were told to do. If we didn't, we'd be in trouble.

A few times, I finished work late. The people who arrived at the canteen before me had eaten my portion of food. I was left to starve. Oh, dear, when that happened I just had to force myself to forget about my hunger. I had to carry on working. If I missed work or was late getting there, I'd lose my work points. If I lost my work points, I'd end up with nothing to eat. I relied on my work points to receive my portion of food.

Over here many people became ill and suffered edema. . . . It was dreadful! Some people's legs became so badly swollen that their skin burst open, and the liquid would ooze out. Eventually they died. In those days, many people died.

When we were really hungry, we would go to the commune's vegetable farm at night to steal vegetables. We added them to the food we received from the canteen. That's how we managed to survive.

Wang Dezheng is Wang Degao's younger brother. Today he lives next door to his brother in a dark and simple room. Because he was so poor, he did not get married until he was in his late thirties. His wife only married him because she is partially blind and was having difficulty finding a husband. Cheerful and more talkative than his brother, Dezheng took great pride in his survival skills.

> I moved to Qingshui when I was three . . . and I lived with my grandfather. He died toward the end of the famine.
>
> My father had a fabric shop in Chengdu, but after the Liberation he abandoned the business because he was a member of I-Kuan Tao. [The government] called I-Kuan Tao a counterrevolutionary organization.
>
> Gradually the government introduced communes in the countryside, and everyone had to eat together at the collective canteen. Each big farming brigade had a collective canteen. Initially I was given the task of preparing vegetables for the canteen. . . . At the beginning we did have enough to eat at the collective canteen. A lot of food was wasted in those days. As time went on no food was left and we started to suffer from starvation. For an entire year, we had no food. Life was terrible. . . . Many people starved to death.
>
> Not far from here, in Pi county near Majia bridge, an entire farming brigade died off except for three families. There had been dozens of families. . . . It was so frightening. I went there to take a look. There was nothing left in the village; no food at all. Some people's legs were very badly swollen. Some also had swollen faces and stomachs.
>
> Our village is quite close to Chengdu, so the situation was a little better. We received a ration of 250 grams of rice a day from the government: 150 grams for lunch, 50 grams for supper, and 50 grams for breakfast. The ration system was

introduced when it was no longer possible to carry on with the collective canteens and the government had absorbed the seriousness of the famine. Here we began to receive a ration of 250 grams of rice a day, but farther afield in other counties, people only got 50 grams of rice rations in a day. At the time, the majority of people in the countryside suffered from edema. At least we were able to go out and come up with some food to fill our stomachs. Those, especially elderly people, who had no means of finding food suffered terribly.

My eldest brother started working in a coal mine in 1958, which was the middle of the Great Leap Forward. I was left on my own to look after myself and my grandfather. At the time, my grandfather was still in good health. I often stole food from our farming brigade and took it home for us to eat. There was no other way. When no one was watching, I would go to the collective canteen to steal food. I was cleverer than most people, and I was never caught stealing. My second brother was caught once. [Laughing proudly] I was never caught.

I was smart. I never tried to keep any food at home. If I managed to find any food I would ask my family to eat it all at once and leave no trace of it. If the cadres had found any food at our home they would have confiscated it. Not only that, but the whole family would have been punished. Some people would steal food and hide it at home. I never did that. We ate everything I stole, and the next day I would go back and steal more. . . . so they couldn't pin anything on me.

After the collective canteen ended, my grandfather died. . . . It was in 1961, the winter of 1961, that he became ill. At the time he was in his eighties.

> After my grandfather died, I became homeless. I started living on my own. . . . In those days even children had to work, not like today. . . . If I didn't work, I couldn't get by. My eldest brother went to work in a coal mine. My second brother [Degao] was working all the time and he had to look after my two sisters. I was on my own. I did everything by myself.

Chef Yan, the friendly street cook from Ziyang county in southern Sichuan, is now in his early sixties. In the course of our conversation, I learned that he was still a young child when the famine took the life of his father and incapacitated his mother.

> After my father died, my mother became very ill and was sent away to an edema clinic. My elder brother was in the army at the time. At home there was only I, my younger brother, and my sister. My sister was a little older than us. We depended on her. She had to take care of the two of us. She did all the house duties as well as having to work for the farming brigade. Because my elder brother was serving in the army, we should have got some subsidies from the government, but we never saw the cash. We were told that the money had been used to pay our debts because we owed money to the brigade. Even years after the famine we were still forced to pay back our debts. It was a terrible time. As a child I shed many tears.
>
> That was the policy then, and there was no alternative. We did not have a strong worker at home, so we just had to suffer. I was very young at the time, but still our local cadres did not like to see me and my younger brother not working.

Every time they saw us, they chased us and forced us to work. So as soon as we saw them coming, we ran away. We often dived into a ditch to hide. If they caught us, they would order us to collect grass. At such a young age picking grass was all that we could do. Even if we were given vegetable seeds, we were too young and we had no physical strength or skill to grow them. Because I wasn't strong enough to carry a hoe, I had to work with a little digger. I could only dig for short periods. It was also hard for me to plow the fields—I didn't have much strength.

My eldest brother was in the army. He sometimes sent money to us. Once he sent us some rice coupons. He sent us over ten kilograms of rice coupons to the commune. We never knew about this. We only heard about it after the commune had ended and the coupons were no longer valid. We were too young at the time, and my mother was ill. To support us my brother saved up everything he earned. He did not get married until he was in his thirties so he could support us.

Zhang Ershu is originally from Jianyang county's Sancha district in Sichuan province. Zhang's mother died in the early 1950s while he was still a young boy. Some years later the Great Famine also took the life of his father. He became an orphan when he was only thirteen. In his village there were nearly thirty orphans like him whose parents had succumbed to the famine. In 1965 Zhang, still a teenager, joined the railroad construction team and moved to Liangshan high up in the mountains between Yunnan and Sichuan. Life was very harsh in Liangshan, and the work was very hard, but as a railroad worker Zhang could at least eat enough food to fill his stomach. When I met him he had already retired, and he relied on his humble retirement salary. Like Hushu he also thought I was a journalist, and he wanted me to write about the problem he and many retired residents in Liangshan are facing: winter in Liangshan can be severely cold. Zhang Ershu and other residents hoped the government would provide them a cold weather heating subsidy. But after several petitions, they had heard nothing from the government. When he heard that I was writing a book about the Great Famine, memories of starvation, horror, and the death of his father flooded back.

> Many people [in my village] suffered from edema. Some had swollen legs, others had swollen faces. Some people's entire bodies swelled up. Lots of people died in our area. In our production brigade, a family of eight lost six members to the famine. There were a lot of orphans in those days. In our brigade alone there were at least twenty to thirty orphans. Conditions were so miserable in our area.
>
> Both my parents died. My mother passed away earlier. . . . During the famine my father starved to death. I was only thirteen at the time. I was a survivor. After my parents died, no one looked after me. In those days no one had the energy to care for anyone else. I became homeless, and I had to find my own way to survive.
>
> Of course I was very sad when my father died. But what could I do? Sadness wasn't going to get me anywhere. At the time my older brother was in the army. When my father was very ill, all he wanted was to drink a bowl of rice soup. My brother sent thirty yuan to us . . . and with the money I ran to the town to buy five catties of rice on the black market. I was caught by an official. He wanted to confiscate my rice,

> but I wouldn't let it go. I held on to it very tightly. There were lots of people at the market that day, and some of them knew me. They surrounded us. . . . I turned around and bit the official so hard that he let me go. I then took the rice and ran. He chased after me, but he gave up when he saw me run into the river. He was afraid of water. The rice got very wet in the river. My father died before he could even finish the rice soup.

I met Zhang Jiujiu in a small roadside restaurant close to his home village in the Chaohu region in central China's Anhui province. To start with, he was shy. But after a few cups of alcohol and a hot meal, he started to talk. He told me that he was only ten when his mother was beaten to death by the local cadre because she had failed to meet the compulsory government poultry procurement quota. In addition to his mother, another thirty-six villagers from the same commune had also been punished and tortured to death. A few months before his mother's death, Zhang's father had fled elsewhere to escape starvation and poverty. Zhang Jiujiu was forced to move in with his eighty-year-old grandfather. Two years earlier the old man had lost his wife—Zhang's grandmother. Three weeks after Zhang moved in with his grandfather, the old man also starved to death. Zhang was left completely alone. He embarked on a journey in search of his runaway father:

> On the day my grandfather passed away, he went out before sunset and took a stool with him to the collective canteen to beg for food. After he had failed to find anything to eat, he died. There was no orphanage in my village, and to earn my food ration I was asked to tend the commune's

cows. Ten days after my grandfather's death, I decided to escape. In the night, I stole some wheat . . . so that I would have something to eat on the trip. The night I left, I walked all the way to the Tongyang River. I carried on walking all night long until the morning came, hoping I could get a train ticket when the station opened.

I had fifty yuan on me. The money had been left to the family by my father before he went away. Originally we had saved two hundred yuan at home, but after my father ran away the canteen manager struck us with a heavy fine. He even confiscated our trees [in our front yard]. . . . However, even though I had money on me, I couldn't buy a train ticket because I didn't have the right papers [or travel documents]. I was only a child. Fortunately, there was a worker next to me who was desperately hungry. I gave him a small bowl of the wheat I had stolen, and in return he bought me a ticket. It cost 1.75 yuan. I took the train to Yuxi first, and then the ferry to Wuhu.

. . .

From Wuhu I planned to head for Jiujiang. Again, without the right papers I couldn't buy a boat ticket. Suddenly I heard a man shouting out: "Who wants to buy a ticket? I can help you if you give me your food rations." It turned out that each boat passenger could use their ticket to purchase one packet of sesame cake and ten packets of dried bean curd. He bought me the ticket and I gave him the food. . . . The boat trip took two nights and three days. We arrived in Jiujiang at night. On the boat we could eat rice porridge plus two different types of pickles, such as pickled green beans and chilies. It cost only half a yuan, and we could eat as much as we wanted. Compared to life at home, this was truly Communism! The first morning I ate eight bowls of porridge. At lunchtime, I spent one yuan on four dishes and filled myself with five bowls of rice. . . .

We arrived in Jiujiang at about eight in the evening. It was already dark. Suddenly some uniformed officers appeared with guns in their hands. They were officers from the Anhui government inspection team. . . . All the passengers on the boat were detained, and only those with the right papers were released. One person from Chen village, not far from ours, was sent back home straight away. . . . I hid myself beneath the decking, and stayed there until everyone had left. . . .

From the boat I ran to Jiujiang train station, but when I got there I was arrested and detained for thirteen days. . . . They made me walk to the detention center. It took an hour. . . . About 130 to 140 people were in the same detention center, some from Anhui, and others from Jiangsu. The detention center was like a prison with high walls. . . . All of us were crowded in the corridor . . . and were not allowed to go out. At one point I got so desperate that I cried. . . . Many people died at the detention center. Their bodies were taken away, wrapped in sheets made from reeds.

I stayed in the detention center for thirteen days. Thirteen whole days! I was the only child. There were many men and a few women. Most of the women had run away to look for their husbands. After thirteen days the officials decided to send us all back to where we had come from. I remember that it was about one o'clock in the afternoon when they put us on to a boat. Since so many people had died in the detention center there were only about fifty or sixty people who ended up on the boat.

> At the detention center I made a friend. He was thirteen at the time, and from Henan province. He was sent on the same boat as me. We both pushed through the fence and got off the boat. We managed to escape. . . . Together we watched the boat leaving. . . . That evening we went to the train station again. We had no other choice. We managed to buy two tickets to Nanchang. Each ticket cost 1.4 yuan. My friend was also looking for his father. When the train reached De'an we got off. From De'an we went to Yongxiu. Yongxiu was like a jungle, covered in tall bushes and wild grass. The roads were very narrow, and we didn't speak the local dialect. Fortunately, we met somebody from Anhui. . . . I knew him because he had married a girl from our village. He took me to my father.
>
> My father was working on a vegetable farm in Yongxiu. . . . When we met I told him about the deaths of my mother and grandfather. His face barely registered the news. Death was normal in those days.

Xiao Bai, who complained about the severe weather and sandstorm in Gansu, is another who lost her parents in the Great Famine. She was eleven at the time and her sister was only six. When it happened, they were in Gansu: a strange land in the far northwest of China, where they had no relatives or friends to turn to. Along with millions of other children in China, they became orphans. Xiao Bai and her sister endured not only hunger but also abuse and hardship. Luckily she survived, and she is now married with three sons. The family lives in a small village in southern Henan's Lushan county in central China. Although Xiao Bai no longer has to endure starvation, her family is still relatively poor. The psychological scars of the famine and being an orphan have continued to affect her. In recent years she has turned to Christianity. She says that she finds solace in her religion, and she enjoys singing hymns. When I asked her about what happened to her and her sister during the Great Famine, she cried.

> It was January 5, 1960, according to the Chinese calendar when my mother died. She was only thirty-nine at the time. She left me and my younger sister to look after each other. I was eleven then, and my sister was only six. When my mother died, my head felt completely empty; I just did whatever people told me to do. I was very young then and I didn't understand much. Someone mentioned about sending us to an orphanage or something like that. There was an orphanage in Dunhuang, but I don't know why they didn't send us there in the end. In Gansu we had no relatives, no aunts or uncles. We had no one to turn to. There was a man whom my parents used to refer to as a brother. He was a little older than my parents, but not a blood relative. After my parents died, we went to live with him at first.
>
> He was—how should I put it—rather reckless. He was quite rough and fierce toward us. To begin with he was OK with me, because I was old enough to go out to work. When I went out to work, my sister stayed at home. This uncle wasn't nice to my sister. Winter in Gansu was very cold, and the temperature often dropped to 20 degrees below zero. Yet even in treacherous weather like this our uncle asked my sister to go out to pick firewood. How could she find any firewood in cold weather like that? One day, when it was dreadfully cold outside, my little sister returned home empty

handed. This uncle got angry and hit her on the head, leaving her bleeding heavily. I didn't know about the incident when it happened. I was working in the field at the time, and as always I had a lot of work to do. When I finally got back, I saw my sister holding her head in her hands. I asked her, "What's wrong with you?" "My head hurts," she answered. I asked again, "Why does your head hurt? Why don't you lie down?" "It still hurts," she replied. She was wearing a thick cotton hat that day. I pulled her hat down, and saw that it was covered in blood.

That day I took my sister with me, and we left. We had nothing and we had no money on us. We left all our belongings at that uncle's place, including things that my father had brought back from the army. Eventually we found somewhere else to live. We lived on our own until October 1962 in the Chinese calendar, and then we moved back to Henan. We lived on our own for a little over two years, from January 1960, when my mother died, until the autumn of 1962.

[During those two years] I went out to work like everyone else. Although I was only eleven, I behaved and worked like an adult, and everyone at our production brigade treated me like a grown-up. I was sent to dig canals and plow fields, and if other adults were assigned to a job, so was I. . . . At the time, I was terrified of the cadres. I worked very hard and did whatever they told me to do: I went anywhere they told me to go and I did whatever task they assigned me to. I have to say the cadres did not bully me. That winter the farming brigade even made two padded jackets for me and my sister. That was the only thing we ever received from the farming brigade.

I often took my sister with me to work. Other people took food with them, but I was too young to think of such a thing. One day while I was working, I heard my sister crying. I looked around and saw her being beaten up [by boys older than her]. . . . Life was really hard for us. No one can imagine how hard it was. In the beginning I cried a lot. But no matter how hard I cried, we continued to suffer. Even if I had cried myself to death, no one would have cared. Gradually, I learned not to cry. Suffering taught me to keep things like that in check. In my adult life I have rarely shed a tear. [She was crying at this point.]

. . .

Later on we decided to return to Henan. It happened that another couple was also planning to return to Henan. In those days the train fare was very cheap: it cost a little over ten yuan. I sold everything we had, including food and whatever, and managed to raise enough money so that my sister and I could return to Henan. We took the train. At the station the couple we traveled with told the ticket officer that we were orphans and that there was no one taking care of us, so they took us with them. That way we got a discount. We paid half price, which was a little over seven yuan. It cost just seven yuan from Hong Liuyuan in Gansu to Henan. The whole trip cost us ten yuan, including the bus fare from Dunhuang to Hong Liuyuan. The distance between Dunhuang and Hong Liuyuan was over 150 kilometers. The fare was very cheap in those days.

We were not the only ones who tried to leave. At the time many Henan immigrants were doing the same thing. Life was very bitter out in Gansu. Apart from the hunger, the weather was also very severe. . . . That's why people wanted to return home [to central China]. As the government did not allow people to leave, some people secretly escaped. I remember that on the way from Dunhuang to Hong Liuyuan [railway station], some people were stopped and banned from taking any buses. But they would not give up—they went by foot. They would have been willing to walk all the way home. Some people died along the way. I remember that two people who were older than us died on the road.

But life wasn't any better in Henan either. Our home village is part of Zhangliang town and the area has very little in the way of land. Limited land meant little food. I remember that we used to receive fifty kilograms of wheat per year for three people. Even now, some places in this area are still poor. At home we lived with my grandmother. My grandfather lived elsewhere with his family. He had another wife, but the first wife did not bear him any children, so he took our grandmother. She was already in her sixties or seventies then. I had to work to support all three of us. I worked hard to earn enough work points to feed us. In those days, I often had to work somewhere far away from the village. I was sent off to build the reservoir, for example. Still we did not have enough food to eat. Life was very bitter. My sister and I came from a family of the wrong class, so we regularly faced hardships and repression. People used to bully us.

. . .

My parents died very early, so it was natural that I went through a lot of hardship. Children with parents had an easier ride through life. I have never stopped dreaming of a better life, even to this day.

While Xiao Bai continues to dream of a better life, thousands of Shanghai orphans who were sent to faraway places because of the famine are still searching for their true identities and their birth parents. I first read about the Shanghai orphans in newspapers. I asked for the telephone number of Mrs. Lü, the founder of the Shanghai Orphans Reunion Association, from a journalist friend of mine. When I called Mrs. Lü, she was not friendly to start with. She told me every day she received hundreds of phone calls, some from former orphans wanting her to help, others from journalists or writers who wanted write a novel or article, or make a program about the Shanghai orphans. She said to me that it is appalling that there were journalists and writers as well as others out there wanting to make money out of such terrible tragedy. She asked me whether I was one of them. I assured her that I did not do it because of money. My intention was to preserve the memory of these orphans and to tell the world their stories. She then told me to do some homework: to check the association's Web site. I spent the next two days browsing through the Web site, until I found the story about Zhang Hu. I called Mrs. Lü again and got a contact number for Zhang Hu.

I decided to visit Zhang Hu in Tongguan, a small county in the east of Shaanxi province, about two hours train ride from Xi'an. While Tongguan was historically an important place for its strategic geographical position, it is now famous for its gold mining. It was a hot summer day. I made a mistake and took the local train. Not only was it slow, it also had no air conditioning and was very dirty. All the way I was constantly tormented by flies. After a miserable two-hour train journey, I arrived at Tongguan station. I was disappointed. The place looked so shabby, and underdeveloped. Gold obviously brought little prosperity to ordinary people in this place. Zhang Hu's eldest son met me at the station. He told me that he was only staying at this backward place because he was the oldest son and had to take care of his parents. But he longed to leave and go to eastern China where his father had originally come from. Zhang Hu lives in a small village outside Tongguan county town. I wanted to take a local taxi, but his son told me not to waste the money. So we took a local bus. It was the longest half-hour journey I have ever taken. When I arrived at Zhang Hu's house, typically built with yellow earth from the region, I was literally covered in yellow dust.

Zhang Hu is a man of few words. In his early fifties, he is one of the luckier Shanghai orphans, compared with his contemporaries. Zhang told me how he eventually managed to find his real parents in Yixing county, Jiangsu province, in eastern China.

> At the time I was too young to understand anything. I only learned what had happened after I found my real mother. My mother told me that she took me to Shanghai and left me on the street. Only when I found my real parents, at a Shanghai orphans reunion meeting, did I learn the full story of how we ended up in Tongguan. I was sent to Tongguan by an orphanage in Shanghai. We took a train from Shanghai to Tongguan. During the time of the famine, there were too many orphans in Shanghai and there was not enough milk to feed [us]. The government had to send milk from other regions. It happened during the hot summer season. Premier Zhou Enlai was concerned that the hot weather might spoil the milk. It was suggested that it might be better to send orphans to other regions where there was a shortage of children. Afterward government agencies counted the number of orphans, and then sent trains to Shanghai to take us away. We arrived in Tongguan by train. My adoptive father came to meet me and took me home.

More than 170 orphans came to Tongguan. I would have to check the exact number. At a reunion meeting for Shanghai orphans we were told that there were 173 orphans who came to Tongguan. It was in 1960. I was just over two years old at the time so I cannot remember anything of what happened.

When I was growing up I had no idea that I was an orphan. I must have been in my teens already when I first learned that we were orphans from Shanghai. The locals called us "Shanghai kids." Until then no one said anything. After I learned about my origins I wanted to look for my birth parents. But I was still very young then and I could not do anything about it. I lost my adoptive mother when I was nine years old, and when I was fifteen I lost my adoptive father. I became an orphan once again. [After that] I lived with my cousin and his wife for several years before I began to live by myself. Eventually I found myself a wife.

A number of orphans went to Shanghai in 2006. Among us we managed to collect three hundred yuan to get our blood tested. That year I didn't go to Shanghai myself but the people who went took my blood sample with them.

It was in 2007 that I first attended a reunion meeting for Shanghai orphans at Yixing county's Guanli township in Jiangsu. When I got there, I met many former Shanghai orphans. More than a thousand people were there, all of us unfortunate orphans. About twenty-three orphans from Tongguan attended the meeting. We each took a photo of ourselves to the meeting. At the meeting, we kept on moving up and down, looking for familiar faces and hoping to find our families. But we didn't know what or whom to look for.

No one from Tongguan found their families at that event. We stayed for three days, and then from Yixing we went on to Shanghai. In Shanghai we had a strong sense that our home was in Tongguan, not Shanghai. Everyone treated us as if we were from Tongguan. As we did not manage to find our original families in Shanghai, we had come to terms with the fact that Tongguan is our home.

In Shanghai we went to look for the orphanage. We were led by our group leader, who had been to Shanghai several times already. We also went to the Bureau of Civil Affairs. But we did not know anyone there, and after fifty years no one knew anyone or anything. In the end we came back to Tongguan. At the Shanghai orphans reunion meeting we left our blood samples. We also took DNA tests, and left our DNA samples.

After a very long time, I got a telephone call informing me that my real parents had been found. That was on November 23, 2009. A week after I received the phone call, I went to Yixing with my eldest son. I was very excited. At Yixing railway station Mrs. Lü and a film crew from the local TV station came to welcome me. My older brother took me to my parents' house. Everyone was excited. My parents and my brothers came out to greet me. My parents are eighty-three now. When they saw me, they were very happy and very excited. My parents had six children, four boys and two girls. At the time they had been afraid that I might not survive the famine, and that's why they sent me away. I was the youngest of the six children. Our family did not endure the worst of the suffering at the time—a number of families suffered terribly and they all died in the famine. My parents told me that many people in the village went as far as eating tree trunks, and quite a few villagers died of starvation. It had been my mother and grandmother who had taken me to Shanghai. They couldn't find the orphanage themselves, so they left me on the street.

I arrived in Tongguan in winter 1960. My adoptive father later told me that when he met me at the station I could barely lift my head up. My head would flop from one side to another. My neck had no strength.

. . . Many orphans from the [same] orphanage came to Tongguan. One entire train carriage was full of orphans. The orphans came off the train at Tongguan railway station. Afterward, the local Bureau of Civil Affairs took down their details and asked any locals who wanted to adopt to come forward.

Besides Tongguan, some orphans went to Hua county [in Shaanxi province]. At the Shanghai orphans reunion meeting I also met orphans who had settled in Shandong province, Tangshan city [in Hebei province], and Inner Mongolia.

Before my arrival, my adoptive parents had lost their only child, and that's why they adopted me. They loved me very much. My father had a nephew whom I called older brother [cousin]. Life was hard in Tongguan too. There was no food to eat at our farming brigade. The main staple in Shaanxi is bread, but there was no bread to eat in those days. We had to fill our stomach with persimmons. We even ate the skin of the fruit. We ate anything as long as we could fill our stomachs.

As a child I was very sick, but we were poor and my adoptive parents had no money to treat my lung disease. I just had to live with it. When I was eight or ten I became severely ill, but I survived. By the time I had reached twelve or thirteen, I was better.

Before my father died, someone told me that I had been a Shanghai orphan. At the time I didn't believe it. I asked my father about it, but he didn't say anything. On his deathbed my father told me the truth. He confirmed that I was an orphan from Shanghai. I felt very sad at the time. I cried. But I had no way of looking for my real parents. Ten years passed, and my desire to look for my birth parents was rekindled, but I had no idea where to start. Since there were so many Shanghai orphans in Tongguan, we decided to get ourselves organized, and begin the search for our real parents together.

After I found my birth parents, I just felt utterly happy. There is nothing else that I now desire. I have only wanted to know where I came from, and who my real parents were. I have a strong sense of belonging to Yixing, but there is no way I can move back there now. Tongguan cannot compare to Yixing. Yixing has developed very quickly over the past few years. There are so many factories in Yixing. Still I don't mind staying here [in Tongguan].

Our generation has suffered a great deal. . . . It is our destiny. I am lucky to have survived. My parents sent me away so that I could survive the famine. I should be happy about it. After all these years I have finally found my real parents, so I am the lucky one. Most orphans have not found theirs. They are still looking. They often gather together to talk about their feelings. They feel very bitter about what happened to them.

I have made a few good friends among the Shanghai orphans in Tongguan. We sometimes get together to discuss the search for our birth parents. We try to help one another. Whenever we hear about any reunion meeting for Shanghai orphans, we let each other know. For the first couple of years, I wanted to attend reunion meetings, but I didn't have enough money. We were quite poor then. It troubled me a great deal. Even now when I think about it I feel pretty sad.

Famine was the result of the government's exaggerations. It brought disaster to the country. Things got so bad because of the exaggerations and the extreme-left policies. If it hadn't been for that, we wouldn't have ended up in this situation. People normally leave poor places to go to places that are better off, but in those years we moved from well-off places to poorer regions. Society was turned upside down.

In Tongguan my name is Zhang Hu. In Yixing my name is Haixiang. When I first heard my real parents call me Haixiang, I felt strange. But now when I hear them call me Haixiang I feel all warm inside.

When I went to Yixing to visit my family, everyone including my nephews came out to greet me. There were thirty of us, plus my parents. [On New Year's Eve] Thirty-two of us sat around the table and had a New Year's family dinner together. . . . I often missed out on the conversations among my family because I cannot understand their dialect. In my family only my nephew and his wife can speak Mandarin. The rest of them speak Yixing dialect. Most of the time we talked about how life is for us now. We rarely spoke about the past.

After my interview with Zhang Hu, I decided to go to Yixing to visit his aged parents. In my mind Yixing was a small county in the east of China famous for its clay and teapots, as well as tea and silkworms. Upon arrival there to my surprise I discovered that this place, about two hours drive from Shanghai Pudong International Airport, is rapidly being transformed into an industrial town. Farming land has become more and more scarce. Along the newly built roads, one can see cement factories and electrical factories everywhere. Zhang Hu's home village is among the few remaining farming villages in Yixing. This is because it is a long way away from the main road. To get to the village I had to walk for almost an hour in the blazing sun. When I finally arrived at the village I felt sick. Ten days later I learned that I was pregnant at the time. My first thought was that I hope my own son will never have to become an orphan like Zhang Hu.

Zhang Hu's parents are now in their late eighties, and they share a crowded house with Zhang Hu's older brother and his family. The house is right in the middle of farming fields. Zhang Hu's older brother and his family are all peasants. They made me sit down and offered me something to drink and eat. In due course they told me how they were overjoyed when they finally found their long-lost brother.

> At the time, he was very young and could barely speak. He didn't know he was from Yixing. I am sixty this year. I was ten years old at the time. I knew about them sending him away. . . . The reason he was given away was because we had nothing to eat at the time. So many people starved to death at the time. In our village alone at least three or four people died in the famine. We didn't want to keep my youngest brother at home and just let him die. In 1960 and

> 1961, the whole country suffered a food shortage. . . . At the time about six children from our village were sent away. Three were sent to Shanghai. Two of them were found. My mother left my brother on the street in Shanghai. We had no idea who took him away or where they took him. There was no address. In 2008 we sent a message to the local "Shanghai orphan hotline" looking for him. We heard about the hotline through Mrs. Lü. I went there with my parents. We then went to Yixing [county town] to take the DNA test. A year later we had a phone call from Mrs. Lü telling us that they had found my brother. Of course we were happy to hear the news.

At this point I turned to Zhang Hu's mother. She told me that for all those years she had never given up hope of finding her youngest son.

> In 1960 we had no money. We had many children, and the youngest one was born in 1958. We had to give him away. He was almost three. I sent him away. I took him to Shanghai, and left him on the street. A trolley bus passed by, and then he was gone. Someone took him away. When we finally found him after more than fifty years, I was very excited. I cried, he cried, and his father also cried.

6
Famine in the Cities

By the winter of 1959, the famine that had killed millions in the Chinese countryside was beginning to extend to the cities. Food queues grew. The mass exodus from the countryside brought millions of hungry peasants into the cities. They could be seen everywhere: on streets, at railway stations, in restaurants and candy stores. Food ran out quickly, but the queues did not ease. In an attempt to contain the problem, the government introduced tough measures to force rural migrants back to the countryside. The migrants were arrested and sent to detention centers. Physical abuse was a regular occurrence in these crowded centers, and tens of thousands of people died during their detention. Within a few days, those who had been sent away would reappear on city streets. Nothing could stop them. Their will to survive was stronger than any government measure.

As food reserves continued to dwindle, many cities started to enforce the ration coupon system. On top of the grain coupon, which was first introduced in 1955, oil, meat, cotton, sugar, and many other daily necessities also were rationed. Only registered urban citizens, government employees, state factory workers, and students could receive these coupons, so those at the bottom of the social ladder, such as poor villagers, started to find their way into the capital, Beijing, and prosperous Shanghai, where it was still possible to eat at restaurants without coupons.

Toward the end of 1960 the food crisis in Beijing and Shanghai reached a critical point. Soon both cities were left with only a few days' food supplies. Telegrams pleading for urgent help arrived at the State Council on an hourly basis. Top leaders including Premier Zhou Enlai were in despair, but they were more concerned that news of the famine should not reach the outside world. A large number of deaths in Beijing and Shanghai would have unimaginable political and economic consequences: what would the world think of China? How the Soviet Union would sneer! A decision had to be made. Sichuan, in the far southwest, was China's biggest province, roughly the size of France, as well as one of its most densely populated. Politically, however, it was not as significant a place as Beijing or Shanghai. The decision was taken at the top: Sichuan's provincial government must send out emergency food supplies to relieve the crisis in Beijing and Shanghai. The order was to be carried out immediately, and there were no grounds for further discussion.[1] By this time famine had already killed several million people in rural Sichuan, and starving peasants could be seen everywhere. There were hardly any food reserves left. Where could Sichuan find the food demanded by the central administration in Beijing?

Li Jingquan, a man with a hard-looking face, a dominating personality, and an extremely thick Jiangxi accent, was the provincial Party head of Sichuan at the time. He was a fervent supporter of the Great Leap Forward. This man, who took pride in styling himself as a new local warlord, insisted that Beijing's request must be fulfilled at any cost. Since there was no food left in Sichuan's state reserves, he decided to eke the amount out of ordinary people's rations. In September 1960, under his instructions, the Sichuan government announced that the provincial grain ration coupon was to become invalid. People in Sichuan's cities and towns lost the equivalent of 2.4 million kilograms of food supplies. This was a bolt from the blue to the masses, who had been saving up their coupons in the hope that one day they could indulge in a feast of plain rice, or so that their children might have more to eat. Those residents who had not been assigned to a collective canteen lost their entire food source. Many were forced to sell everything they had in order to buy food on the black market. Some simply starved to death.

Crime increased in Sichuan's capital city, Chengdu, and in its biggest city Chongqing. Prostitution, which had been banned and as such forced underground, quickly resurfaced. But Chengdu and Chongqing were not the only cities that suffered rising crime rates. Throughout China, train robberies in particular became widespread. Thieves moved from one city to another, causing further upheaval in cities that were already hard pressed.[2]

In the northeast, the home of China's heavy industry, the severe food shortages forced several state factories to close. Food riots were a regular feature. Instead of solving the food crisis, local governments simply suppressed these riots by employing hardcore political pressure.

By the end of 1961, the famine had gradually eased in the countryside, but food shortages in the cities continued into 1962 and 1963. With the situation reversed, urban dwellers began to head off into the countryside in search of food. Although the overall death toll was considerably lower in the cities, malnutrition and other forms of liver disease were widespread. Birth rates dropped sharply. The number of people suffering from edema, hepatitis, tuberculosis, and other illnesses was on the rise. The food situation in the cities began to improve only gradually after 1963, yet food rationing continued until the end of the 1980s, almost thirty years after the end of the famine.

Wuhan, the capital of Hubei province, was one of the most populated cities in central China. It was also the most important political, financial, economic, and transportation hub in the region. Hubei, under the leadership of provincial Party secretary Wang Renzhong, was right at the forefront of the Great Leap Forward. Besides its claim to have achieved very high crop yields, countless road and irrigation sites were set up. Years later, in 1967, Wang Renzhong boasted about his accomplishments during the Great Leap Forward in his confession to the Red Guards. According to him, remarkable achievements were made during those years, and he brushed off any errors as insignificant when compared with the successes.[3] But for many ordinary people living in Wuhan as well as in other parts of Hubei, these were the most horrific times of their lives. There was no food to be seen in Wuhan. Meng Xiansheng, mentioned in Chapter 2, was a student studying in Wuhan when the famine hit the city. He told me that people on the streets of Wuhan faced terrible starvation, and edema was widespread:

> From the beginning of 1959 a compulsory grain coupon system was introduced in Wuhan, and by March it had become obvious that there was famine in the city. All restaurants in Wuhan were closed for one month. . . . Toward the end of 1960, the famine in Wuhan had progressed and become more severe. The term "shooting Sputnik," which had originally referred to achieving high production figures, became an expression for eating a real meal.[4] . . . At the canteen our regular meals consisted of very watery congee mixed with sorghum, corn, and dried sweet potatoes. No other supplementary food, such as cake or fruit, was available. There was no cooking oil either, and the food was indigestible. Many people fell very sick. Although we could see crops and vegetables growing in the nearby countryside,

no one could steal anything from those fields as they were heavily guarded. To ease my hunger I often got up early in the morning to go to the local market in search of discarded, rotten vegetables.

When the famine became very severe, we were encouraged not to move too much. So we lay there and starved. During this time grain coupons were extremely valuable and tradable currency. People suffering from edema, which was caused by starvation, could be seen everywhere in the city. I remember that there was a restaurant near our college that sold soya milk to people suffering from edema. We were told that soya milk could cure edema because of its high protein content. Every day I saw many edema sufferers queuing up outside that restaurant for soy milk.

Yang Ziwei was a health worker at a hygiene and disease prevention station in Wuhan. Although a government employee, Yang Ziwei found herself in no better situation. Besides having to endure starvation, every day she also witnessed countless people suffering terrible illnesses and starving to death. She recounts the time with tears in her eyes:

Between 1959 and 1960 I was pregnant. It was right in the middle of the famine. The only place I could find food was the canteen at the hygiene and disease prevention station. The food was very coarse and rough, very difficult to chew. I couldn't swallow it: my pregnancy constantly made me feel sick. I yearned for some rice or congee. I had to get up extremely early to stand in the queue to secure some congee. The congee was very watery, so I was constantly hungry.

At restaurants or shops, there was no food available for purchase. My first baby was very tiny when she was born. She weighed 1.7 kilograms. Because I had nothing to eat but watery congee and salty bean curd, I did not produce enough breast milk to feed her. I was desperate for food, so I asked my brother to try to get me some from my home village. But he managed to find only a little food in the end. It was so precious that I tried to eat it slowly. My sister-in-law came to my house and she saw the food, so I was obliged to give her some. Instead [of being grateful] she accused me of being selfish: keeping good things for myself and not sharing it among the relatives. After that incident, she created a lot of tension between me and my husband's family.

I remember that during that time all the conversations were about food. We'd queue up for anything. No one wanted to miss out on any food.

I saw many people who died trying to steal food. There is a small island called Tianxingzhou in the middle of the Yangtze River. There used to be some vegetable fields on the island. People from my district could go there by boat. There was no public ferry service in those days, so people had to cross by taking small private boats. Lots of people crossed the river to that island to steal vegetables, but a huge number drowned on their way. The small boats were always overloaded with passengers. Once I also tried to go. While I was waiting for a boat to turn up, I witnessed the sinking of a tiny boat and several people falling into the river. Quite a few struggled to swim to the riverbank, but when they finally reached it they had no strength left to walk because they were so hungry and exhausted. They collapsed, and their bodies were washed away by the current. Seeing what had happened I turned round and went home.

I was working in the hygiene and health station, and I saw lots of people suffering from hepatitis during the famine period. In those days people were not allowed to eat any food that had just been harvested. All of the grain was taken away by the authorities and stored in state granaries. A large quantity of grain rotted in those granaries. The government used the rotten grain to feed those who were starving in the cities. After consuming rotten grain over a long period of time, many people contracted hepatitis.

I will always remember the tears of one of my colleagues at that time. Her mother and young brothers were in Sichuan, and the famine there was even more severe. She had tried to save some grain coupons. The idea was that she could exchange her Hubei grain coupons for Sichuan grain coupons at a higher value. By enduring desperate starvation herself, she eventually managed to save sufficient coupons. Just as she was sending them home by post, the Sichuan government suddenly announced that grain coupons would become invalid in Sichuan. I remember my colleague crying nonstop after she heard the news.

As I listened to Yang Ziwei, I remembered the story my father used to tell me. In 1960 he was a fourth-year medical student at Sichuan Medical University.[5] For nearly two months he ate 150 grams less of grain every day in order to save up his grain coupons in the hope that he would be able to save enough to buy a big bowl of noodles one day. However, things did not work out the way he planned. I decided to interview him formally. First he hesitated, as he did not want me to engage in such a sensitive topic. But I did not give up. I told him that I was simply trying to preserve the memories of those who suffered this terrible famine. As he listened to my reasoning, he began to speak:

> One day our class monitor asked us to attend an emergency meeting. At the meeting he announced that the Sichuan government had decided to cancel the province's existing grain coupons. . . . It was a bolt from the blue. I had been dreaming about filling my stomach with a big bowl of noodles, but now my dream simply vanished like soap bubbles. Suddenly I remembered an incident I had seen not long before in the countryside. One day when villagers were queuing for corn porridge at the brigade's collective canteen, a thirty-something-year-old male villager was handing over his bowl to the person serving in order to receive his family's portion of food. Suddenly someone shouted: "No food for him!" It turned out that the brigade cadre had ordered that this man and his family be denied their share. The server at the canteen stopped serving. I watched as the tears ran down the man's face. In the end he left in great disappointment. When I heard that the grain coupons had been abolished, I felt as sad as the villager who had been deprived of his food.

As famine spread, shortages and starvation also began to reach China's capital city, Beijing. Xian, who appeared in Chapter 2, was a student at the middle school attached to the Central Conservatory of Music, one of the most prestigious institutions for musical studies in China. Like most students from her school, Xian was from a privileged family background. Her parents had joined the Communist revolution in their youth. After the Communists took over, Xian's father was appointed the vice minister of culture, and her mother was a high-ranking official in the Beijing municipal government. Yet even she and her family, as well as her classmates, were not spared from hunger.

> It was in 1962 that I first experienced real hunger. . . . Many of my classmates were from southern China. The reason is simple: in those days only ladies and girls [from privileged and wealthy family backgrounds] had the leisure to study and play the piano and the violin. . . . Quite a few of them were from Guangzhou, as Guangzhou is close to Hong Kong. Some were from Xiamen [in Fujian province, also known as Amoy], as Gulangyu in Xiamen is known as the "city of pianos." There were also some from Shanghai, and just a small number of us from Beijing. Those from southern China found the food in the canteen indigestible. I remember that at the time the canteen used to have a big wok lying on the ground that contained a dark-colored sweet potato soup. We were told that the heavy rain had killed large quantities of cotton crops in the countryside. In rural Hebei, the majority of fields were used to plant cotton. Every year, farmers handed over their cotton to the government, and in return the government would send them food. That year, because hardly any cotton was produced, the villagers received no food. The state had no free food to give away. The only food these villagers had kept in reserve were rotten sweet potatoes. To help the starving peasants, the Beijing municipal government sent them some dried corn, sorghum,

and millet in exchange for their rotten sweet potatoes. These sweet potatoes were then distributed among the schools in Beijing. Every lunch the school canteen served us this dark-colored sweet potato soup. The color of the soup was almost as dark as the wok. It didn't taste sweet like sweet potato should taste because it had gone rotten. But that's the only food we were given for lunch. Many of my classmates from the south went on hunger strike. I nearly joined the hunger strike: I found the sweet potato soup impossible to swallow. But there was no food to eat otherwise, so I had to get it down me in the end. I can never forget that. That was the only thing we got for lunch. Every day was the same. After a while we had to give up. . . . The school knew that we'd be famished by lunchtime, because we needed to fill our stomachs to get through the day. That's why the canteen served the sweet potato soup then, so that we would be forced to eat it. In the morning and evenings the canteen served corn congee. After a while most students in the school started to suffer from edema. Because of that the conservatory canceled our exams that year. I cannot remember much about having edema, but I remember well how happy I was because there were no exams. . . .

I think at the time the amount of rations we received was not that bad. Every month my rations amounted to almost sixteen kilograms of food. All middle-school students received that amount because we were at a growing age. Even my parents didn't get that much food. Their rations were about fourteen kilograms a month. Unemployed people received even less. But in those days the food was cooked with no oil or fat. Even pancakes were steamed.

The conservatory was a boarding school. Every week all students had to attend a meeting. During the meeting we were forced to criticize one another as well as ourselves. The most criticism I got was that I ate too much. Because many of my classmates from the south could not eat the food made from dried corn, I borrowed their coupons to buy the extra food that they could not eat. Although they were as hungry as I was, they could not digest the food in the canteen. . . . I was twelve or thirteen and I was growing; no wonder I was so hungry in those days. Being hungry was my wrong. Try imagining it now. It was so mean to criticize a young girl for eating too much. It was so mean. . . .

One of my classmates from Shanghai had relatives who lived abroad. They sent her some food from Hong Kong—a whole suitcase full of tinned food, milk powder, rice, and cheese. But she didn't dare to touch the food. No one else dared to touch it either. All of us said we would rather suffer along with the rest of the country. I don't know what she did with the food in the end. I only remember that there was a whole suitcase full of food and that it was very heavy. At the time we all had to eat at the canteen. She didn't dare to eat any of the food from the suitcase, even though she wanted to. . . .

Another classmate of mine was from Hong Kong. She joined my class in September 1962. Her family sent her a lot of food, but she did not dare to eat it [at the school]. . . . She hid most of the food at her relatives'. On Sundays, she would ride her British-made bicycle to her relatives' and enjoy a feast there. When she came back to school, she would bring some cheese with her. Although Chinese people did not eat dairy products much in those days, we could not resist the strong buttery and sweet aroma of the cheese. We were all girls, and hunger made us particularly gluttonous. Cheese was like the best food in the world for us at that time. I still have a strong and fond memory [of the taste and aroma].

Because we lived and ate in the school, my classmates from outside Beijing had cake and biscuit coupons, as well as oil coupons, at their disposal. Each month they would get a few cakes and biscuits as a treat. Those of us from Beijing handed over our coupons to our parents. I had to watch my classmates enjoying the sweet things. At home there were five of us children. We were all about the same age: the youngest was nine years old, and the oldest was sixteen. We were all at a growing age. I have no memory of being given biscuits to eat at home. Occasionally I was given a cake or two. I think that's how I started to develop my sweet tooth. I yearned for sweet things because I could not have them. [Laugh.] Later on, when I could buy sweet cakes, I would eat half a kilo of them in one go. The sweet taste made me so happy! . . . Even now my family remembers how I have a special weakness for sweet things. Every time I go back to visit, my brothers and sister buy lots of cakes for me. They all know what I love. They fill up the cake tin before I get home. Unfortunately for health reasons I am not supposed to eat too many sweet things. Still I have a reputation for enjoying and eating sweet things. . . .

It was then that I learned to steal food. I was so hungry all the time, and that made me very gluttonous. Watching my classmates eating cakes made me [envious]. As I mentioned already my coupons had to be handed over to my parents at home. At home we used a tin to store cakes and biscuits. . . . Every weekend when I went home I would get up in the middle of the night and go to search out the cake tin. I could not resist. I would try my best not to make a sound when I was taking out biscuits and cakes. But everyone knew as there weren't that many biscuits or cakes in the tin. . . . I remember that occasionally my mother also bought some candies. For me it was a real pleasure to be able to steal a candy or two. Every time I went home the first thing I'd do is to find out where my mum had hidden the candies. The candies were sold at a very high price in those days. I don't think any ordinary people on the street could afford them. Most people's salary was only a little over twenty yuan per month. . . .

. . . Since all five of us were growing children, the food we received was never going to be enough. I remember that at home we used a green-colored plastic bowl to measure rice. It was my elder brother's idea. Sunday lunch was the only time we got to eat rice because Sunday was the only day that all of us were at home together. The rice was measured out carefully: my two elder brothers got 200 grams each, I got 150 grams, my younger sister and my parents and grandparents all got 100 grams each. It wasn't much at all. We steamed our own individual portions of rice in our own bowls, so we all knew which one belonged to whom. We added a lot of water to the rice, hoping that the amount would expand to fill the entire bowl. . . .

We never got to eat meat in those days. The meat rations were even less than the amount of grain we received. I cannot remember the exact amount. In fact every month my meat coupons would be handed over to the school. I think they were something like 100 grams per month. At home they used their meat coupons to buy canned pork ribs. The Chinese are good at this sort of thing. That's why many people in China like to cook with pork fat. The canned pork ribs were full of pork fat—white-colored pork fat. In those days the only vegetables available were white cabbage and radish. So at home we'd cook up a big pot of white cabbage with one can of pork ribs. The vegetables were covered in a layer of grease. The taste of fat made our stomachs happy. That accompanied by a bowl of thick congee-like rice was the most perfect Sunday lunch we could get. I cannot remember how many vegetables we were allocated in those days. From memory, every month each family would receive a total amount of vegetable rations. This was divided into thirty days and according to the number of people in the family. . . . It was something like 36 grams per person [per day]. It was too little to give each individual person as a fixed amount, so [the government] assigned a total amount for the whole family. Besides pickled vegetables, the most common, and often the only fresh vegetable in those days was cabbage. Even potatoes were scarce. Potato was in fact considered a superior food staple in those days. No vegetables, no cooking oil, no candies, no cakes—there was hardly anything to eat in those days. My parents were cadres, so they received extra meat coupons. That's how we got to buy canned ribs. We did not dare to buy any fresh meat. There were too many mouths to feed at home, so we made a huge pot of vegetable soup. It was covered in pork fat. This left a deep impression on me. I can still taste it. . . . We ate that for two years. It was so delicious!

My mother was a cadre at the Beijing municipal government, one of the most powerful institutions in Beijing. Even there a lot of cadres suffered from edema. I remember that my mother's legs were all puffed up and that if we put pressure on them it would leave deep recesses. My mother also suffered from anemia. The government was afraid that government cadres might die [of edema], as this would damage China's political image. So they sent all edema patients from various ministries, including those from the Beijing municipal government, to a special rehabilitation center. They did not care if ordinary people were dying elsewhere—only government officials in Beijing were taken care of. That's called privilege. It was during that period that my mother learned to play Mahjong. They had nothing to do at the rehabilitation center but play Mahjong. As the government had no food to feed them, the Beijing municipal government sent a lot of people off to Inner Mongolia with the army to hunt for yellow sheep. . . . They went by Jeep over all Inner Mongolia on the hunt for yellow sheep. They also went to Qinghai to hunt the animal. At the center the other thing that my mother was given to eat were buns made out of chaff. It was supposed to be very nutritious. My mother didn't eat them herself. She hid them in her clothes, and every Sunday when she came home she would bring them to us. That must have been toward the end of 1962. I remember it clearly. . . . Beijing was the last to experience the famine because it was on the priority list for supplies.

. . .

Apart from food, cloth fabric was also rationed in those days. The ration lasted for years and years. Everyone got coupons for sixty-six centimeters of cotton per year. This was barely enough to make patches out of. . . . In my family our clothes were all full of patches. When I first went to the conservatory school, there was a rule that each year we had to go to the army, to a factory, or to the countryside for reeducation. Because most of my classmates were from the south, they did not have any dark-colored clothes to wear for occasions such as these, so I borrowed some from my brothers and sister and brought them into school for my classmates to wear. Once we went to a tank corps. When the soldiers saw us, they could not believe their eyes: how could these students dress so poorly? All the clothes had been repaired so many times and were full of patches. We got the same reaction when we went to a factory in Shijingshan just west of Beijing. . . . The only exception was the time when I was chosen to attend the October National Day parade. My mother used up all of the cotton coupons she had saved for the whole family and bought three meters of fabric to make a dress for me. It was an unforgettable event as I had not seen any new clothes for years. My mum made the dress with her own hands. She sewed all night long until I had to leave for the parade. Later this dress was passed on to my sister. After my sister grew out of it, we cut the dress open and used it to make a quilt cover. I will always remember that dress. . . . My grandmother was still alive in those days. She kept any badly torn clothes and . . . would use them to make soles for shoes. She made shoes for all of us. All five of us wore shoes made by my grandmother. . . . As a child what I hated most were my socks. They had been repaired so many times. They were covered in ugly patches.

. . .

> But I must say that things were still a lot better in Beijing. I think that for ordinary people, especially those not working in government work units, life must have been terrible during those years.

The late Zhao Tielin came from a similar family background. I first met him in 2007 at a small restaurant just south of Tiananmen Square in Beijing. He smoked and drank hard liquor throughout the entire meal. He was a well-known local photographer. His subjects were mostly marginal figures or stigmatized groups, and his work often depicted the ugliness and the dark side of Chinese society. Over the years we became good friends, and slowly I began to understand those depressing elements of his work. Although both his parents were high-ranking Communist cadres, his father usually found himself on the wrong side politically and suffered repeated purges throughout most of his political career. His mother was beaten to death during the Cultural Revolution. At the time he was still just a middle-school student, and he was also beaten so badly by Red Guards that his ribs were broken. In his adolescence he suffered a great deal both emotionally and physically. It made him strong but at the same time it also made him very critical, as well as pessimistic. Almost every time we met, we would share a meal together. By his choice, we always went to dirt-cheap places where he still haggled about the price and the portions. When I asked him why, he told me that food had always been precious to him, and that he could never forget the feeling of hunger during the Great Famine.

> Between 1959 and 1962 were the most difficult years. There was nothing to eat. Both my parents were high-ranking Communist cadres, but I did not escape hunger:

> not even for a day. In those years, my father got into trouble politically. My mother was also a cadre, and her salary was 138 yuan per month, but still we could not get enough food to eat. You can imagine what the ordinary people had to suffer. At the time there was a slogan: "The countryside can be sacrificed, but no one should die in the city [Beijing]." People went almost crazy [for food] in those days. I only managed to eat one meal a day. I was a growing teenager at the time, and I would get very hungry. When I got really desperate, I'd go to the countryside to steal corn stalks. In the springtime, I'd climb the trees to pick the leaves. I would mix the leaves with corn flour, and make cakes to fill my stomach. That was the situation in the city. In the countryside it was even worse.

At the other end of the social spectrum, Erjie is a ninety-year-old illiterate grandmother living in Chengdu, Sichuan province. She is one of millions upon millions of ordinary people [*lao baixing*] in China.[6] In 1945, at the end of the Sino-Japanese War, she walked many miles from her home village in the countryside of northern Sichuan to the provincial capital, Chengdu, in search of a better life. But the Communist Liberation in 1949 brought little improvement to her life. Soon the famine broke out. She watched her children suffering from constant starvation and fighting fierce battles over food, while her husband coped with severe illness. With the same strength and remarkable courage that she had taken in leaving her village, she and her family survived the famine. When I told her my intention, she was more than willing to help. The interview with her lasted for nearly four hours, and she told me:

In 1958 I gave birth to my youngest daughter. It was in the middle of the Great Leap Forward. . . . Because we were poor and we had no food to give her, we talked about giving her away. . . . Actually, to begin with, I had considered having an abortion, but that didn't work out. There were condoms on sale at the shop but we couldn't afford them. They cost five yuan each.[7] . . . My husband also considered having a vasectomy. In those days the government encouraged people to get vasectomies. But my husband was already quite old by then. . . . A number of people warned us that a vasectomy might damage his health. They didn't think it was suitable for him. We did not have anything of an education and we simply didn't understand such things. Not knowing what to do, I tried a tonic made up of *sanqi* [panax notoginseng] and alcohol. I was told that the tonic could induce abortion, but it didn't work. Then I tried to jump off a construction site, hoping to get rid of the fetus that way. That didn't work either. People stopped me. They warned me that if I didn't abort successfully I might end up with a disabled child. I wouldn't know what to do with a disabled child, so in the end I thought I'd give her away. . . . My sister was against it. Since she had no daughter of her own, and her son had already grown up . . ., she said that she would adopt my second daughter. That's how I gave her my second daughter and kept the newborn.

. . .

In the beginning of 1959 . . . I found a temporary job in the university canteen. . . . If I hadn't worked at the canteen, I would have died of starvation during the famine. My husband suffered from edema as well as tuberculosis at the time. . . . When I first started to work in the canteen, the food was not rationed. . . . There was always rice on the table. [In those days] each table had two big yellow wooden buckets filled with rice or porridge for students to eat. You could eat as much as you wanted. In [1960], 1961, and 1962, however, life became very difficult. We didn't eat any pork for over three years, and there was no cooking oil available. Ten kilos of rice [per person] was all we received each month. . . . In those days peasants in the countryside suffered terribly, and many starved to death. So many of them died! People like us who lived in the city at least had ten kilos rice to eat. . . .

My sister and her family received fewer food rations than us. At the time her mother-in-law was living with them. . . . One day when my sister was not at home, I heard the mother-in-law cursing my second daughter. "We have no food to eat for ourselves, why should we keep another little bitch?" she said. Hearing her words I felt terribly hurt. . . . On one occasion my sister spent thirty yuan buying a chicken on the black market—in those days my salary was only twenty-one yuan per month. Her mother-in-law had a grandson who stole the chicken and devoured it raw. It's hard for me to imagine how he could eat a whole raw chicken. He didn't leave so much as a morsel. He was punished of course, but it did not stop him stealing. My sister also bought some cakes at some exorbitant price. She tried to hide them in a jar, but again this boy found the cakes and ate them all. His grandmother blamed my daughter for stealing the cakes. . . . She insisted that my daughter pay for what had been stolen. She always accused my daughter of stealing food, and was always trying to protect her own grandson. . . .

My sister told me to give our grain coupons to them in order to avoid my second daughter being mistreated by her mother-in-law. So we did. . . . My sister gave half of the coupons to her mother-in-law. She put them in a bag and hung this over her neck. At the time, the mother-in-law shared a bed with her grandson. One day after she had gone to sleep, the grandson cut open the bag and stole the coupons. He spent them all on food, and ate it all in one go. My sister watched her mother-in-law starving, but she could not do anything. . . . The mother-in-law kept on moaning to me about how hungry she was. When I asked her about the coupons, she told me what had happened. It was the first time I had heard her say anything bad about her grandson: she wished for him to die young. I looked at her face and remembered the time when she helped me with my baby. I went home and managed to fill a bowl with some rice to give it to her. I told her to use the rice for herself. I don't know what happened to it. A few days later, she died of hunger. . . .

The worst year was 1961. In the canteen I witnessed [university] students suffering from starvation. At the time food was served from a big bowl, with each student receiving a portion that was never big enough. The food served had no nutritional value and tasted terrible. . . . Because of the food shortage, the canteen ended up adding wood dust to the wheat flour, and used this mixture to make steamed buns. After eating the buns students suffered from terrible constipation. The canteen also fed students human urine. . . . Because many people suffered from famine-related edema, someone came up with the idea that fungi growing out of fermented urine could cure the disease. Each day buckets of human urine were carried into the canteen, and these were added to the vegetables that were served to the students. The food consumed by the canteen staff was always kept in a separate bowl so that the chefs never ate any food contaminated with urine. . . . At the time I thought the whole thing was very cruel. . . .

In those days each family received two hundred grams in vegetable rations, but vegetables were very hard to come by. My second daughter, who was only four at the time, was sent [by my sister's family] to stand in a queue to try to buy vegetables. She had to walk all the way to the other side of the campus, but in the end she only managed to get in at the back of the queue. She never had a chance of getting anything. Vegetables were only sold to the university professors as they could afford cigarettes and they were able to bribe the vegetable sellers with these cigarettes. . . . Fortunately I had the job of delivering vegetables for the university canteen. I was able to pick up leftover cabbage leaves from the fields in the countryside [and take them home].

. . . I remember four days when we received no food at all. . . . My husband quarreled with me: he accused me of being selfish and not caring for my children. It was true that I could eat rice and vegetables at the canteen, but I could not bring them home. So I bought some sweet potatoes from a boat—occasionally there was a boat selling sweet potatoes on the river. I don't know where it had come from. The sweet potatoes were extremely expensive: half a kilo cost as much as forty to fifty yuan in today's money. I also asked the buyer in our canteen to buy some radishes for me. He bought two kilos for us. Each meal, we cut two or three sweet potatoes and put these together with a few slices of radish. That's how my family survived over those four days. Without sweet potatoes and radish, my family would have died.

To get by we ate almost anything there was, including wood dust. My husband also ate tree bark and radish stems. . . . My youngest daughter was just over one year old. When she saw the canteen staff peeling carrots and discarding the peels by the waste sewer, she picked them up and brought it over to me. She asked me: "Mum, can you wash this for me?" Hearing what she said, tears welled up in my eyes. As I washed the dirt off the carrot peel, the tears streamed down my face. After that whenever I was sent to collect vegetables for the canteen, I always went into the fields to pull out some carrot stalks for my daughter. . . . I washed them carefully in water so that my daughter could chew them. She was always feeling hungry, as her stomach was empty most of the time. Sometimes I would pickle some old cabbage or mustard leaves and boil them up to feed the children. Sometimes that was all they had to eat. What could they do but fill their stomachs with whatever there was to hand? When they were hungry, I could hear their hearts beating: dong dong, dong dong.

. . . My two sons fought every day over food. They fought fiercely. It was awful to watch. Even my youngest daughter suffered from hunger. Being the youngest child, she received the smallest amount of rations, but she always cried out for the biggest bowl. She cried very loudly in order to get her way. My other children cursed her for that and they still talk about it even now. . . .

My husband suffered from tuberculosis. He was sent to Ya'an to cut bamboo. The reason they sent him was that the university construction unit had failed to secure their order for bamboo, as most of the peasants who had done the job previously had died of starvation. Even the few who had managed to survive did not have enough strength left to do the job. . . . So my husband was sent by the head of his unit to cut bamboo in Ya'an's Tianquan. For a whole year he would go up to Tianquan, for up to forty days each time. He lived and ate with the local peasants. Their daily diet consisted of a small flour pancake and a bowl of watery soup made of radish stalks. . . . After being in Tianquan for a while, he was diagnosed with tuberculosis and edema. His condition was already quite severe by that time. His body became badly swollen, and the skin on his legs turned yellow. Both his lungs were infected and turned a dark color. When he coughed he spat blood. When his sickness reached a critical point he went to the university clinic for a check-up, and they sent him to the rehabilitation center straight away. At the time, the center was full of sick people suffering from edema and tuberculosis. My husband stayed there for nearly two years. . . .

After my husband had gone to the rehabilitation center, there was no one at home to look after the children. Life became impossible for us. My husband used all his salary to buy expensive cakes for himself. He no longer cared for the children. I had no other means, so I began to raise rabbits. I bought one big fat rabbit first. After three months she gave us a few babies. My sons helped me to dig a few pits in our kitchen and we made a home for the rabbits. My sons also went out to collect grass to feed them. The rabbits grew very quickly. After three or four months the babies were big enough to sell. With that money I was able to buy some food for the children. . . .

My neighbor Mrs. Liu's family was better off because several members of her family were chefs. . . . Mrs. Liu's brother was the manager at one of the canteens, and a large amount of food from the canteen ended up at their home. They even had rice left over to lend to others. While their youngest daughter had excessive amounts of food to eat, my two sons were fighting over scraps day in, day out. . . .

Someone I knew used to sell food on the black market. He was managing the catering for a children's nursery. He always managed to find food and to sell it off on the black market. Until now I have never told anyone about this. I sometimes bought food from him, so that when my oldest daughter came home, there was food for her to eat. She was at college at the time, and her rations were not at home but at the college. Every time when my oldest daughter came home, my younger son, who was always hungry, would accuse her of stealing his food. He even cursed her for eating his salt ration. . . . If the famine had gone on for any longer, my family and I would have died eventually.

After saying goodbye to Erjie, I decided to call on Mrs. Liu, who lives a few doors away. Like Erjie, she too is an ordinary, illiterate woman. When I asked her about what I had heard—that her family was relatively better off during the famine because some family members worked in the university canteen—she groaned:

Life was miserable in those days. Even in Chengdu, the situation was really awful. To survive, a number of people from my family ran away. My nephews and nieces fled to Xinjiang. They became farmers there. One of my nieces has raised her three children in Xinjiang. They have all graduated from universities now. All my nephews and nieces ran away. . . . Life was tough in those days. We were really miserable. My husband's salary was twenty-eight yuan per month. It was not enough to feed my entire family. In those days we ate very cheap food: plain rice plus one vegetable dish. All the meals were like that. But during the famine years, we could not even afford to buy chard. How miserable! Even chard was selling at almost one yuan per kilogram. Very occasionally we would buy some to cook. One bowl of chard would empty very quickly. Today is so different—vegetables are abundant.

. . .

During the famine, we had no choice but to endure hunger. There was nothing we could do. It was the same for everyone. In my family, adults drank alcohol to stave off their hunger. My brother and husband, along with my brother's wife, all worked in the university canteen. When they came home they just drank alcohol to combat their hunger, so they could save the food for the children to eat. Oh, it was dreadful. I feel ashamed to talk about it. Life is good now. My memory is not so good. All I remember is that life was miserable then, and that we did not have enough food. We just dragged on day after day. I remember that red liquor [made from sorghum] was the only thing on sale over here. . . . We had to queue up for the liquor. My husband, my brother, and his wife lived off that. They have suffered ill health years later because of it.

> Life was particularly dreadful in 1961 and 1962. I gave birth to my youngest child a couple of years before that. She was born in 1958. After that life was continuously miserable. I ate . . . whatever I could find. In 1958, when I gave birth, a bowl of rice congee was the best thing I got to eat. But I had to eat less. If I did not eat less, how could we get by? Even to this day, I still deprive myself of food. Sometimes I would eat less so that my children could have more to eat. Even when I was very hungry, I just had to bear it. Many people suffered from hunger in those days. Sometimes I fainted, but there was nothing I could do. If that happened, I would drink boiled water. What a miserable time. I don't want speak about it any more.

This was not the first time, in my interviews for this book, that I heard people say they drank alcohol to combat their hunger. Xiuying is an old neighbor of my family. I knew her when I was still little. She looks like a happy woman, always with a smile on her face. One day when I was visiting my grandmother, she happened to be there too. We started to chat, and I was surprised to hear that this cheerful-looking woman had endured so much hardship in her life. When I asked her about the famine period, she frowned, and the smile disappeared from her face.

> The Great Leap Forward: what difficult years those were. I had already moved back to Chengdu by then and was working full time. There was no food to eat. Every Sunday, we drank sorghum liquor to fill our stomachs. We drank that instead of having food, so that we could save the rice for the children and the elderly people at home. I began to suffer from edema. That was during the Great Leap Forward—there

was no food to eat. I was sent to the hospital, because I was a worker. At the hospital the doctor gave me some medicine to help replenish my blood because I also suffered from severe anemia. At home, my family bought some chard for me to eat. My little nephews and nieces fought over it. They fought over chard! They even attacked each other physically. They were only small children at the time. The older one is over fifty now. He has already retired. The younger one is still working. In the end the older one gave way, and let the younger one eat the chard. Whenever I could find some rice from the canteen, I would bring it back to feed the family elders. . . . Apart from chard, we also supplemented our diet with chaff. We used grain chaff to make cakes. Some of us became terribly constipated after eating it. It was awful!

. . .

I remember one day after work, I bought a cake for my elderly mother-in-law. On the way home I was robbed and lost the cake. . . . People were very fierce in those days. That's because there was no food. . . .

. . . What a terrible life [we had to endure]. We only managed to eat one meal a day. From lunch one day, we would have to wait till the next day at lunchtime before we'd get fed again. There was hardly anything to eat. . . . How could we celebrate the Chinese New Year? We had nothing to eat, and we had no money. Today I have money to buy food, but I am too old to enjoy it. My health is not that good. I am suffering from quite a few physical problems.

Nearly a thousand kilometers west of Chengdu, Guiyang in the southwest of China is the capital of Guizhou province. Situated in the east of the Yunnan-Guizhou plateau, Guiyang was once surrounded by thick forest. During the Great Leap Forward, large-scale deforestation was carried out to make way for irrigation projects, for the mining industry, and for converting forest into farming fields. The damage was enormous. It took many years for the region to recover. Even well into 1963 and 1964, Guiyang city and the nearby areas continued to suffer from a shortage of supplies. Mr. Po was a doctor of Chinese medicine in Guiyang. Trying to raise a young family was extremely difficult for him and his wife.

> During the famine years, malnutrition was extremely widespread. My first child was born in 1963 when officially the famine was over, but my wife still couldn't get enough to eat. The state rations remained very mean, not much better than previous years during the famine. The monthly rations we received consisted mainly of corn and wheat. There was a small amount of rice. On top of that each month we received one kilogram of pork, four pieces of bean curd, and five hundred grams of sugar. That was for the entire family. We were also given some coupons for cooking oil and vegetables, but we could hardly find any oil or vegetables to buy. My kids never saw any apples or oranges while they were growing up. They only learned about these fruits from their primary school textbooks later on. I often went out to look for some apples or oranges for my kids, but it was impossible to find them. These were the most ordinary fruits. I felt extremely sad for my children.

7

Surviving the Famine

A history of famine is as much a history of survival as it is of starvation, destruction, and death. Humans are able to endure extreme conditions, and our ingenuity in coping with terrible crises is a great reflection of human strength.

The world over, most human beings would do anything in order to survive, and this includes stealing and killing. During China's Great Famine, to scrape together the currency to barter for food, people sold everything they had, from furniture to clothing, children and sex. The ability to cheat and steal became essential tools of survival. Anything edible was swallowed, from wild herbs to tree trunks, snakes, rats, insects, earth, and even human flesh. One of the greatest slaughters of wild animals in history took place during this time. Even the giant panda, lauded as China's "national treasure," was not spared.[1] Grazing on raw food growing in the fields was widespread. While famine claimed millions of lives, many people were killed or became sick by ingesting toxic herbs, plants, or poisonous and indigestible foods. White clay, also known as "immortal earth," magically relieved the feelings of hunger, but it also caused severe constipation, potentially leading to death.

In times of extreme scarcity, selfishness was normal. Surviving meant taking food out of someone else's mouth. Cadres and canteen staff ate up the ordinary villagers' rations. The serving spoon became a symbol of power. Fights over food were regular occurrences within families: husbands fought with their wives, brothers and sisters beat each other up over a piece of bread.

Escape was another common strategy for surviving the famine. As early as the spring of 1958, in some parts of the country where there were already signs of famine, migration became the way to avoid food shortages. Still Mao went on to declare the People's Commune to be the "Communist Paradise." As the situation of famine escalated, so the mass exodus grew into a nationwide movement. Apart from those who were too ill to leave, almost the entire rural population in China was on the move. People crammed themselves into the cities like ants. Many worked excruciatingly hard in order to fill their stomachs. Often they had to endure appalling conditions and extreme humiliation. However, the meager hope of being able to get a mouthful of food kept them going.

In many ways, it is more grueling and more painful to try to survive than it is to die. To many survivors of the Great Famine survival meant coping on a day-to-day basis, since no one knew how long the famine was going to continue, and how long they were going to be able to last. While most survivors considered themselves lucky, they often found the experience of survival extremely painful. More than fifty years after the famine, many survivors still struggle to equate the swift changes in this new era of economic boom with the painful recent past that they endured.

Sun Po, the housewife from Xushui mentioned in Chapter 3, is now in her nineties and still in good health. This talkative peasant woman has lived in Hebei province's Xushui county, in central China, all her life. She says that although Xushui was one of the first counties in the country to boast of having produced more food than its inhabitants consumed, it was badly hit by the famine. Many people died of starvation in this model county for the Great Leap Forward. Polio was a common disease among children in the area at the time of the famine, and one of Sun Po's sons suffered from it. After two children in her village died of the disease, Sun Po was determined to keep her sons alive and not to let anyone in her family die. She succeeded. Both of her sons are now fairly successful in what they do, but Sun Po lives on her own by picking rubbish. She is not ashamed of it. But even more so she is very proud of her skill in surviving the famine.

> I was a bit canny. I hid a metal bucket underneath the well. Sometimes I went to the fields to steal food and I then used the metal bucket to cook it up. But I had to be very careful. I did not dare to do it very often in case the smoke attracted the attention of the other villagers. If anybody saw me, I could have been arrested and I would have had nothing to eat. I only cooked in emergency situations, for example when someone in my family became very sick. When I did, I used a quilt to try and cover up the smoke. When my neighbors were desperately in need of help, I also cooked to help them out.

During the famine, starvation often was not caused by lack of food but resulted instead from political punishment. Zuo Rong is a retired teacher from Shayang county in Jingmen municipality, Hubei province. In 1958 he was denounced as a rightist, and was sent to the Shayang Labor Camp. Shayang Labor Camp is famous in China for the brutal torturing methods used there. This place is sometimes described as "Hell on Earth." Between 1959 and 1962 Zuo Rong toiled at the camp. Besides being constantly tortured and having to engage in hard labor, he and his fellow prisoners also had to endure the terrible hunger. He remembers how they, as well as people from his home village, struggled to survive.

> In 1959, I lost my job. I was sent to Shayang Labor Camp to do hard labor. The labor camp was like a prison without the four walls. I stayed there for three years, until 1962. That was during the time of the Great Famine. The food in the camp was not fit for human consumption. There was one guy from the northeast [of China]. He was a big man, with a big appetite. He had a university education and could speak Japanese. He didn't care to correct his inner thoughts. Each day he focused his mind on finding food to eat. The camp had two canteens. One was for inmates like us, and the other for the camp cadres. The cadres' canteen served food made with wheat. Every evening, this guy stood by the window of the cadre's canteen and used a wire to try to steal a steamed wheat bun to eat. After a while someone found out what he was doing. He was banned from going near the canteen. But that didn't stop him. He started to go to the storeroom to steal raw wheat. He used to fill his socks and trousers with wheat. When no one was around, he took out some of it to eat. There was no fire, so he would eat it raw. Once after he had eaten too much raw wheat, he suffered a terrible stomach pain. I was in charge of a small study group at the time. He called out to me for help. He told me what had happened and said he was going to die. I reported this to the camp cadres, and they sent him to the nearby hospital to have his stomach pumped.
>
> . . .

> In my home village too a low-ranking cadre named Xu Xianqing literally stuffed himself to death. He was so hungry that he ate too much chaff in one go. . . . For the villagers it was lucky that there were many lakes in our area, so they could always fish things out of the lake to eat. Many of them avoided death by starvation in this way. Complain? In those days ordinary people didn't dare to say anything even if we were very angry indeed. We just had to find ways to survive. It's human nature to try to survive.

Pan Zhenghui, the former Great Leap Forward Worker from a small village in Peng county, Sichuan province, now lives on her own in a filthy two-room house made of earth. Having survived real hardships in her youth and in the prime of her life, the dirt does not bother her. It's nothing compared with what she had to endure earlier.

> During the time of the famine we struggled to survive each day. What could we do otherwise? If there was no food to eat, we had to find other ways to survive. I told myself that as long as I worked hard I would not starve to death. I had to leave early in the morning to go to work, and at night I would come home very late. When I saw a space by the trees near the riverbank, I would try to open it up [in order to grow some food]. To open up this plot of land I broke many hoes and two blades. I could only do it by the light of the moon. During the day, I had to go to work. I had to do farming work for the brigade. I could not just let myself die of hunger though. I had to try to find a way of growing some food. That's how I survived, little by little.

I was only twenty-five years old. "Like the morning sun,"[2] I was not afraid of fatigue. I worked really hard. I always took on the toughest job in the brigade. I never failed to accomplish any task. When there was no one to carry the human waste—to be used as fertilizer—I would volunteer to do it by carrying a bamboo rod on my shoulder. I also made good friends with the villagers. When they had no food to eat, or when there was no rice for the New Year, what did I do? In 1962, just before the [Chinese] New Year, I crossed over to another farming brigade, which had some extra food left over, and I borrowed some rice from them. That way everyone in my village got rice for the New Year.

My first two children died soon after they were born. My third child was born in 1962. . . . At the time, the government was encouraging us to have children. When I gave birth to my third child I got one and a half kilograms of eggs, one and a half kilograms of brown sugar, and fifteen kilograms of rice as a reward. The eggs were from the commune's storeroom. Everything was still rationed. Fifteen kilograms of rice was simply not enough, but we just had to manage. I added other things to supplement the rice. What could I do otherwise? I struggled through. At the time I looked as thin as a monkey. Soon after I gave birth I went back to work, carrying my baby on my back. I was given forty days of maternity leave with a price to pay. I got no work points for those forty days. Without work points, I had nothing. No food. . . . One day I saw . . . some big radishes in the field. So I took a big bamboo basket with me and went into the field to pick a few radishes. I carried them home on my back, and then washed and cleaned them. There was a creek in front of our house, and I washed them in there. Afterward I chopped them up. Even today I cannot forget the scene: the whole kitchen full of radishes.

In 1959 Huang Manyi, the woman from a small village in Dingyuan county, Anhui province, who compared life at the time to that of beasts of burden, had just reached nineteen. The famine took the life of her father. On his deathbed he urged her to survive and to take care of her mother and younger brother. Manyi lived up to her father's last words and did her best to survive. Tears flooded her eyes as she recalls what she had to endure in order to survive.

The Great Leap Forward happened in 1958. Toward the end of that year, the food began to run out. In those days hardly any grain had been harvested—one mu of land could yield only a handful or so of grain, that's all. The cadres lied. They exaggerated the amount of grain produced. By 1959 nothing was growing in the fields except for a few sad-looking withered crops. There were no chickens or pigs either. In our area, people were not allowed to leave. The militia were always trying to catch people who were attempting to flee the famine. Those who got caught were taken back and beaten to death. Starvation had become prevalent. To survive, people were forced to steal.

By the end of 1959 we didn't see any grain for almost half a year. We went to the fields to steal radishes and to look for wild herbs to eat in order to keep alive. At the time, my aunt who was living in another village said that she had some dried vegetables left over. She told me to go over and take some. When I left her place, I saw some militiamen standing by the roadside. They were trying to catch people escaping from the canal construction site. They had a dog with them. I was afraid that the dog would bark, but I managed to run away without them seeing me. I left in the dark, and by the time I got back to my village it was already broad daylight. Just before I reached our house, the Party secretary of our brigade saw me. He asked me what I was doing. I told him that I had gone to my aunt's place to get some dried vegetables. He accused me of making a big deal of the food shortages in order to disgrace our county, and informed the general secretary of the Youth League [in the commune]. The Youth League held a meeting to denounce me. They asked me to confess. I refused. I told them they could kill me if they wished. I told them I had done nothing wrong. In the end they let me go.

If we had not had those dried vegetables, everyone in my family would have starved to death. Very soon it began to snow heavily, and we were housebound for a while. I used those dried vegetables to make soup for the family. Whenever it was possible to step out I also went out to fetch some dried straw that the brigade used to feed the cows. I boiled this in water. I would drink it when it was first boiled. Then I would boil it again and give the second round to my brother to drink. My mother would drink the final round. When the snow stopped I would go out to dig some wild herbs again.

Sometimes I would even go out to look for wild herbs in the rain and snow. I didn't care whether they were poisonous or not. As long as they were herbs, I would dig them up and take them home to cook. Every time I went out, my younger brother would stand by the door waiting for me to come back. When he saw me coming he would start saying: "How come it took you so long? How come it took you so long?" He would say it over and over again. That's the only thing he would say to me. He was so desperately hungry.

[At the time] my mother was in very poor health, and my father was suffering from schistosomiasis. . . . They were sent to build the dam and canal near Hefei. After a while, they ran away. My father went to my brother's place near Hefei, and my mother came home. My mother had to hide for fear that the cadres would come looking for her. Later on my brother [in Hefei] was sent away to do hard labor, so my father returned home. On his way back he was caught. The officials treated him as a vagrant. My father was detained for over a month, and he was badly beaten and regularly starved. After a month, someone who knew my father saw him, and told my uncle. My uncle got my father out of detention. On his way back, my father collapsed. Fortunately a former classmate of my brother's saw him, and carried him home. After that incident, my father's health deteriorated. Eventually, he became completely bed-bound and he could no longer move. Even when he was lying on his bed he still said to my younger brother, "Wait till I have recovered—I will work very hard and make a good living so that you can eat a whole bowl of rice." That's how he used to comfort my brother. Oh, I cannot continue—my heart aches.

One day my father said to me, "My child, I am not going to last very long. You must look after your brother, and try your best to survive. You must do what you can not to die. The bad times won't last forever. . . . Things will get better." That's what my father told me. That day it was snowing outside, and it was extremely cold. I could see my father's heart was aching as his tears fell. My father was so thin and so weak that he could barely speak. I told myself that even if I had to crawl to get it, I had to go out and find some food to feed him.

I went to the brigade office and asked them to lend me some food. They refused. They told me that many people were asking for food and that there just wasn't enough food to go around. So I went to the head of the militia. He was about the same age as my father and they were on good terms. I asked him to give me some food so that I could save my father's life. I told him, "When my [older] brother comes back, we will repay you." He told me to ask the head of brigade. I explained that they had already refused my request. He did not give me any either, so I followed him around from one village to the next. I followed him around for half the night until daybreak. In those days there were no roosters crowing any more. In the end, the head of the militia went to the canteen and got a handful of rice from the staff there. He put it in my hand. I ran home and cooked the rice up with a big bowl of water. I tried to feed my father, but he couldn't swallow it. My father died while I was feeding him. It was in 1959. He was only in his forties. [She wept at this point]

After my father died, I told myself that I must honor my father's words and do what I could to survive. I remembered that there was a pile of straw in our school's sports ground. I went back to the school and found some dried grain shells there. I took them home. At the time my second brother was working in Hefei. My oldest brother, who had returned from doing hard labor in Fujian, was also living in Hefei. At home there was only my mother, myself, and my younger brother. One day I went to Hefei to look for my brothers. We had no money, and it was more than fifty kilometers from our home village to the provincial capital. I walked all day and managed to cover half of the journey. Then I sold some of my mother's clothes, and with that money I managed to get on the train that took me to Hefei.

I went to my second brother's place first. He was working and I had to wait till the evening to see him. At the time his monthly salary was twelve yuan. He could barely fill his own stomach and he had no food to give to me. I started to cry. I was afraid that after having gone all the way there I was just going to die. And if I was going to die, my mother and my younger brother were not going to be able to survive either. That's three lives. I was so hungry and thirsty. I went to my cousin's home but no one was there. I sat on the doorstep until three in the morning, without eating anything for the whole day. I was also afraid I might get caught and sent to the detention center, just like my father. In the end my older brother turned up. He told me I must try to survive, if only for the sake of my mother and younger brother. He gave me one coupon for 500 grams of rice, and with that I bought 250 grams of cooked rice, 250 grams of uncooked rice, and a few pieces of bread. I took them with me and made the journey home.

On my way back I was followed by a man. He had an axe behind his back. I knew that he wanted to kill me and chop me into pieces. He asked whether I had any food in my pockets, and I said no. I told him that my brother was in Hefei, and that if he went there he'd find some food to eat. I also told him that my brother was looking to pay someone to help him carry a film projector back to the countryside, and that he should go to Hefei straight away to look him up. So he left. But after a while he turned back and tried to catch up with me. He was very thin and hungry, and he barely had the energy to run. Fortunately I ate some rice before I left Hefei, so I could run faster than he could. After I got rid of him, I tried to avoid running into anyone else, so I turned away from the main road and walked on a small country path. Oh, what a terrible time! It was so dangerous in those days—I could have died. There were many crimes back then. On my way to Hefei I saw people being robbed and beaten to death. But I was quite fearless and cautious, and kept looking around to see whether I was being followed.

When I got home both my mother and younger brother were lying on the bed. They could barely talk. For two days and two nights they had nothing to eat, and they were dying. I took out the rice I bought from Hefei and cooked it up to feed them. That saved their lives.

Guangzhong, the seventy-year-old farmer from Dinglou village in Pingdingshan region, central south Henan, who talked about how villagers cheated in order to meet the sand collection target imposed by local cadres and to achieve the high figure in iron and steel production, remembers that between 1959 and 1961, Henan province's champion region in iron and steel production also experienced some of the highest death figures. Guangzhong turns out to be one of the very few survivors of the famine in his village.

In the middle of the famine my father starved to death. He was quite ill at first and eventually he died. Not far from here, in Lushan county, they had the highest death figures [for the region]. In our village many people got ill because of starvation. Edema was widespread. [To survive] people ate anything, from leaves of Pagoda trees to Elm trees. [After a while] trees over here became totally barren. The leaves had all been eaten by starving villagers. . . .

We only managed to survive because of my mother. She was very hardworking and thrifty. She searched everywhere for wild herbs, tree leaves, dried sweet potato, and corncobs to feed us. Near our home there was a mountain, and inside the mountain you could find a type of special stone. We used to mill the stone into fine powder and mix it with wild herbs. We made pancakes with the mixture. We thought it was quite tasty, but after eating it we suffered from terrible constipation. Our stomachs became bloated, and the pain was unbearable. In the beginning the grown-ups would use a wooden stick to help the children scoop out the hard lumps one by one. Later on the villagers also operated on one another. At the time we called it noodle stones. These days the stone is an essential material in rubber auxiliary manufacturing. It helps to solidify and glue ingredients together.

Qiu Wenhua, from the same village as Guangzhong, was a young boy at the time of the famine. In Chapters 1 and 2 he spoke about how his family lost its home during collectivization and how in his village people were forced to dig sand in the nearby river during the freezing winter and were starved to death. Now in his sixties, he is still unable to forget the intense hunger and humiliation he endured some fifty years ago. He talks about how he and others in his village struggled to survive.

> In those days even the cows could barely stand up because they had nothing to eat. Quite a number of cows in our brigade starved to death. When no one was looking, some brave people would cut off a piece of meat from the dead animal to eat. . . . We hardly consumed any proper food and many people suffered edema, which was caused by starvation. In our village a huge number of people starved to death. At least twenty people died, and most of these were elderly people. Younger ones could last longer. The cadres did nothing to help. The government didn't give us any food or medicine either. They gave us nothing.
>
> My grandfather died of starvation. He was in his sixties. It was in spring 1959. My parents were away working at the time and they left me at home to look after my grandfather. It was really horrible. I really don't want to talk about it. . . .
>
> In the autumn of 1959, desperate hunger drove me to the fields where I stole a corncob. It was very tough, too tough to chew, so I lit a fire to cook it. While I was cooking, some cadres caught me. They tied the corncob to my shoulder and paraded me through the village. I felt so humiliated, but the villagers all understood that I had done it because I was so desperately hungry.
>
> Stealing was very common. When autumn came round, any young wheat sprouts would disappear as soon as they came out. . . . The famine lasted until 1962. The head of our brigade was punished by the government because he was cruel to the villagers. . . . He was given a ten-year sentence. . . .

> Things began to improve only in 1963. That year we harvested mung beans. I still remember it clearly. . . . For three years we had hardly anything to eat. Every day I dreamed of having a mouthful of food.

As a chef, Yan from Ziyang county in Sichuan is very fond of food. During my interview with him, he recalls vividly a whole host of things that he and his fellow villagers consumed in order to survive the famine.

> I was about ten in 1958, and I was still at school. From the school we had to walk a long way to the collective canteen. The canteen was so far away, and quite often I didn't go. My family pickled radishes in those days. At mealtimes we soaked some in hot water, and then drank the water. What else did we eat? We also ate wild celery and banana stalks. We used to peel the outer part of the stalks and chew up the hearts—in the same way as one would chew up sugar cane. We also ate cakes made from pea stalks. First we milled the stalks into flour. Then we would sieve the flour and use it to make cakes. There would only be one cake per person. [Laugh]
>
> At the time, there were seven of us in the family. Each of us would only get a small bowl of food from the canteen, so one person would end up getting just one serving-spoonful of food, and that consisted of mostly liquid.
>
> Even as a young boy, I could barely fill my stomach with the food we received from the canteen. So I went up the hill with other children of my age to collect rape stalks. We took the stalks home, and blanched them in water. After

blanching we squeezed out the excess water and cooked the stalks in a pan. We cooked them until they turned into a thick stew. We ate that to stave off the hunger.

We also ate insects, such as crickets. Whenever I caught a cricket I would just put it straight into my mouth. It was still alive, but I ate it like that. We also ate little worms. The worms lived in the earth. After plowing, they would come to the surface. We used to light a fire and cook them over the fire. Some people also ate toads, but I didn't. I was frightened of them. Even now I am still frightened of them.

I did eat snake, however. My father was still alive then. Once he cooked a snake and I ate some of it. The snake bones were so hard that I couldn't chew them. I only remember that the snake soup was very white. It was so greasy that even now I can still feel the grease when I touch the things I wore at the time. I can't wash away that greasy feeling. My wife teases me about it sometimes. She says that I suffer now because I was so fond of food that I would eat anything.

I also ate water celery. This was a wild vegetable that grew on the edge of the farming fields. I ate it either pickled or cooked. The worst thing we ate were cakes made of "immortal earth": a type of white clay. It came in a pure white color, and people used it to make porcelain. They called it "immortal earth." It had a sandy texture. Since we were so hungry back then, people often mixed the white clay with water to make pancakes. We used to fill our stomachs with that. One old lady got severely constipated after eating it. She had to use her fingers to scoop out the hard stool. We also ate ramie leaves. These were used to make shoes, but during the time of the famine we would chop them up

> finely and make pancakes to feed ourselves. . . . That was in 1959—it was the most difficult time.

The first time I met Huang Mama, the woman from a small village on the western Sichuan plain who watched her own child succumbing to the famine, she was selling wild herbs on the street and carrying a huge rattan basket on her back. I was intrigued and wanted to find out what herbs she was selling, so we ended up getting into a discussion about edible herbs. During the course of our conversation I asked her whether she and the local villagers consumed wild herbs during the time of the Great Famine. She paused for a minute and then started to reminisce about the past:

> [In those days] many villagers grazed on raw peas and broad beans. They also stole and ate wheat grains. The child from the family opposite ours once ate some raw peas and his stomach swelled up afterward. He was too young to be able to digest raw peas. I still have a strong memory of him eating unshelled raw peas and running around wearing no clothes. Sometimes people roasted wheat grain[s] and peas in the stove. These were unshelled peas and wheat. They first pushed them into the stove and once they were roasted they used a shovel to fish them out. They would also use a sieve to separate the peas and wheat from the ash. That's the way they ate them.
>
> When people could no longer bear the hunger, they also went to the local market to buy black taro to make black bean curd.[3] They would cook up an entire bowl of it and eat it all in one go. Lots of people got sick afterward. In less than half a day, many people died: their dead bodies lying around all over the place. I saw them with my own eyes.

> People also consumed castor beans. I watched them collapsing after eating them. When there was nothing to eat, some people filled their stomachs with roasted castor beans. The beans tasted delicious roasted, but lots of people got ill after eating them. They fainted and collapsed one after the other: they lost their balance and fell to the floor. Their vision also became blurred: the sky became murky and the earth turned dark. Gradually they lost consciousness. Over here people also ate juanzi berries. These are small, white-colored berries that grow wild in the countryside. Juanzi berries are very tasty, but they are also poisonous. Many people became unconscious after eating them. Again, people collapsed all over the place.

While ordinary people consumed insects, earth, and wild herbs, those with guns and power hunted down wild animals. Coming from a high-ranking cadre family, Xian shed some light on how the privileged classes in Beijing filled their stomachs.

> [In Beijing] there were special shops serving high-class cadres. Army cadres were the best off. The army sent soldiers to hunt yellow sheep as well as wild deer and wild horses. They hunted any wild animal. They slaughtered the animals and took the meat back to Beijing. They then distributed the meat among various government and army units. In those days, in order to survive, human beings became almost crazy in their hunt for food. This must rank as one of the first incidents organized on such a large scale of humans hunting and slaughtering wild animals to survive.

The privileged and those with guns hunted wild animals in order to survive; others searched for food in faraway and strange places. In the course of the interview Xian told me how her two brothers went on an adventure to the countryside to search for some food. At the time they were just middle-school students.

> I remember that by 1963 things got better in the countryside because of some changes in government policy. Farmers were allowed to have a plot of land for growing their own vegetables and keeping pigs and chickens. . . . My aunt's husband was from Liangxiang in the western suburbs of Beijing, but we had never had any contact with his family. . . . My two brothers were middle-school students then, and they decided to go to Liangxiang to search out these distant relatives of ours. Their hope was that they might find some food with these relatives. My brothers took a long-distance bus to the nearby town and walked the rest of the way to the village where the relatives lived. When they got to the village they told villagers that they were looking for relatives and hoped to find some food. None of the villagers had met my brothers before; they could have been imposters. However, the villagers were extremely kind, since they saw that my brothers were just children. [They asked them] how they had got there and on which bus. My brothers did find the relatives at last. The relatives' family took my brothers in and made a feast for them. Afterward, they sent them away with dried corn, dried sorghum, millet, and a freshly slaughtered chicken. I seem to remember they also got potatoes. They took with them all the food they could carry: their school bags were filled with food. . . . They

> didn't take any buses back—they wanted to save money. On their way back they passed through some farming fields. They picked up discarded corn cobs and potato stalks and they stuffed those into their school bags, too. They walked all the way home carrying all the food. After they got home they milled the corn cobs and potato stalks and mixed these with wheat flour. The mixture made for a substantial meal. Since we didn't have much wheat, we always tried to add other things to it to make up for the quantity. Sometimes we added some flowers from the Pagoda tree, sometimes other wild herbs. We added anything we could find. We used the mixture to make cakes and bread. It was more substantial. I always remember this.

Chen Gu, the talkative woman who told me about what happened during the Anti-Hiding Campaign in her village in Pengshan county, Sichuan province, also spoke about how she and her family as well as her fellow villagers endured the misery and tried to survive the famine. As she spoke, she broke into tears.

> In 1958 I was only three and I was sent to the collective nursery. But I often ran away from the nursery because I was constantly starving there. I was desperately hungry in those days. Each time my mother would take me back to the nursery and the staff would lock the door. Watching my mother leaving, I would run after her. But by the time I reached the gate, it was already shut. Whenever I spotted the nursery gate left open, I'd run out and try to steal some food.
>
> Once I even stole my brother's chaff cake. I was eating at the nursery at the time, and my brother ate at the collective

canteen with other villagers. He was treated as an adult laborer, so he received a bigger portion than me. His amount was twice as much. When I saw that my mother and brother received bigger [chaff] cakes, . . . I tried to steal theirs. Once I grabbed my brother's chaff cake in my hand and ran off like a shot. I ran into a shelter that my neighbor used to store rubbish. I hid myself in there and tried to eat the cake. But before I managed to take a bite, my brother caught up with me. He took the cake out of my hand and slapped me really hard in the face.

Talking about my brother, he too stole food. When the ox died in our village, each family received a piece of meat. When the adults were not looking, my brother put a small piece of raw meat into his mouth. He gulped it down quickly and the meat got stuck in his chest. My mother gave him some wild cotton roots to eat in order to save his life. Wild cotton root was supposed to aid digestion. My brother was a little older than me. Sometimes he took a basket with him to pick up discarded vegetable leaves in the fields. On those days I waited for him outside our house, wanting to see whether he had managed to bring back any vegetable leaves. My mother was pregnant at the time. If my brother didn't bring anything back, my mother and I would have nothing to eat. Each day I waited for him to bring home some vegetables so that we'd have something on the table. I could spot my brother from far away. When I saw him walking toward our house, I would run to see whether there were any vegetable leaves in his basket. If the basket was empty, tears would fall from my eyes because I knew I would have nothing to eat. If I saw anything in his basket, I'd be so happy. What a great feeling that was! I cannot talk about it now. Each time I talk about it, tears fill my eyes. [She begins to weep.] Once, seeing people washing vegetables, my brother tried to pick up some discarded leaves. They asked him, "Child, why are you picking up those leaves? They have been discarded." My brother replied, "My mother is pregnant and she needs to eat, so I'll pick anything up." In the end these people gave him a lot of yellow or withered leaves. When we saw him carrying the leaves back, we were over the moon. We went through the leaves carefully. When I saw carrots attached to some of those leaves, I put them in my mouth straight away.

When my mother was in the advanced stages of her pregnancy she received twenty kilograms of sweet potatoes from the government. The total amount was supposed to cover her for forty days: that's five hundred grams per day. My brother and I always wanted take a bite of her sweet potato. We were still young and didn't understand things, and we expected to eat her food. If we saw her eating sweet potato, we would run to her and stand by her. If she gave me a few pieces, I would hold them in my hands and run off into the corner where we took our shit. I would chew them all up very quickly. I had no idea how to behave in those days. I only knew that if my father came in and saw me, he'd scold my mother. . . . Sometimes my brother and I also stole my mother's food. . . .

My family had a stone mill, and people used to come to our place to mill food for the pigs. Sometimes people showed pity on us children and gave us dried maize to eat, so my brother and I often stood by the mill hoping that someone would give us some maize. Soon the person in charge of taking care of the pigs discovered what we were doing, so he deliberately mixed cow shit with the maize. When people came to our mill, we went as usual to beg for the maize. We were told, "Look—there is cow shit in the maize. Do you still want to eat it?" I was dying of hunger in those days, so I ate it. Be it cow shit or pig's shit, I would eat anything!

There were also lots of insects and worms that would be dredged up after people plowed the fields. My brother and I used to take a pot with us to the fields when the adults were plowing. We followed them. If we saw an insect jumping, we would try and catch it. Even if it jumped very fast, we could still do it. After we caught insects we cooked them up. We then peeled off the legs and ate the rest of the body in a mouthful, including the intestines. We'd eat anything in those days. There was really nothing we didn't eat.

People also searched for and ate zajuer, a kind of earth fungus. It was considered a good thing then. After the rain it grew from the spot where a goat had done its dump. . . . Zajuer grew naturally. You can't find them now. In those years things like that were like gifts from heaven—they saved peoples' lives. We called this "immortal rice." It's odd that such things saved peoples' lives.

In our village, thieves constantly came across other thieves. In those days the village kept some sweet potatoes in a storage room. One day a thief made his way in and bent down to help himself to some of the sweet potatoes. As he stood up, he bumped his head on another thief who had also come to the storeroom looking for sweet potatoes. If you didn't steal, you could never have survived the famine.

The canteen staff and cadres from the inspection teams stole, too. They always saved all the goodies for themselves. Sometimes they took food home so that they could eat slowly at their own pace. Ordinary villagers, however, had nothing to eat. . . . Once my mother went to my aunt's place because my aunt's son was ill. When my mother came back, the canteen staff refused to serve her any food. The reason was that she had missed her work that day. My father beat my mother up because she didn't get her portion of food. . . . He pulled her hair and pushed her head against the ground. Afterward, my mother's eyes became swollen and red. They looked like light bulbs. Her hair was in a huge mess too. All this trouble just because she had not got back in time to do the farming work and she was deprived of her portion of food.

There was a woman in our village. She was a big woman, and able to walk for miles carrying very heavy loads. The food at the canteen was not adequate for her, and she was often desperately hungry. One day she hid some pickled snake beans in her trousers. She did not put them anywhere else but in her trousers. Her sister-in-law reported this to her mother-in-law, saying that "someone had stolen a load of pickled snake beans to feed herself." The sister-in-law then took the snake beans out from this woman's trousers. This riled the woman's husband. He yelled at the mother and the sister-in-law: "Stop complaining to me. Just give me a gun and I will finish her off in one shot." On hearing this, the woman ran away. All these years she never showed her face again.

. . .

> Even today when I think about life back then I still feel very miserable.

Yang Mang is from small village in Qianjiang county, Hubei province. He was a middle-school student when the famine hit his village. He remembers how villagers tried to survive by taking food from other people's mouths.

> There are few things I want to tell you. One is about the lotus roots that grew in the pond near the dwarf Bangda's home. After the lotus roots had been harvested by the commune, lots of children went into the pond to try and pick out the leftovers. It was winter, and those children had no shoes. Their feet were frozen and became completely numb. Bangda's mother-in-law was a mean woman. She poured human manure all over the pond in order to prevent others going near it, so that she could dig up all the leftover lotus roots to feed her own grandson. . . .
>
> Another thing is about the daughter-in-law of the ironmonger, Mr. Tang. Once when she was making rice cakes for her baby, she was so hungry that she could not resist eating the cakes while she was making them. In the end she finished all the cakes herself. The baby was so thin. There was no flesh on him but for his bare bones. He screamed, but there was nothing left for him to eat. The child's nickname was Eda [which means to grow up starving.]
>
> . . .
>
> In those days people with power had a relatively good life. In our village, for example, Wu Zhen, an ex-army soldier, never had to suffer starvation. Weijin was the bookkeeper

> for the collective canteen. One day I saw his family sitting in the dark eating white rice. That was the day that the canteen claimed that it didn't have any food to feed us.

In times of starvation and death, selfishness became normal. The ironmonger Tang's daughter-in-law was not the only one who ate her own child's food. Mrs. Luo, the villager from northwest of Sichuan who watched her own son and mother succumbing to the famine, told me of a relative of hers who refused to feed her own grandson in order to save a mouthful for herself.

> I remember that my sister's mother-in-law had a grandson. He was ten years old at the time. He was only about this tall but his grandmother asked him to tend the sheep. She also refused to give him any food to eat. I told her that she was very mean not to feed him, but she replied: "I have hardly anything to eat myself. I have to work to get my food, so where am I supposed to find food for him?" I told her: "But he is not old enough to work and he has been tending sheep for you." She replied: "Why don't you feed him yourself?" The boy died not long afterward.

Xie Mou is from a remote village in Mianyang region in northern Sichuan. He was eleven when the famine broke out. Although he and his family survived it, life did not improve much for them. It seemed to him that the only way out was to join the army. He left his home village in 1965, as soon as he was old enough to sign up. He was stationed as far away as Liangshan, a mountainous region bordering Sichuan and Yunnan. This is one of the poorest areas in China, but for Xie Mou life in Liangshan was still better than in his home village.

In 2008 the Sichuan earthquake wiped out his home village. Having settled in faraway Liangshan, Xie Mou escaped the devastation. He regards himself as doubly lucky.

> I was still a child then, but I remember that in our brigade many people starved to death. Everyone tried to fill their stomachs before they died. Family members regularly fought each other over food. Wives and husbands fought each other all the time. The fighting could be very fierce.
>
> I remember that one night I was woken up by the hunger. I was so hungry that I couldn't go back to sleep and started to cry. My parents could do nothing to comfort me except to give me a few sweet potato leaves to chew on.
>
> Although I was only a child then, I understood [that in order to survive] we had to steal food. One night after we children went to sleep, my parents went out and stole a piece of pigskin. In those days, after pigs had been slaughtered the butcher would hang the pigskin outside to let it dry. My parents took a piece home. It was covered in black-colored bristles. They burned the skin and cleaned off the bristles before cooking it. After it was cooked they woke us up to eat it. My parents did all this in the dark. If the brigade head had found it out, he'd have confiscated our cooking pot. If he ever saw smoke rising from people's houses he would go to that family and smash up their pots and pans.
>
> No one died in my family. My elder brother joined the army during the Korean War and was able to send some money back every month. If we hadn't had his support, we'd never have been able to escape death.

Lao Yu, mentioned in Chapter 2, also lives in Liangshan. Originally he was from a small village in Fushun county in southern Sichuan. In 1957 he went to study at Chengdu Agriculture Machinery College. After his graduation two years later he was sent to work in Liangshan. That was at the height of the famine. Life was harsh but at least as a government employee he received a monthly salary and nine kilos of food per month. In his home village many people starved to death, including seven entire families. Those who survived turned to theft.

> In 1961 I went home for a visit. My father told me that everyone in the village had become thieves. I asked him how this had come about. He said that the villagers had built hidden compartments into the bottom of their grain baskets. When they were sent off to transport grain, they'd take some grain and hide it in these compartments. . . . This was their survival strategy. I suppose you could call it stealing. Almost everyone in our village did that, so you might say that everyone was a thief in those days.
>
> . . .
>
> My aunt's son was a minor cadre at the time. . . . As a cadre he was allowed to grow some sweet corn for himself. When my father and two uncles were suffering from edema because of starvation, they went to visit my aunt. Seeing my aunt was just an excuse—what they really wanted was to get some food from my aunt and her family. My aunt gave them some dried sweet corn, but the three men hardly had the strength to mill the corn. When they finally managed, they cooked up the milled corn meal. My father ate two big bowlfuls. "Even though I was full to the bursting point, still

> I wanted to eat more," he told me. . . . "In the end I was so bloated that I could barely walk."
>
> . . .
>
> For the entire Great Leap Forward period, life had been very hard. Over here I was supposed to get nine kilograms of rice a month, but in reality the rice was mixed with other coarse food. I never understood why things could be so bad. . . . What did I do to survive the hunger? In the beginning I tried just to grin and bear it, but later when I could no longer handle it, I just forced myself to sleep through it. That is if I was able to get to sleep. . . . Back in my village things were even worse. For over a year, the collective [canteen] served nothing but sweet potatoes: sweet potato for breakfast, sweet potato for lunch, and sweet potato for dinner. When there were no sweet potatoes left, the villagers resorted to food substitutes such as sweet potato leaves and wild herbs. You could fill your stomach with such things. Villagers even ate chaff and white clay. This clay was called "immortal earth." Those who could not find food substitutes died. . . .

On my way to see Liushu, the upright man from Wengong district in Renshou county in central Sichuan who called radical collectivization a "pipe dream," I was struck by how fertile the land was in the surrounding countryside. The lush green hills were covered with loquat trees. It is hard to believe that more than two hundred thousand people died in Renshou during the Great Famine, many of whom were from Wengong. At the time the hills were barren, and the loquat trees stood naked with no leaves or bark. They had been consumed by the villagers. "Anything edible was eaten," Liushu told me, while trying to remember how he and his fellow villagers had struggled to survive.

> One could see people trying to steal food wherever one turned. At the time there was a saying that ordinary villagers ate whatever they could find, while cadres ate—I cannot remember the exact words now, but it was something like "villagers steal what's grown out there while cadres enjoy food from the storeroom." People grazed on anything that grew in the fields—from peas to corn and sweet potato. Theft was extremely prevalent. I remember that I was given the job by the brigade to guard the cornfield when the corn was ready for harvest. Guess what happened? Before I took up my duty, someone had already stolen all the corn. The production team leader told me off, saying, "It was your job to guard the corn—how come you let people steal it all?" and then he deducted my food rations. I knew the thief was from our production brigade, so I cursed loudly, shouting, "Who is the heartless culprit? You stole the corn without paying for it, and now here I am with nothing to eat." Someone told me not to get so angry, that the person who stole the corn couldn't help himself—he did it out of desperation. The thief must have been very hungry, and stealing would have been his last resort.
>
> In those days when the peas sprouted people stole them, and when the wheat started sprouting they stole that as well. Some people also managed to get into the storeroom to steal the food that was kept in there. If they were caught in the act, they were beaten up or given a lesson in morality. I remember that the commune used to hold meetings to beat up those villagers caught stealing. . . .

My youngest brother is now a local cadre. He was still a child during the time of the famine. I remember that he always filled up his bowl first, even if it was only sweet potatoes. At the time, each person received less than half a kilo of sweet potatoes per meal. After my brother had filled up his bowl we were left with nothing to eat. He screamed loudly every meal. It was like that every time. And because he screamed, he was often beaten. At the time, life was really hard. People often fought over food. For just a mouthful of food, family members turned hostile toward each other. . . . Families didn't feel like families. Some of them split up as a result—some family members had to leave their homes because they couldn't get enough to eat there. Over here lots of people ran away.

At the time I was going to a school in the county town. At the school my food rations were nine kilograms per month. I was so hungry that I ended up trying to swallow my own saliva. There was nothing else I could do. Each day during siesta time, all the students in my class went up the hill to look for wild-growing sweet potato. We had to fight over it. Once, after I had taken back some sweet potato, I couldn't even bring myself to eat it because it was so precious. I hid it inside my suitcase and waited until I could no longer bear the hunger. Only then would I take it out and bite off just a couple of mouthfuls. That was my survival strategy.

At one point we were sent to the countryside to support the agricultural work, and the amount of food rations remained the same at nine kilos. Because we were doing hard labor, the feeling of hunger was more intense. One of my classmates came and told me, "I really cannot bear this anymore—I am

> going home." At the time I was the team leader. When he informed me of his decision, I replied, "If you want to go home, that's fine. I won't stop you." He said to me, "Since I am leaving, I don't need my food coupons any more, I am giving them to you." So I got double portions of food. That's how I survived the most difficult time.

As the famine progressed, in parts of China there was simply nothing left to steal. Desperately hungry villagers resorted to eating dead human flesh. Although I had read of the prevalence of cannibalism in Gansu province at the time,[4] when I traveled to Hui county in southern Gansu I just could not picture cannibalism there. Surrounded by rich forest and natural resources, Hui county is known as Gansu's "little Jiangnan," meaning that it was as rich as the Yangtze River delta. Rice, wheat, and cornfields stretch for acres, and every year the area also produces an abundance of walnuts, gingko nuts, chestnuts, and many different types of precious medicinal plants. How could Hui county have run out of food to sustain its population? But during the Great Leap Forward, Hui county was also one of the major sites for iron and steel production. Deforestation was rampant. The destruction was catastrophic. This was accompanied by a severe famine. Local villagers not only consumed all the geese, dogs, and cats in the area, but they also ate tree bark and grass roots to appease their hunger. Chen Apo and Chen Gonggong, the old couple who were introduced to me by their grandson studying in Chengdu, recount the horror of the time and how villagers struggled to survive.

> When they were desperately hungry, some people tried to steal food to fill their stomachs. There was nothing much

> to steal. Occasionally you might find some coarse food and rice to steal. My children cried all the time because they were hungry. People even consumed human flesh. It happened in Haiyaba, a village not far from here. One poor peasant ate the flesh of his own child. He was arrested and convicted. Afterward the entire family also died of starvation.

Cannibalism did not occur only in one village; it happened in different parts of the country as well. Far from Gansu, in Wu Yongkang's village in Guangshan county, Henan province, similar incidents also took place. Unlike Hui county, Guangshan does not boast pretty scenery or natural resources. The county town in Guangshan looks shabby and soulless, and is surrounded by flat countryside. There are many of these kinds of towns in China. "Poor" and "tacky" are the words to describe them. This unremarkable place was a famous site in the history of the Great Famine, however, because of the high numbers of deaths that occurred here: one-third of its population was wiped out, including many entire families. Among them were thousands of people who were tortured to death. Some were even buried alive. At the time there were 120 people in Wu Yongkang's village, and 74 were killed by starvation or beating. I had often read about cannibalism being widespread in the area, so I asked Wu about it. He turned his head and looked into the distance, and said:

> Yes, there were cases of people eating human flesh. In our village there was a man named Wu Xiaofan. After his daughter died, he consumed her body because there was nothing else to eat. Over here almost every village had cases like that. You see, in those days there were no dogs or cows

> left. Even if there were cows, they belonged to the commune and no one was allowed to slaughter them or consume them. People had to fill their stomachs with something.

Indeed, in many places it seemed that dead human flesh was the only food available not only for human consumption but also for animals. This happened in an area called Doumen in Zhongshan, Guangdong province, just a couple of hours drive from the then Portuguese colony of Macau. A former villager, Liang Xiansheng, recalls:

> The commune didn't care whether we were hungry or not. We were worse off than pigs. In those days pigs were hungry, too. In our area [one could see] hungry pigs scavenging and consuming dead human flesh.
>
> . . . My home village was in southern China. It's very close to Macau—it takes only a few hours from our area to Macau by boat. So many people escaped to Macau.

Like in Liang Xiansheng's village, elsewhere in China, those who had the strength left or the means to run away tried to escape the famine. Lao Liu and his brother, from Fushun county in southern Sichuan, were among those who ran away. When they were in their early twenties, they walked over a thousand miles to Zhaojue in Liangshan Yi Autonomous Region, where Lao Liu lives today. Although the two brothers escaped death, Liangshan, high up in the mountains, was not exactly "heaven on earth." Today in his seventies, Lao Liu still struggles to try to make ends meet.

> I fled here in 1959. Why? Because I was starving at home. I had no other option but to flee. I walked here on my own

two feet. In those days there was no transportation to these parts. I walked for seven days, covering more than one thousand kilometers. I was with my brother. Before we left we borrowed a basket of sweet potatoes from a relative. We cooked them up and took them on our journey. When we felt hungry we would eat one of them. This lasted us for seven days. At night we would rest at road construction sites. All the way we kept on meeting workers constructing the road. They were Han Chinese. We did not meet any Yi people. We could not even get close to them. The [Yi] uprising had just been quashed by the Chinese government. Although the uprising was suppressed by the government in 1959 and 1960, the trouble in the region continued. It took many more years till things finally settled down.[5]

I decided to come because Liangshan is far away from home, and I knew people working here. I was told that I could find a job here. So I did. I did many jobs here, from being a loading-bay worker to being a presser at an oil-pressing factory. All of the jobs I did were very hard work, but at least I could fill my stomach. . . . Because I had to do a lot of hard work, my health is very poor now. As factory workers we were promised free health care, but in reality I pay for most of my medical expenses. Five hundred yuan is the most I can get back from the government—that is if I am admitted into the hospital. I pay a consultation fee each time. When I challenged the government's Medical Insurance Unit, they pushed the responsibility elsewhere. . . . Furthermore, I have never seen the government subsidy that was promised to those of us who live in mountainous regions and frontier areas. When I asked about it, I was told our work unit has no

> money to pay us. Since I am retired, no one gives a damn. I don't understand the government policy at all.

Wang Yeye is a ninety-year-old peasant from a small village in Puxi township, Jimo county, northeast of Shandong province. It was his grandson—a graduate student at Shanghai Jiaotong University—who introduced me to him. During the interview I learned that Wang Yeye was one of the millions from Shandong and Henan who escaped to northeast China to survive the famine. Locals called this mass exodus *chuang guandong*, which translates literally as "brave the journey to the northeast" and means "to leave one's country or home in order to survive" or "to try to make a new life in no-man's land." Many years after the famine, Wang Yeye still felt ashamed about having deserted his family when he ran away. He has never talked about it with his children and grandchildren. I was the first person to ask him about it.

> One of my relatives worked in a hydropower station in Shenyang, and [through him] I got a job working on a dam construction site. After working there for one month, I managed to run away despite the fact they didn't allow me to leave. I ran off to Harbin and worked as a loading-bay worker. The pay was quite good—I could earn up to fifty yuan per month. But I had to work day and night, often with no rest at all. I told myself that I mustn't die of exhaustion in this strange land, given that I had run away from home in order to survive. When the thought of still having young children and elderly parents at home hit me, I decided that I had to leave. I begged all the way until I reached the railway station. For five or six days I helped to load and

> unload goods at the station, and then I moved on to other parts. In the end I found a job in a factory in Liushu tun [in Heilongjiang province, northeastern China]. The factory did not allow any families, so I stayed there on my own until the spring of 1962. When I got back to my village, I saw many starving villagers here who could barely stand. . . .
>
> Under the Nationalists I ran away in order to avoid military service. I was still a young man then. [During the famine,] many people starved to death over here. When someone died of starvation, all other villagers helped to bury the body or to throw the body away. . . . We were all scared since we did not know when it would be our turn to die.
>
> . . . Nevertheless I didn't want to stay in the northeast. I wanted to come home. . . . The place where I was [in the northeast] was very cold and deserted. There wasn't much food around. I was in a place close to what is known as Badahuang [Great Northeastern Wildness].[6]

Xiao Mama is another who left her native land in 1960 at the height of the famine. She and her husband plus their two children moved from Qiyang county in Hunan province, central China, to a small village outside Mengding township in Yunnan province in the far southwest corner of China, on the border with Burma. Unlike Wang Yeye, who ran away by himself, the Xiaos were drafted by the government to go to Yunnan. They were given no choice.

> In 1960 we left our home in Qiyang and migrated to Mengding. We were drafted into leaving because there were too many people and not enough land at home. We were sent to Yunnan to open up the wasteland.

At the time conditions were terrible back home. Whenever I think about it now tears fill my eyes. There was nothing to eat, except for a few sweet potatoes. Everything we grew was taken by the collective. . . . It started in 1958 at the time of the mass production of steel and iron. Many people died. Nothing grew in the fields in those days, and there was no food to eat. People were starving all the time, and no one had any strength left to work. Still we were forced to do heavy jobs such as carrying coal. Some people stole food to survive, but if they were caught they would be beaten to death. One of my relatives once stole two bowls of rice. He was very tall and he could no longer stand the hunger—that's why he tried to steal. He was caught and was beaten to death that very evening. . . . People fought each other over food. It was like a war. We didn't want to go to Yunnan, but if we stayed at home our children would have had nothing to eat. . . . In 1961, a year after we arrived in Mengding, we got a letter from home saying that there was still no food to eat and that more and more people were starving to death. In one small brigade more than ten people died. A small brigade normally consisted of forty to fifty families, and more than ten people had died of starvation. That's a huge number.

Coming to Yunnan was the Chairman [Mao]'s order. We would never have come otherwise. Life over here was very tough at the beginning. There weren't even proper roads over here. . . . Initially the situation looked a lot worse than at home. . . . One person [who came with us] cried. He couldn't believe how terrible the conditions were over here. . . . Some did return to Hunan, but in 1961, a year later, they found

> themselves back in Mengding again because there was no food to eat at home.
>
> When we first got here there were no chopsticks, so we cut down some bamboo to make our own. We desperately needed fat in our diet so we went to the Dai villagers and bought some snake oil from them.[7] Each meal we added a little snake oil to the vegetables. We had to queue up for salt in those days. The line used to be very long. In 1961 and '62 we built a road, and gradually goods from outside were able to reach us here. . . . But high up in the mountains there is still no road, and people are still very poor even today. They still can't afford rice there.

In southern China, close to the border, many people tried to escape the hardships by going abroad. Chen Xiansheng, the teenager living in Nanning city, Guangxi province, whose family had lost everything during radical collectivization, as mentioned in Chapter 1, then escaped to Hong Kong toward the end of the famine. Now in his seventies, living comfortably in Hong Kong, he recalls vividly how he and his family survived the famine.

> To survive I ate everything. As Muslims, our religion forbids us to eat pork. But in those days I even ate pork. It tasted so good to me. . . .
>
> When things were really bad, we went to the countryside [to look for food]. Sometimes we secretly crossed the border into Vietnam to fill up with foodstuffs and other goods. . . . From Nanning to the Vietnamese border we had to pass through Pengchang county. We did the entire journey on foot. On the road I saw dead bodies everywhere. No one took

care of the bodies. They were simply covered up with banana leaves. The bodies looked totally wasted, and some were completely deformed. I can never forget that horrible scene.

Eventually I left Guangxi and moved to Taishan county in Guangdong. I had no papers, no permit, and no grain coupons. A relative took me in, and I stayed there for more than half a year. Finally I could eat rice grain. Not white rice, but rice with the outer husks. Being close to Hong Kong, life in Guangdong was much better. Those with families in Hong Kong also got lard. It was sent from Hong Kong by post. . . .

In those days even very basic everyday supplies were hard to come by. Everything was rationed. You needed coupons for everything, from soap to oil to food, fabric, meat, and sugar. You even needed coupons for soy sauce. But there was no soy sauce to be found. One of my relatives worked in the chemical department of a government unit. He knew a bit of chemistry, so he mixed human hair and hydrochloric acid together. Guess what—it turned into amino acid. Purified amino acid is MSG. Add some salt water and a bit of color, and it became homemade soy sauce. We collected a lot of empty bottles and started our clandestine soy sauce factory. We also went around to all the barbers in the city and collected as much human hair as we could find. Besides human hair, we also used ox bones, pigs' bones, and pigs' skin. Anything with a high calcium content would do. That's how we made soy sauce.

From Taishan county Chen Xiansheng escaped to Hong Kong. He was one of many. Between April and May 1962, thousands of people in southern China embarked on a mass exodus. Hong Kong, situated next to Guangdong province, was a relatively easier escape geographically. More than sixty thousand people pitched up here, but forty thousand were sent back to China by the British colonial government. Subsequently the British colonial government expanded the Frontier Closed Area in the northern part of Hong Kong along the border with mainland China. Like Chen, Deng Xiansheng from Dongguan in Guangdong province was one of the luckier ones who managed to stay in Hong Kong. As mentioned in previous chapters, in Deng Xiansheng's village the mass production of iron and steel as well as "deep plowing" led to crop failure and terrible famine. As a result many villagers suffered edema and died. Deng Xiansheng survived by escaping to Hong Kong. Now in his seventies, he has two grown-up sons and lives a relatively comfortable life in Hong Kong.

> When there was no food to eat, I survived by eating sugar-cane fiber. After squeezing out all the juice to make sugar, cane fiber was what was left. I chewed on that to stave off my hunger. . . . Once I caught a pair of frogs. I shared them with my mother and my two younger sisters. Just one pair [of frogs] for four of us, but we felt so satisfied after eating them. . . .
>
> In 1962 there was a mass exodus to Hong Kong [from the mainland]. That's when I came to Hong Kong. It was in May 1962. I was only twenty when I made my escape. Because I couldn't swim, I just followed the crowds and crossed over to Hong Kong by foot. I was the only one in my family who managed to escape. . . . Coming to Hong Kong was my destiny. I have never regretted it. . . .

Lau Tinpo from a village in Bao'an county in Guangdong province was another among the thousands who escaped to Hong Kong in 1962. He was in his twenties at the time. He remembers that in his home village many people died from illnesses caused by starvation. He compared it to the plague. Historically plague was a major health threat in the area, and it took many lives. During the famine, the locals consumed everything that grew there, and after they had eaten up all including the papaya fruit, they also ate every part of the papaya trees. In the end Lau Tinpo was faced with two choices: to die or to survive. He chose the latter and escaped to Hong Kong. He recalls his journey to Hong Kong:

> Many people were trying to escape to Hong Kong. We crowded into fishing boats. I'd have crawled all the way to Hong Kong. . . . The government did not permit us to leave. But we fooled the officials because they thought we were on a fishing expedition. After the fishing boat sailed out to sea, we jumped into the water and swam toward speedboats. We climbed on to these speedboats, and it is these that took us to Hong Kong. Many people escaped to Hong Kong in this way.
>
> I first came to Hong Kong in 1962. Life was good here, and I even found a job. . . . In the beginning I earned thirty Hong Kong dollars per month. I tried to save as much money as I could. After two months I saved fifty Hong Kong dollars and I bought myself a watch. Later I saved even more and I bought myself a suit for ten dollars. Month after month life became better and better.

8

Memories of the Famine

On January 25, 2005, two days before the sixtieth anniversary of the liberation of Auschwitz, Zuzana Ruzickova, one of Europe's most respected harpsichordists and a Holocaust survivor, spoke about the importance of remembering such human tragedies.

> The most important thing is that these events are held up as a warning against dictators or terrorists repeating these mistakes.
>
> The second thing is of course to warn against things such as the Auschwitz lie. As more of us survivors die out, so the Auschwitz lie will spread, because it's such a terrible thing for humanity to remember. So these memorial days are for me very, very important.[1]

Seven years later, on April 27, 2012, Wen Jiabao, then premier of China, visited Auschwitz-Birkenau in Poland, the site of the largest concentration camp and extermination camp under Nazi Germany. On his visit, the Chinese premier was quoted as saying: "This is an unforgettable, dark page in the history of humankind which cannot be forgotten," and "Only those who remember history can build a good future."[2] Under the Third Reich 1.5 million people were exterminated at the Auschwitz-Birkenau concentration camp. Between

1958 and 1962, according to a recent estimate, some 45 million were killed in Mao's China during the Great Famine.[3] Unlike the Holocaust or any of the other major human catastrophes of the twentieth century, there is no place in China's collective public memory for the Great Famine—the worst famine in human history, one that killed millions. In today's China, Mao Zedong is still revered as the great leader of the Chinese nation, and his portrait still hangs at Tiananmen—the Gate of Heavenly Peace—outside the former Forbidden City in Beijing. With the economic boom in major Chinese cities and the staggering, if rather suspicious, GDP growth, it looks as if Mao's vision of the Great Leap Forward has finally come to pass. There seems little need to remember a famine—another dark page in the history of humankind—that occurred more than half a century ago.

As the generation of famine survivors grows older, and many have since died, so the private memories of the famine are slowly fading away. To preserve their dignity, which enabled them to survive, few survivors have talked to anyone, not even their children, about their experiences of the long-since forgotten Great Leap Famine. Why trouble the younger generation with such anguish and suffering? It is all still too painful to think about. It is simply too upsetting. However, the memories continue to torment those who went through it. People still taste the bitterness of those dreadful years. As Judith Herman observed in her study *Trauma and Recovery*, "atrocity, however, refused to be buried. Equally as powerful as the desire to deny the atrocity is the conviction that denial does not work."[4] On a number of occasions during my interview with survivors, when I asked them to talk about what happened to them in the Great Famine, they immediately fell into silence. After a short pause, however, they began to talk and were unable to stop. For many of them to be able to tell someone the terrible events that happened to them some fifty years ago was a form of healing.[5]

Loss is perhaps the most sensitive subject to raise. Among nearly one hundred survivors I interviewed, whenever death was evoked, especially that of close family members, embarrassed laughter was a common disguise. Others simply stared into the distance in silence. "What could we do? We could barely take care of ourselves. No one had the capacity or energy to care for others," was a response I heard often. Occasionally, people also admitted the emptiness that they felt as they watched family members die.

For a number of survivors, especially those who lived through the famine as children, it is not death, however, but the intense feeling of hunger that haunts them most. Many of them speak of how hungry they were all the time, and how hunger had made them very anxious. Conversely, they tend to speak about food or even food substitutes with very strong emotions. Be it dried straw on the roof, white clay from the hills, or a live insect in the field, they remember these as utterly delicious, and they describe their experience of obtaining such things with great excitement.

Since the Great Famine has been written out of the official historiography, and the Party has made a real effort to distance itself from any sense of blame or any feeling that such dark forces could ever be unleashed again, few people I spoke to linked the famine with the government or the Communist Party, even those who considered that their policies were misplaced. Some blamed the local cadres. The larger number of survivors accepted it as their own fate. "That's how things were in those days" and "we had to follow orders" are two commonplace expressions among survivors. It seems there is still little that one could do about it today. Fifty years after the famine, the lives of many survivors in rural China have barely improved. China's current economic miracle has brought very few benefits to these people. As I traveled across China to interview famine survivors, the more I saw and the more I heard, the more I felt how important it was that the voices of the survivors be heard and their memories not forgotten, in order that their children and their children's children will never have to live with the same fate again. For the rest of humanity, it's about time that all learn about what happened in China more than fifty years ago—the worst famine in history—so that this may be a warning against such a tragedy ever happening again. It is my hope that one day the government in China and the Chinese Communist Party will engage in an open discussion of this dark episode in China's recent history and dedicate a public memorial day to the remembrance of famine victims. To quote Premier Wen again: "Only those who remember history can build a good future."

When I read in a Hong Kong newspaper that Wu Yongkuan, a peasant and famine survivor in Guangshan county in Henan province, had put up two private memorial stones in his village to honor those who had died during the famine, I was very excited. In October 2010, on a bright sunny day, I set out for Guangshan to visit Wu Yongkuan and his memorial stone. I was accompanied by two friends. We started in Xinyang city. Xinyang city is the regional capital of Xinyang region. As pointed out in Chapter 2, under the extreme leadership of Lu Xianwen, Xinyang region was badly hit by the famine. Here, out of a total population of 8 million, 1 million perished during the famine.[6] Guangshan is a small county in Xinyang region, but the death toll here was high. In the previous chapter it was noted that one-third of the population in Guangshan was killed by the famine, and many were tortured to death or buried alive. The dead bodies were thrown into mass graves. In 1961, after witnessing the horror in Guangshan, Li Xiannian, China's vice premier at the time, broke into tears. "The defeat of the Western Route Army was so cruel yet I did not shed a tear, but after seeing such horror in Guangshan, even I am unable to control myself," he wept.[7]

Initially I wanted to take public transport from Xinyang city to Guangshan, and a local scooter or mini van to the village. Having traveled all over rural China over the preceding four years, experience had taught me this was the best way to get into the remote villages. But as I was four months pregnant and my travel companions had quite a lot to carry, they insisted that we hire a taxi from Xinyang. This turned out to be a major mistake. The taxi driver, who had boasted of his knowledge of Guangshan, turned out to be rather clueless once off the main road. The Google map we had in our hands was completely useless: it pointed us to a small river from where there was no road ahead. After wasting half a day we gave up and decided to stop for lunch. We stumbled into a small roadside cafe that was packed with local factory workers. Instead of turning us away, the kind owner opened up his own apartment above the cafe and served us a simple but memorable meal. In due course I got into a friendly conversation with him. With Wu Yongkuan still on my mind, I asked the owner whether he had heard of Wu Weizi village and the villager Wu Yongkuan. This time it was like I had won the jackpot. The restaurant owner turned out to know one of Wu Yongkuan's relatives. A few minutes later he came to me with Wu Yongkuan's son's phone number. An hour later, we met with Wu Yongkuan's son, who took us to his father's home. Wu Weizi—Wu Yongkuan's village—was not far from the main road, though it was well hidden. We had to pass through overgrown bushes, and the road into the village was narrow and muddy, a real contrast to the asphalt main road. This contrast is very common in today's China, and it has been my constant experience over the past four years.

Wu Yongkuan, in his late sixties, has a typical Chinese peasant face: square and creased with winkled eyes and forehead, with a friendly smile. Since I had already lost half a day searching for him, I wasted no time with formalities. I explained to him straight away that I wanted to visit the memorial stones. The stones are situated in the middle of an overgrown field, about five minutes walk from Wu's house. As we walked I asked him about his motivation in putting up the memorial. He told me:

> The reason I built the memorial stones is so that the young people in our village will know about what happened, and they will never follow the same path again. The "Wind of Exaggeration" killed many lives. I want more and more people to know what happened so that they will never permit anything so foolish to happen again. . . . One should be responsible to people and to one's country. That's why I set up the memorial stones. . . .
>
> Many people died in the famine. In our little village, seventy out of just over a hundred people died. . . .
>
> [The inscription] on the top of this stone reads: "In 1959, during the food crisis." Around here we call the famine "the food crisis." Below are the names of 42 villagers who died in the famine. My father's name, Wu Dejin, is on this one. The top of the next stone also reads: "In 1959, during the food crisis." Below are the names of a further 29 villagers who died in the famine. . . . I set up these two stones in 2004 during the Qingming festival.[8] Some villagers helped me to build them. We paid for them out of our own pockets. . . . There are 71 names altogether [on these two stones]. Before the famine there used to be 121 villagers here, and 71 of them

> died during the famine. Only 50 villagers, including adults and children, survived. . . .
>
> These days very few people give much thought to the tragic events that took place in 1959. I always tried to talk to my children about what happened. One of my sons, who now lives in the United States, was very supportive of what I have done. In fact he was the one who suggested that I put up a memorial stone. I had no money, so he made a contribution. It cost a few thousand yuan to put up these two stones. It's important to preserve the memory of the 1959 famine. It's the only way that we can avoid similar incidents happening again. I did this for the sake of our society and mankind. Future generations must learn how terrible it was. . . .

Among survivors I interviewed, Wu Yongkuan was unique. Unlike him, many survivors simply try to keep the memory of the horror to themselves. Others find it too hard to bear, and try to forget it. Mrs. Zhou, the villager from Anyue county in northern Sichuan who spoke about the damage caused by the "Wind of Exaggeration" to the local area in Chapter 3, is in her seventies now, with three grown-up children. After all these years, she has never spoken a word to her children about what happened during the famine.

> I never want to remember the famine years. Thinking about it makes me feel very miserable. In those days people like us who were born in the wrong class had no right to speak. We could only hope secretly that one day government policy would change and we'd be treated equally with others. We also hoped that one day there would be plenty

> of sweet potatoes. I remember that I used to think that I'd do anything as long as I could have sweet potatoes to eat. Things are better now. Since Deng Xiaoping took over, our life has improved a great deal. The famine lasted for three years. Those were bitterest years of my entire life.

Bai Daniang, whom I introduced in Chapter 1, the peasant woman I met in a small market town in the western Sichuan plain who told me how she was deprived of her portion of food by the collective canteen because she had to take care of children, first caught my eye as she was sitting against a wall stroking a couple of rabbits in a basket. She looked incredibly peaceful, and I found her presence overwhelming. I asked her what she thought of the famine years. For a moment she looked at me in silence. I paused for a while and said nothing. I have learned that in a situation such as this the best thing to do is to keep quiet and wait to see what happens. After a couple of minutes, Bai Daniang began to speak:

> Life was absolutely horrible during the time of the famine. Whenever I think about what happened, tears start to fall from my eyes and I just can't stop crying. No, I don't want to talk about it. If I start I will cry. I don't want to have that bitter taste in my mouth again. [She pauses for a little while but does not stop.] Yes, life was really horrible then. We ate coarse chaff, vegetables, sweet potato leaves and stalks. We also ate carrot leaves. No matter how rough the leaves were, we never threw anything away. . . . Life was horrible then! Whenever I think about what we had to endure in those days, the tears just start to pour out. What a horrible time.

After saying goodbye to Bai Daniang I traveled northward to a scenic village in Langzhong county, northern Sichuan. Li Anyuan, the eighty-year-old villager who lives alone in a dark wooden house and who helped me to fan away mosquitoes during the interview, was rather curious that I wanted to know about what happened more than fifty years ago. I told him my intention was to record history. When I turned around and asked him how he and his fellow villagers feel about the famine, he hesitated for a moment before going on to explain:

> Nowadays people here don't think about those times anymore. Things were pretty miserable back then. These days life is not too bad for many people. What do I think about that time? Who wants to think about what happened then and why it happened? There was no need for me to talk of those dreadful years [to my children]. Under Chairman Mao, we learned to appreciate life by eating bitter food. The food tasted as terrible as pig's feed. It was made of wild herbs or grass plus some sorghum flour. Before the Liberation [in 1949] . . . only the desperately hungry ate such things. Most people could not stomach them. Today's younger generation—like you—has never tasted such bitter food.

Faraway from Langzhong, in a small village in Hebei province's Xushui county, Lao Sun is an old villager who goes around collecting rubbish in factories and selling it to recycling companies each day. He has three sons, all of whom are doing well financially, and give him plenty of money, but he says he does not want to forget the hardships in the past and he is proud of the fact that he can make a living by himself.

> During the famine life was very harsh—as harsh as under the Japanese. Under the Japanese we were scared all the time, but at least we had food to eat. During the famine, we starved. Almost every village had people who were starving to death. At the time I believed that everyone should overcome his or her hunger for the sake of the nation. But I must say what we had to endure was too harsh to bear, that's why many old and sick villagers did not survive. . . . I am proud of the fact that I and my family survived such severe hardships. I have no regret about the past. I have done nothing wrong to the Party.

Unlike Lao Sun, most survivors I came across do not want to remember the hard times. Wang Qibing, an eighty-year-old villager from Chaohu in central Anhui who told me in Chapter 2 how the local cadres used to trick villagers to report on each other during the Anti-Hiding Campaign, is one of them. He tells me:

> In those days too many people starved to death, and we didn't know why. As a peasant, I don't think about it anymore—that time is long gone. There is no need to keep it in my head. What's gone is gone. . . . The hardship lasted from 1960 to 1961. You cannot image how many people died in our village. Too many people died.

West of Chaohu, in Hunan province's Junshan region, Wang Deming, the seventy-year-old villager bedbound because of the chronic disease bilharzia, says similar things about the past:

> Life was very tough in those days, but I have no ability to record what happened at that time. . . . I was only in my

> teens. I had to do what I was told. I had no rights or power. If I didn't follow orders, I'd be denounced and punished. Cadres used to beat people up. Some people were even beaten to death. We never knew why—they didn't give us reasons. . . . Life was very bitter then and we had no food to eat. . . . Things are better now with the "One Child" policy. It's a good policy. We had too many children in those days and we had no means to feed them. My youngest child is forty-one now. I have four children, and they are all doing well. One is a teacher and another is a cadre. I am grateful to the Party and the People's Government.

Huang Manyi, the woman from Dingyuan county in northern Anhui, does not find it easy to override the past. Despite the fact that she finds it too painful to remember those terrible years of famine, the intense feeling of hunger and the horror of watching people die has haunted her for many years. As I listen to her words I feel strongly that for the sake of those who died and those who survived, like Manyi herself, it's important to tell the world what happened and not forget the past.

> For me the famine only ended in the 1980s. It was only then that I stopped feeling hungry. Only then did we have enough food to eat. . . . In 1961, people were dying on a daily basis. We were so hungry. When there was food, people would stuff themselves to death. . . . My memory is a little confused, as I rarely talk about those days. I cannot bear to think about it. It's even worse trying to talk about it. . . . At the time no one was allowed to keep a tally of how many people died. I know that quite a number of entire families

> were wiped out in our area. Today people are still afraid of talking about what happened, and we still don't know how many people died.

As with Manyi, hunger is a theme that came up constantly during my interviews. A number of survivors told me that hunger and the horror of being without food is what they remember the most. Qiaoer, the woman from Huang county in Shandong province, whose parents refused to comply with an order of the commune, is now in her late sixties. She has two grown-up sons, one of whom has a successful business in Beijing. Although hunger and being without food is no longer an issue for her, when I asked her what she remembered most of the famine years, she told me:

> I often cried because I was very hungry. At the time, even if we did have food, it tasted terrible. We searched everywhere for leftovers or wild plants. Cornmeal was the best thing that we got to eat. There was no rice or wheat growing in our area. We were so happy just to get a little cornmeal! As there wasn't enough of it to eat, we added wild plants to it. . . . I could never forget the time I dropped our portion of food when I went to fetch it from the collective canteen—I still remember it so clearly. I burst out crying because I was so angry at myself. My entire family was waiting for me to bring them something to eat. I couldn't leave food on the ground like that, so I tried my best to pick it up bit by bit, even though it was covered in sand.

Wei Dengyu, the friendly villager from a remote village in the northern Sichuan hills who talked about how he and his neighbors used to waste their time chasing sparrows during the Great Leap Forward in Chapter 2, is now in his eighties. His village is far away from anywhere else and is still very poor. The Wei family is one of the most prosperous families in the area. Their newly built two-story house sticks out like a tower in the village. But any newly gained prosperity still does not diminish the painful memory of hunger, starvation, and having to watch people die. As we spoke, he nearly wept telling me of the misery he and his family endured:

> Many people died of edema. In our area more than twenty people died of it. I watched them dying. It was terrible. Their legs were all swollen. One of my sons was born in 1958. My wife was so thin that there was hardly any flesh on her body. Throughout her pregnancy we had no food to give her. Everyone in the family was starving—our stomachs were constantly empty. After she gave birth, all she got to eat was ten kilograms of rice—that was for the entire month. . . . Not surprisingly, she barely produced any milk to feed the baby. . . .
>
> I wish the famine had not happened. Look at everything today—the world is so much better. My goodness! Today's children have so much. Even little kids celebrate their birthdays. They have so much food to choose from—yoghurt, milk, soy milk. We could never have dreamed of such things in those years. . . . Today people are too happy and they often forget the past.

When I asked Lao Yu, the retired man who lives deep in the mountains of Liangshan and who was originally from Fushun county in southern Sichuan, how he remembers the famine, he told me a story about food.

> [At the time of the famine] my mother once came home and told me: "I could smell someone cooking rice—it was so delicious. If I could have a bowl of rice to eat, I'd die happy." Years later our life began to improve because of the economic reforms. Life got a lot better. My mother lived to see that. She was already in her nineties. One day I asked her, "Mother, during the time of the famine you told me you'd die happy if you could get a bowl of rice to eat. Now you not only have rice, you also have meat to eat. Do you want to die now?" "No! I swear in my mother's name I no longer wish to die," she answered. [He and people around laughed at this point.]
>
> That's how life was at the time. . . . Too many people died at the time. Because a huge number of people were dying all the time, it's not possible to keep count how many died. I watched with my own eyes. I saw many people die.

Xiao Bai, the survivor whose parents were killed by the famine when she and her sister were still young children, cannot forget the intense feeling of hunger, and how miserable life was during the famine. She blames the terrible hardship that she and her sister endured simply on bad luck. Still yearning for a better life, she has turned to Christianity.

> One day I was so ravenously hungry that I could no longer bear it, and in the end I used a ladder to climb up on to the roof. The roof was covered with dried cornstalks. I pulled one off and started to chew on it. It tasted utterly delicious! I was so hungry and nothing could have tasted more delicious than dried cornstalk. I chewed on one after the

> other. There were at least a couple of times that I remember feeling hunger that was as desperate as that. In those days, I was often starving to the point that I could no longer bear it. From the second half of 1959 to the first half of 1960, life became completely unbearable. For almost a year we literally had nothing to eat. . . .
>
> I never blamed anyone for the hardships I had to endure—I only blamed myself for not being good enough. I never resented Chairman Mao for those difficult years that I went through. I just believed that it was my fate. . . . [But] I have never stopped dreaming of a better life, even to this day.

Xiuying, the old neighbor of my family who lives in Sichuan province's capital Chengdu, is now in her eighties. She too puts the famine and starvation down to bad luck.

> Those years we went through was not living. Every day we just struggled on and drifted along. I never questioned government policy—I blamed it all on my fate. Some say that Chairman Mao was too old [and that he made mistakes]. But I don't think of it like that. If it wasn't for Chairman Mao, who liberated us, we would not be able to enjoy today's good life. . . . The past is more or less buried in my head—too many things happened, I cannot remember them all. My husband and I are getting old each day, and we rarely go out these days. We only go out when we are called to attend meetings. That's all.

Xiuying is not unique. While the memory of famine is slowly fading, Mao, meanwhile, is still heralded as an idol by a great number of survivors throughout China. In many of the villages I visited, I was struck by the presence of Mao's portrait hanging on the walls of villagers' homes. When I asked Chen Gonggong, the old man in Gansu province's Hui county, why his family had hung a portrait of Mao on their wall, his answer was very simple:

> Chairman Mao was like an emperor. His portrait can dispel evil.

In Henan province's Suiping county, where China's first commune—the Chayashan People's Commune—was founded, I noticed that in almost every home there was a portrait of Chairman Mao. This region was one of the worst hit by the famine. When I asked Liu Laoshi, the retired village teacher in Suiping county's Yicheng district whom you have met in Chapter 2, why he had hung up Mao's portrait, he told me:

> We have strong feelings for Chairman Mao. . . . It was Chairman Mao who founded the New China. To use another word, he liberated us. Our life changed and improved a lot after the Liberation [in 1949]. Young people today did not experience the change at the time, that's why the younger generation doesn't share the same strong feeling [for Chairman Mao] as we older people.
>
> It's true that life was very difficult in 1958, 1959, and 1960. The entire country experienced terrible hardship in those three years. I was a primary school teacher then, but I suffered the same hardship as peasants in the countryside. Life was hard for all of us. Anyone who had a little education understood that the country was going through a

> difficult time, and individual hardship was part of it. It was by bearing that in mind that we endured and survived this most difficult period.

In Mao's home region, Xiangtan, in Hunan province, villagers like Tang Xianping feel the same about Mao:

> When Chairman Mao was still alive, those of us from Xiangtan were very proud that the chairman was also from Xiangtan. It was our fortune. I worshiped him. It was his idea to turn the entire rural countryside into military organizations. During the time of the famine, people never thought that Chairman Mao could be wrong. No one thought about things like that.

Similarly, in Hunan province's Hengyang region, Wang Wenchun, the veteran of the Korean War who complained in Chapter 1 about how collectivization destroyed normal family life, says that Mao was, however, blameless:

> I have to say that Mao Zedong's policy was correct. Even if some things did not work out, we cannot blame him. We all know that Mao Zedong did a lot for us, that he even sacrificed his son [Mao Anying] for the country. Mao Anying was sent to fight in the Korean War, where he was killed in battle. I was also in Korea at the time, and we held a memorial service for him. You have to admit that Mao Zedong had a good heart. The mistake he made in his old age was that he could not think clearly. Old people don't think clearly. They are no good for anything. . . . In our village, those

who are now in their sixties and seventies all think like that. Although most of them suffered terrible hardship, they all praise Mao Zedong for the good things he did. I am telling you the truth. I don't tell lies.

. . .

Let me tell you some of the things Liu Boweng [also known as Liu Ji, a fourteenth-century military strategist, politician, and scholar] predicted in his [divination poem] "Shaobing Song": "There will be hardship: people will have to eat at the canteen for one thousand days, ..."[9] It says. Not only so, Liu Boweng also predicted that "the back of the hand holds the fortune." This means that if you turn the Chinese character for "hand" around, you can see it looks like the character "Mao." Mao is for Mao Zedong. All this was predicted by Liu Boweng.

My deepest memory of the famine years was the communal life and the collective canteen. Let me tell you that life became much better under Chairman Mao. . . . One of Chairman Mao's achievements was that he got rid of the landlords. Not only that, he also led us to "Land Reform" and "Mutual Aid Group." But the People's Commune, which came afterward, was not a wise move. It did not work out. . . .

Life is better now, people are grateful to the Communist Party, but I have to say today's cadres are very corrupt.

Barber Feng, mentioned in Chapter 1, the former barber for the collectives, lives in the same village as Wei Dengyu in the northern Sichuan hills. In contrast to Wei, the Feng family is one of the poorest in this very poor village. More than fifty years ago, collectivization deprived him and his family of their livelihood and brought them massive debts. Life has not improved much for them. No wonder Barber Feng is less optimistic about Party policies and present-day China:

> Under the commune, we had to use all our money to repay the debts that we owed. Every year was like that. We had to pay back our debts year after year. Even last year, we were still paying back the money that we used to owe. The debts are still not cleared. We owed more than ten thousand yuan in total. In those days, that was a lot of money. . . .
>
> Life was so difficult at that time—it's hard for me to describe. . . . I only have one thought: that one day—that is, if the Communist Party continues to rule—someone [in the leadership] might be willing to do some good. If that happens, then maybe there will be justice for us.

Mr. Liu, a retired practitioner of Chinese medicine, is now in his seventies. He lives in Wenjiang, a suburban district of Chengdu, Sichuan province. During the famine years, he took charge of the clinic in a small village in Anyue, northern Sichuan. To this day, the horror of watching people dying continues to trouble him. Talking to Mr. Liu reminded me how important it is for the voices of the survivors to be heard, so the terrible tragedy of the Great Famine of Maoist China is not forgotten.

> As a doctor, the hardest and most unforgettable thing was watching so many people die. There are many things that still disturb me about what happened during those years of the Great Famine, but I shall take my memories with me to

the grave. One thing in particular made a very deep impression on me. It upsets me terribly to this day: although my immediate family survived, the majority of my relatives and friends were killed by the famine. Many people lost their entire families. I have seen a whole family wiped out by starvation. That image is fixed in my mind forever: watching so many people starving to death and there being nothing that I could do about it. My heart really ached. It was because of this experience in the famine that I decided to work hard and to improve my skills as a medical practitioner. That's why I went to study Chinese medicine at college. . . . All these years my overriding desire has been to save lives.

Notes

Introduction

1. Liao Bokang, "Lishi changhe li de yige xuanwo: Sichuan Xiao, Li, Liao shijian huimou" [A Whirlpool in History: Recounting the "Xiao, Li, Liao Incident" in Sichuan], in *Dangdai Sichuan Yaoshi shilu* [Major Historical Events in Contemporary Sichuan], by the Contemporary Oral History Editorial Office (Chengdu: Sichuan Renmin chubanshe, 2005), p. 170.

2. "Documents of the Sixth Plenum of the Eighth Central Committee of the Communist Party Congress," November 1958, from Hunan Provincial Archive, file number 141–2–76.

3. *Lao baixing* literally means "old hundred surnames." In Chinese it is used to mean "ordinary folks."

Chapter 1. The Tragedy of Collectivization

1. Patricia Buckley Ebrey, *Chinese Civilization: A Sourcebook*, 2nd ed. (New York: The Free Press, 2009), p. 458.

2. Chairman Mao's second speech at the Session of the Eighth Communist Party Congress, May 17, 1958, from Chishui County Party Committee Archive, file 1-A9–42, pp. 24–25.

3. "Walking on two legs" referred to developing both agriculture and industry.

4. Benjamin A. Valentino, *Final Solutions: Mass Killing and Genocide in the Twentieth Century* (Ithaca: Cornell University Press, 2004), pp. 121–22.

5. Hannah Arendt, *The Life of the Mind* (New York: Harcourt Brace Jovanovich, 1978), p. 180.

6. The Central Committee of the Communist Party and the Southwest Bureau's instruction to carry out Land Reform, 1950–1952, from Western Sichuan Party Committee Archive, file CX 1–882, pp. 21, 156–58, 284–85.

7. The Southwest China Public Security Bureau's instruction on how to carry out the Campaign to Suppress Counterrevolutionaries, 1950–1952, from Western Sichuan Party Committee Archive, file CX 1–839, pp. 127–28.

8. Valentino, *Final Solutions*, p. 121.

9. Zhou Xun, *The Great Famine in China, 1958–1962: A Documentary History* (New Haven: Yale University Press, 2012), pp. 17–18.

10. Didi Kirsten Tatlow, "Dead Reckoning," *South China Morning Post Magazine*, April 29, 2007, pp. 16–20.

11. Ya'an is a region in the west of Sichuan, bordering Tibet. It was strategically significant because it linked China to western Asia. It was also the first place in the world to plant tea artificially, and was an important center for the tea trade until the Communist liberation in the early 1950s. For further reading on the tea trade in Ya'an see Andre Migot, *Tibetan Marches*, trans. Peter Fleming (London: Rupert Hart-Davis, 1955), pp. 63–64. Besides tea, the region is also home to the Giant Panda, and is famous for its rich natural resources and thick forestry. In the Great Leap Forward of 1958, Ya'an was converted into a giant iron and steel factory. Millions of farmers from all over Sichuan were sent there to assist in the work. Trees were felled. Tianquan county became an epicenter of deforestation. Logs from Tianquan were sent to many different parts of China.

12. For further reading see Frank Dikötter, *Mao's Great Famine: The History of China's Most Devastating Catastrophe, 1958–1962* (New York: Walker, 2010), chapter 33.

13. Mao's speech at the enlarged Politburo conference in Beidaihe, August 17, 1958, from Hunan Province Party Committee Archive, file 141–1–1036, p. 15.

14. For more information on Xie Fuzhi see the Introduction of this book.

15. It means those who served food at the canteen treated people differently. They often served more food to cadres and those they liked, and less to those they disliked.

16. Yi, also known as Lolo, are people who live in what is now southwestern China. In 1949 the Communist army took over Liangshan, where a large number of Lolo lived, and suppressed the "Black Yi"—the highest rank of Yi society—and made Lolo an ethic group in China. The name Lolo was made redundant, and Yi ethnic group became the official name for these people. The Communist Party claimed to have also abolished the slavery system (hierarchical structure) of the Yi society. When this was introduced in 1956, it encountered resistance by the "Black Yi." The Yi uprising was eventually put down by the Communist army between 1959

and 1960, and Liangshan was turned into the Yi Autonomous Region, under the administration of Sichuan province.

Chapter 2. Endless Campaigns and Political Pressures

1. The Lushan plenum, officially the eighth plenum of the Eighth Central Committee of the CCP, began on July 23, 1959. The original objective of the conference was to review the developments in China during 1958 and to solve some practical issues brought about by those developments. During the conference, Peng Dehuai, then China's defense minister, and Zhang Wentian, the minister of foreign affairs, criticized some elements of the Great Leap Forward, and a few Party leaders supported them. This angered Mao, who launched an attack on Peng, Zhang, and three other ministers, and insisted on pushing ahead with the Great Leap. The conference marked a key turning point in Mao's rule: criticism of Party actions and policies became equated with criticism of Mao himself.

2. That was more than 10 percent of the total local population.

3. "The time of extreme hardship" is a local term used in Chaohu region to describe the Great Famine.

4. These classifications were first introduced during the Land Reform in the beginning of the 1950s. The four bad classes were landlords, rich peasants, counterrevolutionaries, and other bad people. Others were classified as upper middle, middle, lower middle, poor peasants, and landless laborers.

Chapter 3. Unnatural Disasters

1. Comrade Li Jingquan's speeches at Sichuan province cadres' meeting, March 11–19, 1959, from Sichuan Provincial Party Committee Archive, file JC1–1553, p. 160.

2. For further readings see Dikötter, *Mao's Great Famine*, pp. 25–33, 174–84. Also see Zhou, *The Great Famine in China*, chapter 5.

3. Zhou, *The Great Famine in China*.

Chapter 4. Starvation and Death

1. The investigation was conducted by Xiao Feng, a senior journalist and the former Party secretary for the official newspaper *People's Daily*. After spending nearly a month in Sichuan, Xiao compiled a nineteen-thousand-word report in September 1962 titled "The Situation in Sichuan." The report went astray, and during the Cultural Revolution Xiao was purged as a "capitalist roader." After the Cultural

Revolution, a copy of the report was passed to Liao Bokang, the former Party secretary of Chongqing municipality and former chairman of the United Front for Sichuan province. See Liao Bokang, "Lishi changhe li de yige xuanwo: Sichuan Xiao, Li, Liao shijian huimou" [A Whirlpool in History: Recounting the "Xiao, Li, Liao Incident" in Sichuan], in *Dangdai Sichuan Yaoshi shilu* [Major Historical Events in Contemporary Sichuan], by the Contemporary Oral History Editorial Office (Chengdu: Sichuan Renmin chubanshe, 2005), p. 170. Also cf. 1954–61 Sichuan province census, September 1962–February 1963, from Sichuan Province Statistic Office Archive, file JC67–1003, p. 4.

2. "Fuyang Dayuejin shimo" [The Great Leap Forward in Fuyang], in *Zhengtu: Fuyang shehui zhuyi shiqi dangshi zhuanti huibian* [Zhengtu: A Special Collection on Party History in Fuyang During the Socialist Period], vol. 1, by Fuyang Party History Research Office, 2006, p. 155.

3. "Documentations Regarding Comrades Zhang Jie, Hao Quanren, and Guo Zhaorong's Errors," March 20, 1961, from Fuyang Region Party Committee Archive, file J 3–2–0278, pp. 45, 64.

4. Comrade Zhou Enlai's report at the government meeting for planning, commerce, and agriculture, December 4, 1961, from the Hunan Provincial Party Committee Archive, file 141–2–138, pp. 3–6; a summary report from the Central Committee of the Chinese Communist Party General Office regarding food shortages and riots throughout sixteen provinces and autonomous regions, as well as proposed measures to resolve the problem by local Party committees, April 25, 1958, from the Hunan Provincial Party Committee Archive, file 141–1–1055, pp. 66, 68.

5. For further reading on cannibalism see Zhou, *The Great Famine in China*, chapter 4.

6. Kashin-Beck disease is prevalent in poor regions of China among the rural population.

7. Smoking could help dull the appetite. Tobacco is often used to ease the pangs of hunger.

8. Yantai is also known in the West as Chefoo.

Chapter 5. Orphans of the Famine

1. For further reading on the practice of wives going to other provinces and getting new husbands as meal tickets see Zhou, *The Great Famine in China*, pp. 114, 133, 135–37.

2. Reports and correspondences on how to distribute relief funds by Sichuan Province Bureau of Civil Affairs, February 1–December 15, 1962, from the Sichuan Province Bureau of Civil Affairs Archive, file JC 44–1442, no page number.

3. Sang Ye, "Fifty Thousand Orphans and the Road Home: An Oral History Account of the Legacy of the Great Leap Forward," in *The Rings of Beijing: China's Global Aura*, ed. Sang Ye and Geremie R. Barmé (forthcoming).

4. Ibid.

5. Report on relief work by [Sichuan Province] Bureau of Civil Affairs Famine Relief Department, February 2–December 1961, from Sichuan Province Bureau of Civil Affairs Archive, file JC 44–824, p. 199.

6. The I-Kuan Tao religious movement incorporates elements of Taoist practices, Confucian teachings, and Chinese Buddhism. It originated in mainland China in the first half of the twentieth century. After being banned by the Communist government in the early 1950s, many of its members moved to Taiwan and overseas. I-Kuan Tao is now the third biggest religion in Taiwan, with an estimated 2 million members throughout the world. In mainland China, it is still banned as an illegal secret society.

Chapter 6. Famine in the Cities

1. Liao Zhigao, "Guanyu Sichuan diaoliang de huigu fansi" [Sichuan Grain Dispatch Review (to support the rest of country)], in *Dangdai Sichuan yaoshi shilu*, vol. 1 (Chengdu: Sichuan Renmin chubanshe, 2005), p. 72. Between 1956 and 1965 Liao Zhigao was head of the Secretariat in Sichuan province. He was the second most powerful man in Sichuan, after Li Jingquan.

2. For further discussion see Zhou, *The Great Famine in China*, pp. 125–29, 135.

3. See *The Crimes of the Counter-Revolutionary Revisionist Wang Renzhong*, vol. 1, a publication of the headquarters office of the Hubei province Red Guards, September 1967.

4. In other words it was almost unrealistic.

5. Formerly China West University, and now part of Sichuan University.

6. Many people I interviewed in this book call themselves *lao baixing*, which translates as "ordinary folks" in English. Literally, it means "a person with a surname"—that is, not a noble or a slave.

7. Erjie's monthly salary was twenty-one yuan between 1958 and 1962.

Chapter 7. Surviving the Famine

1. Richard Spencer, "Eat, Shoots and Lives," *Daily Telegraph Magazine*, December 18, 2004, p. 21.

2. On November 17, 1957, Mao, on his trip to Moscow, met with Chinese students studying there. He told them: "You young people, full of vigour and vitality, are in the bloom of life, like the morning sun. Our hope is placed on you." The "morning sun" became a phrase widely cited by the Red Guards during the Cultural Revolution.

3. Black-colored konjac jelly made of the konjac plant. It can be toxic if not treated properly or if eaten in large quantities.

4. Zhou, *The Great Famine in China*, pp. 59–71.

5. For further details on the Yi uprising and the Communist takeover of the region see Chapter 1.

6. This refers to the uncultivated lands of northern China.

7. The Dai are an ethnic group living on China's southwest frontier.

Chapter 8. Memories of the Famine

1. "Zuzana Ruzickova: Surviving the Horrors of the Holocaust," an interview conducted by Ian Willoughby and broadcast on Prague Radio in English on January 25,2005(www.radio.cz/en/section/one-on-one/zuzana-ruzickova-surviving-the-horrors-of-the-holocaust).

2. "Wen Jiabao at Auschwitz: 'This Cannot Be Forgotten,' " *GlobalPost* (www.globalpost.com/dispatch/news/regions/europe/poland/120427/wen-jiabao-at-auschwitz-cannot-be-forgotten).

3. Dikötter, *Mao's Great Famine*.

4. Judith Lewis Herman, *Trauma and Recovery* (New York: Basic Books, 1997), p. 1.

5. This was also experienced by the interviewers who taped the memories of Holocaust survivors. See, in interviews in Germany, Cathy Gelbin, Eva Lezzi, Geoffrey H. Hartman, Julius H. Schoeps, eds. *Archiv der Erinnerung: Interviews mit Überlebenden der Shoah* (Potsdam: Verlag für Berlin-Brandenburg, 1998), and in interviews in the United States, Roberta R. Greene, *Studies in the Holocaust: Lessons in Survivorship* (New York: Taylor and Francis, 2011).

6. Xinyang diwei zuzhi chuli banggongshi, "Guanyu diwei changwushuji Wang Dafu tongzhi suofan cuowu ji shishi cailiao" [The Truth Regarding Regional Party Secretary Comrade Wang Dafu's Errors], 1962, pp. 1–2.

7. Zhang Zhong, "Xinyang shijian jiemi" [The Truth About Xinyang Incident], *Dangshi tiandi*, 2004, no. 4, p. 42; see also Qiao Peihua, *Xinyang shijian* [The Xinyang Incident] (Hong Kong: Kaifang chubanshe, 2009).

8. Qingming is a traditional Chinese festival that occurs each year on April 5 in the Western calendar. In China this is the day for the family to offer prayers to ancestors and to sweep tombstones.

9. "Shaobing Song" or "Pancake Poem" (1368) was a poem presented to the first Ming emperor, Zhu Yuanzhang (1328–1398). It is now widely regarded as a poem of divination, for some of the lines in the poem are said to refer to events that took place in China later.

Index

Names of famine survivors are pseudonyms, marked here with an asterisk